Selling Globalization

SELLING

GLOBALIZATION

The Myth of the Global Economy

MICHAEL VESETH

LYNNE
RIENNER
PUBLISHERS

BOULDER
LONDON

Published in the United States of America in 1998 by
Lynne Rienner Publishers, Inc.
1800 30th Street, Boulder, Colorado 80301

and in the United Kingdom by
Lynne Rienner Publishers, Inc.
3 Henrietta Street, Covent Garden, London WC2E 8LU

Library of Congress Cataloging-in-Publication Data
Veseth, Michael.
   Selling globalization : the myth of the global economy / Michael
Veseth.
    p. cm.
   Includes bibliographical references and index.
   ISBN 1-55587-797-4 (alk. paper)
   1. International finance. 2. International economic relations.
3. Competition, International. 4. Economic history—1990–
I. Title.
HG3881.V396   1998
337—dc21   98-11073
                                                                                CIP

British Cataloguing in Publication Data
A Cataloguing in Publication record for this book
is available from the British Library.

Printed and bound in the United States of America

      The paper used in this publication meets the requirements
       of the American National Standard for Permanence of
       Paper for Printed Library Materials Z39.48-1984.

    5   4   3   2   1

Contents

Preface

This book began as a project to explore the application of chaos theory—the analysis of nonlinear dynamical processes—to international political economy, especially to the study of international financial movements. For a variety of reasons, I thought that international capital flows might be an especially interesting area to hunt for nonlinear dynamics. This hunch was correct. In fact, exchange rates and international capital flows display elements of both crisis and chaos, which are analyzed, illustrated, and discussed in the critical central chapters of this book.

Once the case for chaos in international finance was established, the question I faced was, "so what?" One answer was *globalization*. Many people tell the story that global financial markets are the driving force behind the globalization of production, consumption, culture, politics, and more. The existence of crisis and chaos, however, makes truly global finance impossible, as a close study of the data indicates. This drew me into the globalization literature, which I found in need of a critical analysis. Much of what is written about globalization turns out to be nonsense and is accepted mostly because the story is appealing and because there are strong political and intellectual interests supporting it. Globalization, at least as it is conceived by some, is a myth. But like good myths, it is difficult to forget even after its illusive properties are revealed.

The notion that globalization is a myth, at least on some level, and that international financial chaos necessarily limits globalization was a very radical idea when I first began talking about it to friends and colleagues. They thought I was nuts. As I began the final revisions of this book, however, the full impact of the financial collapse in Asia was beginning to be realized. And my ideas no longer seemed so outrageous. The globalization myth, however, lives on. It seems to have a life of its own—quite apart from the new information about the financial structures that simultaneously make global expansion possible and limit its growth. Why?

In trying to explain the persistence of the globalization myth, I have found myself moving in two directions. One path leads to the concrete world of case study. Case studies of four "global" firms—Boeing, Microsoft, Nike, and the world's largest pension fund management company, the Frank Russell Company—let me think creatively about what actual globalization is and what it means, which led me to the truth behind the myth.

But I am also concerned about the interests that are served by the myth of globalization and those interests that are threatened by its debunking. These concerns led me to the political economy of global finance. Here I discuss which political interests are furthered by the threat of global business and what intellectual interests within the economics profession are threatened by the possibility that something so important as global financial markets might not behave according to the simple laws of supply and demand.

I have intentionally tried to avoid an academic writing style in this book. I have tried to make the text interesting and the opinions clear and provocative. I have tried to prompt reaction and dialogue. I hope readers are not put off by my occasional brashness. I have spent a lot of time reading authors who try to "sell globalization," and I guess a bit of their style has rubbed off on my work.

Although the focus of *Selling Globalization* has shifted, its real core is still chaos theory. International political economy is complex and dynamic. It is tempting to oversimplify issues that are multidimensional and complex, but it is often wrong to do so. We need to be wary of what we "buy" when simplified visions of complex processes like globalization are presented to us.

◆ ◆ ◆

I am an authority on debt, and I have run up more than the usual number of professional debts in writing this book. I am grateful to the University of Puget Sound, which has supported my work for many years, and to the Bologna Center of the Johns Hopkins University School of Advanced International Studies, where work on Chapters 5, 6, and 7 took place. David Balaam deserves special thanks for the help he provided me during the process of revising the manuscript. I am also grateful to an anonymous reviewer for a number of useful revision ideas. Finally, I would like to thank Leon Grunberg, Sunil Kukreja, David Sousa, Matt Warning, Ed Greenberg, Felix Martin, Jamie Ledford, Jon Westerman, Aadip Desai, and most of all, Sue Veseth. The errors and outrages that remain are all mine.

I dedicate this book to Ernie Combs—teacher, colleague, and friend.

1

Global Visions

Globalisation is a trend that has spawned many conventional wisdoms. The freedom of employers to locate factories wherever labour costs are cheapest is said to have reduced the power of labour. The ability of companies to choose countries with user-friendly tax and regulatory regimes is alleged to have undermined the power of the nation state. Income inequality in the developed world is often attributed to the globalisation of production. While there is an element of truth in each of these assertions, they are all potentially misleading.

—Financial Times[1]

This book is about the G-word: Globalization. Globalization is one of the most powerful and persuasive images of today's world. The image of globalization—as promise or as threat—is invoked daily to justify actions and to rationalize policy. Managers are encouraged to "think global." Investors sink their cash into "global" mutual funds. Politicians at every level in every country push to plug into the global web. Globalization is big and it is hot.

But is globalization more than an image? What is the real nature of this process and what does it hold as promise or as threat? I believe that the "globe" is experiencing real and important change, but it is not *globalization*. Or at least the most important element is not the *global* element.

In this book I argue that globalization is badly misunderstood. It is quantitatively and qualitatively different from the conventional wisdom. In particular, it is fundamentally different from the extreme visions of globalization—hyperglobalization—with which we are constantly bombarded in newspapers, on television, in popular books, and in scholarly journals.[2]

In fact, I argue, the popular hyperglobalization images of seamless global markets and a borderless world are impossible from a practical point of view, whatever their theoretical or emotional appeal may be. Global financial markets have a built-in tendency toward chaos and crisis, and the instability worsens as the markets expand. Without a stable financial base, an integrated global economy is out of the question. Truly global firms are rare animals in this world of chaos and crisis. The emerging "global economy" that we hear so much about is really something else.

If globalization as we commonly think of it does not exist, then how did we come to think of it this way? My answer is that hyperglobalization and its image of the seamless global economy are useful. Many people are able to further their own economic, political, and intellectual interests by painting in vivid, memorable colors a picture of hyperglobalization at work. Globalization is sold, and we buy it. But globalization is really a delivery system, not a final product. When we accept the image of hyperglobalization, we simultaneously accept, usually without question, a number of other images—political, economic, and intellectual.

Globalization is the Marlboro Man of international political economy. People are attracted to the advertised image and buy the product associated with it. It makes them feel good and look cool, and they are soon addicted. Then one day they wake up with emphysema. This process is misleading and potentially dangerous. It is time that this globalization business was more closely scrutinized.

This first chapter presents short case studies of how globalization is understood, misunderstood, and used to sell a variety of policies, programs, and ideas. I then outline the argument that I make in the main part of the book, so that you will know what you are getting into and will be better prepared to put specific analysis and particular case studies into a broader context. After I have convinced you that actual globalization is different from what the conventional wisdom suggests, I sketch my own image of globalization. But I save that for Chapter 8.

FOUR FACES OF GLOBALIZATION

Globalization has many faces. It is in fact a complex dynamic process. Because it is so complex, however, its true image is hard to grasp, and it is easy—too easy—to see what you want or have been conditioned to see. To a certain extent *globalization* is a mirror that shows us the face we are looking for, not the one that's really there. Much of this book is devoted to a more detailed analysis of what globalization is versus how it is perceived and why.

Let me show you four faces of globalization that made the news in the dog days of summer 1997 when I was writing the first draft of this chapter. It seemed as if whenever I picked up the newspapers, I found advertisements for globalization among the news stories and editorials. These stories were mundane—the sort of stories that you find in daily newspapers during any month of any year. (I have saved the best cases for more extensive treatment in other parts of the book.) The mundane regularity with which globalization gets sold is important. Globalization is so widely marketed for so many different reasons that it has infiltrated our understanding of the world in a fundamental way. We no longer really think about globalization in assessing an argument that is based on it. This is a fundamental error. If we are interested in understanding the changes that the world is experiencing today, it is a fatal error.

So I am going to tell you four stories from the summer of 1997. In the first story, which features Nike, I want you to see how the threat of globalization can be used effectively to promote *private* interests even in a situation in which the global connection is clearly irrelevant. In the second story, I want to show how the image of globalization can be manipulated and used to promote *public* policies that are at best tangentially related to global markets. These two stories should help you understand how powerful the image of globalization is and how important it is to "sell" globalization in order to sell other things.

The third story, which is about the Boeing–McDonnell Douglas merger, shows how the consequences of actual globalization do not always follow the hyperglobalization model. Bigger markets do not necessarily mean the end of the state, for example. This almost makes you wonder if the bigger market/smaller state mindset is not missing something. And finally, the fourth story looks to the prodemocracy movement in Indonesia to provide an example of how globalization can be used to promote all sides of an issue. These two stories question whether globalization is really what it is advertised to be—or if, in fact, it is something entirely different.

In short, my goal in this first chapter is to create a context that questions the common understanding of globalization.

Case 1: Globalization and the New Nike Factory

Nike, the company that makes shoes and equipment for the likes of Michael Jordan and Tiger Woods, is the quintessential "global firm." Of the four business case studies I present in Chapter 3, it is, in fact, the only company that satisfies my definition of a truly global firm. In the summer of 1997, Nike announced that it wanted to construct a major U.S. production facility outside of its Oregon home (where little actual manufacturing takes place). Who wants our business? Who will make us the best deal? What will you give us to build the factory in your town, Nike seemed to ask.

Nike's announcement fits the conventional picture of how global firms are supposed to operate. They can produce anywhere and sell everywhere, the story goes, so local governments must bid for their business. This is the classic case of the footloose global firm versus the intimidated, powerless state.

I became aware of the event because Nike's plans involved the Puget Sound region of Washington state, where I live and work. The *News Tribune* reported on August 10, 1997, that

Representatives of Nike Inc. are scheduled to meet with officials in Pierce and Thurston counties next week about possibly building a manufacturing plant and offices for up to 5,000 employees.

Snohomish County economic development officials confirmed that they, too, are courting Nike for what may be a major Puget Sound expansion outside of the sports equipment company's Beaverton, Ore., world headquarters.

At this point, any talks with Nike are considered very preliminary. Washington is competing with sites in Colorado, New Mexico, Nevada and British Columbia, and it isn't certain Nike will select any of them.

"We've been in contact with a number of states and have asked them to look at a particular tax scenario," Nike spokesman Lee Weinstein said. "How could it affect us and our taxes?"[3]

Nike seemed to be playing the various state and local governments against one another, looking for the best deal. They could build their factory anywhere—even in Canada—bringing jobs and revenues to whatever location they might choose. This mobility gave them power to extract concessions from state and local officials. A related *News Tribune* article provided context.

The immediate catalyst behind Nike's current search for a second campus site, one outside Oregon, is a land-use dispute the company is having with Metro, the Portland-area regional government. Metro wants Nike to have housing built on part of its campus adjacent to a light-rail station; Nike wants to put more offices there.

Also at issue is Nike's growing sense that it has done a lot for Oregon, while the state hasn't offered it anything in the way of tax cuts. Tax incentives played a major role in building the "Silicon forest" around Portland. In comments to *The Oregonian,* Clarke wondered why Intel and other semiconductor companies get tax deals and Nike is ignored.

Knight's inquiry isn't a guarantee a second Nike campus will be built outside Oregon. Metro and the state of Oregon could patch things up with Nike. Knight, a native Oregonian, might decide to continue to keep the bulk of his operations there.

It's possible, some Washington officials say, that Nike is turning to other states solely as a bargaining chip to use in its struggle with Metro.[4]

When I first read these articles, I recognized Nike's strategy as a variation on the hyperglobalization theme. The idea that global corporations are free to move about in a "borderless" world and can therefore dominate and coerce geography-bound states is an important aspect of the conventional wisdom about globalization.

As I thought about it some more, however, I realized that the article was also about something else. Nike was basically asking governmental units to compete for their investment funds. The fact that these governments *can* compete shows that they have power to at least control scarce and valuable resources. These governments control something that Nike wanted. Interesting. The much-heralded death of the state may be exaggerated after all. The state is not dead; that is not what is new here. What is new is the degree of competition among different governments, which has nothing to do with the conventional wisdom. To a certain extent, what we misinterpret as "globalization" is often increased intergovernmental competition, which attenuates the power of individual governments without necessarily reducing state power overall.

What is also new is the fact that Nike can shape this competition to its corporate advantage. It was able to do so, of course, because the image of hyperglobalization makes everyone believe that Nike could or would build a new factory just about anywhere. This image gives Nike power over governments—not limitless power, but power just the same. Power and authority are no longer so concentrated in the state, but diffused unequally throughout a more competitive international political economy of governments, firms, and other institutions. Oregon has some power and so does Nike; neither can rule, and both can bargain in a competitive environment. This is an interesting new environment, but there is nothing fundamentally "global" about it.

What should we make of the fact that Nike invited offers from only a few states? That doesn't seem very *global*. Perhaps these states are known as the most competitive and willing to make concessions. This would put more pressure on Oregon officials to make concessions of their own, which seems to have been Nike's strategy in this situation. About the only thing that the targeted states have in common with each other (and with Oregon) is the availability of excellent winter skiing. If this is indeed the key factor in Nike's global plan, then I guess the image of globalization as the "end of geography" will need to be revised.

Nike's plan worked, by the way. And it worked fast. The *News Tribune* reported on August 20 that

> It was a day to schmooze the swoosh.
> When Nike Inc. representatives—clad in shorts, athletic shirts and hiking boots with those trademark swooshes—came to the South Sound on Tuesday to scout a home for a new manufacturing plant, they were met by men and women in business suits, crisp white shirts and heels.
> They were served Snapple in wine glasses, cookies on platters and Starbucks Colombian blend coffee. They had breakfast at the Tacoma Club in Pierce County and lunch at the Indian Summer Golf Course in Thurston County.
> And they heard local representatives' best sales pitches, all meant to persuade the athletic-shoe giant to tap them on the shoulder with its magic wand when the time comes.[5]

The very next day, The *News Tribune* reported that

Nike got half of what it wanted from the Beaverton City Council this week.

The athletic shoe giant objected to Beaverton's plans to designate 15 acres of Nike property north of the light-rail line for residential use.

Nike also opposed plans requiring it to provide a public access road across its land to the new Beaverton Creek station of the light-rail line.

The City Council has decided to absolve Nike of any responsibility to use part of its property for housing. But it required Nike to provide the public access road.[6]

The moral of the story? "I should have worn shorts," according to one of the jilted local government suitors that Nike used to extract concessions from Beaverton.[7] No, it probably wasn't a question of style, although it must have been hard to interpret the Nike style of business dress as a serious statement of interest in making a multimillion dollar investment.

No, the moral of the Nike story is this. Nike was able to bargain with local governments for concessions in part because of its image as a footloose global firm. Although Nike is footloose and global in many respects, the image is probably wrongly applied to this specific case. But the belief in footloose globalization as a general feature of corporate behavior was enough to induce local governments to scramble to offer concessions to Nike, which improved Nike's position in bargaining for its Oregon home turf. Hyperglobalization (swoosh!) was a useful image that served Nike well in these negotiations.

Case 2: Globalization and the World Trade Center Luncheon

Globalization is a powerful tool for private interests, but its use is not limited to "global" business firms like Nike. Globalization is equally useful in the public sector. The real beauty of globalization is that it can be made to seem relevant at all levels of analysis, even at the local Rotary Club or Chamber of Commerce luncheon. The *News Tribune,* my source for local news here in Tacoma, commented on one such luncheon in its July 23, 1997, editorial column.

The downtown luncheon held Tuesday by the World Trade Center Tacoma was a signal event in Pierce County's economic history.

It wasn't merely the fact that Gov. Gary Locke was the keynote speaker, although his presence—and what he had to say—were both significant.

Most impressive was the unprecedented, community-wide focus the event brought to bear on the need to make Tacoma and Pierce County a genuine player in the global marketplace.

For much too long the concept of international trade in Pierce County has centered mainly on the Port of Tacoma. The port, blessed with deep water, a handy proximity to the Pacific Rim and an abundance of terminal space, has grown dramatically as a handler of container cargo.

But the South Sound region must look "beyond the boxes," as a City Club of Tacoma report once put it, to truly make a place for itself in the burgeoning global economy. More small and medium-sized local businesses—not just the Boeings and Weyerhaeusers—must seek new markets abroad. And if the region fails to capitalize on the present opportunity, it risks losing its best chance to build an enduring prosperity.[8]

The key to Tacoma's success, the *News Tribune* opined, is globalization. If Tacoma can become "a genuine player in the global marketplace" it will grow and prosper. If it does not, it is doomed to a stagnant backwater fate. This idea is not ridiculous when applied to Tacoma, since historically its existence has been based on international trade and finance. Still, the same argument is made at civic luncheons everywhere, it seems. Every town with a port, railroad, airport, satellite dish, or fax machine thinks it sits, at least potentially, at the center of the earth. Probably you have heard civic leaders in your town say the same thing.

The publisher of the *News Tribune* thought the matter important enough to have his own luncheon remarks published in full a few days later. We have reached a point where participation in the global economy is critical, he said.

Why is this moment historically special? Part of the reason is the legacy we have inherited:

- Great harbors and ports forged from the vision of the pioneers of trade.
- Huge international businesses dominating aerospace and software spawned by the vision of Northwest entrepreneurs Bill Boeing and Bill Gates.
- The fortuitous accident of geography that places us at the American gateway to the explosive new markets to the west— markets whose growth will dominate the world stage for generations to come.
- The wonderful coincidence that we are in one of the most gorgeous places in the world, situated in a time zone halfway between the great markets of the past 100 years and the great markets of the next 100.
- And transcendent changes in communications technology that will transform the way we do business.[9]

All correct so far. Tacoma *is* relatively well prepared to enter the global world of the twenty-first century. This isn't an accident, however. Tacoma was originally built to take advantage of the global economy that existed one hundred years ago, when the nations of the world were in some respects even more economically integrated than they are today.

So what are the implications of globalization? Where does the logic of global markets lead? Surprisingly, I think, global logic calls for policies that have an extremely local focus, according to the *News Tribune* publisher.

We are beginning to shape the vision but we haven't done the real work yet:

- Our education systems are too weak and our standards too low.

- Our public higher education system serves too few students and is mired in 18th-century governance mechanisms that make them desperately slow in responding to new educational and training needs.
- We have become complacent congratulating ourselves about our preeminent trade record—highest in the country in per capita exports, after all. But we're pretty mediocre once you look past Boeing and a couple of others.
- We have squandered too much time watching our waterfront decay.
- We have seen our neighborhoods suffer because they are arrayed on the fringes of a dilapidated core.
- We've wasted a lot of time and resources focusing on interregional competitive issues rather than on the regional collaboration essential to face the world.
- We have sometimes elected too many officials who see the world as a place to erect walls rather than extend arms.

But we are fixing those things.[10]

I agree with everything that the publisher put on his list. These are all serious local problems that need to be addressed in my city and state, and the sooner the better. But are they globalization problems? No. Is globalization a reason for reforming university governance or dealing with neighborhood decay? Not really. Or rather, if globalization is the *only* reason or the best reason, then the case cannot be very strong.

I understand the logic that connects the two parts of the speech, local problems and global markets. Urban neighborhood redevelopment is related to globalization in the following way. To compete in global markets, you need to attract global investment. To attract global firms, you need to be able to offer an attractive business and living environment. Neighborhoods that "suffer because they are arrayed on the fringes of a dilapidated core" make Tacoma's living environment less desirable, discouraging the people who work for the firms who compete on the global markets who make the footloose investments—who live in the house that Jack built. If you've got suffering neighborhoods, you can kiss global investment good-bye. Simple as that.

I am intentionally being overly critical of this argument, not because it is especially offensive, but because it is such a common way of thinking and arguing. The argument works, too, I think.

Globalization, international trade, and competitiveness *may* be reasons to confront issues such as education, neighborhoods, and the environment for small and medium-sized businesses. But there are probably ten or twelve *better* reasons. These issues and globalization are important, but they have little to do with one another.

The publisher's speech uses something that is *hot*—globalization—to promote something that is *not*—urban neighborhood redevelopment. By linking this local issue with a global one, the local issue becomes more attractive and easier to sell to public officials and private taxpayers. Selling globalization is the key to selling everything else.

Case 3: Globalization and the Boeing Merger

People look at globalization and tend to see what they want to see—or, perhaps, what they have been conditioned to see. For many people, globalization is the triumph of the market and the death of the state. But if you want to believe that global firms are running amuck and national interests are being trampled to bits, do not read about the merger of Boeing and McDonnell Douglas, which was finalized at the end of July 1997.

At first glance, the merger of two global industrial and technological giants, creating the largest aerospace and defense manufacturer in the world, seems to be quintessential hyperglobalization. The advent of global firms to fill global markets is a fundamental feature of the conventional wisdom. These global firms are more powerful than any government, it is said, and can pretty much do as they please.

What a surprise, then, that regulatory questions about the merger's competitive consequences were sticking points as the merger deadline neared. Stunningly, it was not the U.S. government that questioned the merger, but the European Union (EU). The EU threatened to impose crippling fines and sanctions on Boeing if the merger with McDonnell Douglas went through as planned.

This is a puzzling development, especially if you have bought the hyperglobalization argument. Globalization is supposed to be about the extension of private *market* power, not public *regulatory* power. States are supposed to have *lost* the ability to regulate global markets. It is hard to make sense of a globalization that produces global regulatory power.

The specific issue that raised EU concern over the merger was the fact that Boeing had signed exclusive twenty-year supply arrangements with three U.S.–based airlines. The EU said that it was concerned that the merger unfairly limited competitive prospects for Airbus, Europe's own commercial aircraft producer. In fact, this issue was a red herring. McDonnell Douglas is no longer a major player in the commercial aircraft market, so the merger could not possibly concentrate market power. The issue was really Boeing—Boeing versus Airbus, and the United States versus the state interests of the EU. In this supposed face-off between "market" and "state," the *Financial Times* reported that

> In the end, it was Boeing that blinked. A last-minute concession by the U.S. aerospace manufacturer yesterday on the terms of its planned merger with McDonnell Douglas ended months of brinkmanship with Brussels,

which had threatened to turn into the most bruising transatlantic confrontation for decades.

The Boeing offer was faxed to Mr. Karel Van Miert, the EU competition commissioner, on the eve of a Commission meeting which was widely expected to outlaw the merger. The offer met the last of Mr. Van Miert's main objections by proposing to scrap the exclusive 20-year supply agreements which Boeing has signed with three U.S. airlines.

By dint of bluff, bluster and browbeating, Mr. Van Miert had already persuaded Boeing to yield on two other points. It had agreed to limit defence technology "spillovers" into the merged group's commercial operations and to publish separate accounts for the Douglas civil aircraft business.

Boeing had also offered to shorten the exclusive supply agreements to 13 years, and to sign no more for a decade. But the company had refused, almost to the end, to abandon exclusivity altogether. Unless that happened, Mr. Van Miert insisted, Brussels would veto the merger.

Had the Commission done so, it would have unleashed a potentially uncontrollable chain reaction. Mr. Van Miert had said that if the companies then pushed ahead with the merger, which U.S. anti-trust authorities cleared last month, the EU would impose swingeing fines and business restrictions on them.

Such penalties would almost certainly have prompted U.S. retaliation. Washington has been considering measures, ranging from filing a complaint against the EU in the World Trade Organisation to imposing anti-dumping or countervailing duties on exports of European Airbuses to the U.S.[11]

The merger did nothing to alter the competitive dynamics of the commercial aircraft market, but it gave the EU a convenient opportunity to impose some constraints on Boeing and thereby give Airbus a modest competitive boost. The EU action was not about monopoly power; rather, it was about national interest. The Boeing–McDonnell Douglas merger pushed the United States and the EU to the verge of a trade war.

Does this case illustrate the power of the market, a point that those who promote globalization like to stress, or the surprisingly potent authority of the state? Both stories can be told here. In fact, state and market almost reverse their roles in some markets, such as aerospace and military hardware.

Firms (like Boeing) behave almost like states, adopting foreign policies, engaging in diplomacy, and negotiating with other states. All these activities highlight state power, which is an unexpected theme of the case studies I present in Chapter 3. States, on the other hand, act more like firms, promoting products and using their influence to seal profitable deals. Although the state hasn't been slain by the market, things have definitely changed.

Case 4: Globalization and Democracy in Indonesia

Globalization is the death of democracy, according to many who write on this issue. As global firms and markets gain power, citizens lose it. My colleague

David Sousa has authored an exceptionally clear-headed statement of this idea. The issue, he writes, concerns

> the conflict between the *logics* of the market and democracy. The democratic impulse is to bring decisions on issues affecting the society at large under popular, or *public*, control. But in free market systems, a whole range of decisions with important public consequences are *private*, held in the hands of rational, profit-seeking business leaders. Citizens may prefer more government spending for universal health care, or tighter environmental and workplace safety regulations. They may organize to win higher wages and better working conditions. But these popular impulses may undermine profitability in ways that are unacceptable to business managers—democratic claims often violate the logic of the market.[12]

In hyperglobalization analysis, the rise of the private market unambiguously shrinks the domain of democratic public controls. Globalization is dollar dictatorship.

Given this aspect of the conventional wisdom, I was surprised on July 24, 1997, to come across a *New York Times* op-ed column by Thomas L. Friedman about *globalutionaries*—democratic revolution through globalization. The focus of Friedman's column was the struggle for power in Indonesia, where the Suharto regime has held tightly to power for thirty years. A democracy movement has appeared, but those involved do not seek to extend democracy by pushing back the market, as hyperglobalization rhetoric suggests. These revolutionaries are different, Friedman writes, and

> What's interesting is their strategy. The Suharto regime allows no space for a democratic opposition to emerge. So what the pro-democracy, pro-clean government forces are relying on is not a revolution from below, not a revolution from above, but a revolution from beyond.
>
> Their strategy is to do everything they can to integrate Indonesia into the global economy on the conviction that the more Indonesia is tied into the global system, the more its government will be exposed to the rules, standards, laws, pressures, scrutiny and regulations of global institutions, and the less arbitrary, corrupt and autocratic it will be able to be. Their strategy, in short, is to Gulliverize the Suharto regime by globalizing Indonesian society. As a military analyst, Juwono Sudarsono, put it: "The global market will force upon us business practices and disciplines that we cannot generate internally." Or as another reformer here remarked to me: "My son and I get our revenge on Suharto every day by eating at McDonald's."[13]

The issue of globalization and democracy seems complicated and more than a bit fuzzy. On one hand, I do believe that market forces impose constraints on public policy, affecting the range of choices from which democracies can choose. On the other hand, the *threat* of globalization can be used by political entrepreneurs to gain power—globalization is an attractive foe that one can run *against* as well as run *from.* Political entrepreneurs can exploit what we call *globalphobia,* a term used to refer to a fear of globalization: "Globalphobia is proving a potent force in US politics and foreign policy. The administration has tried to ignore it, confident that bombarding the public with good economic figures—the best growth, inflation and unemployment for a generation—would cure it. But globalphobia is holding its own against the statistical barrage, and even gathering strength."[14]

The public threat of global markets can be used to promote the private interests of candidates. Ross Perot, for example, used the fear of global competition to fuel his run for the U.S. presidency in 1992. And now I read that globalization, or the threat of globalization, can also be a tool of globalutionaries to promote democracy when the status quo is a nonmarket dictator such as Suharto.

Globalization can apparently destroy democracy, create it, and be used by political enterpreneurs to manipulate democracy. This globalization must be a terrible, wonderful thing.

A UNIVERSAL ELIXIR

The fascinating thing about globalization is its versatility, acting as a universal elixir. It can be used as an excuse or reason to do almost anything. I have shown four faces of globalization, but it really has a thousand faces, many of which I examine in later chapters. I cannot think of a public policy or private interest that could not be justified in some way as a response to globalization's positive or negative perceived effects. Selling globalization makes it possible to sell anything. No wonder globalization has been so thoroughly and successfully marketed by so many for so long.

The selling of globalization occurs at all levels. However, it is an especially well-developed enterprise in the business world. Business consultants advise their clients to "think global, act local" and promote the global market as "Prometheus unleashed." The business of selling globalization (and associated consulting services) is itself a global business.

Selling globalization is also an important academic industry. At about the same time as the events in the four cases just discussed, the scholarly journal *New Political Economy* published a special issue devoted to globalization and the politics of resistance.[15] Fourteen articles manipulated globalization in various ways, mostly promoting various forms of political, social, economic, or intellectual "resistance."

In the Preface to this issue, John Kenneth Galbraith writes emphatically in defense of the welfare state.

> Capitalism in its original form was an insufferably cruel thing. Only with trade unions, pensions for the old, compensation for the unemployed, public health care, lower-cost housing, a safety net for the unfortunate and the deprived and public action to mitigate capitalism's commitment to boom and slump did it become socially and politically acceptable. Let us not be reticent: we are the custodians of a political tradition that saved classical capitalism from itself.[16]

Globalization, Galbraith writes, is not the death of the welfare state, but a reason to extend it *globally*. At precisely the time when the relevance of the nation-state is being seriously questioned, Galbraith looks ahead to a return of Camelot. "We can even have a measure of sympathy for those who oppose us," he concludes in an almost Marxian tone. "We, not they, are in step with history."[17]

Only days after *New Political Economy* appeared, the *Review of International Political Economy* published a special issue devoted to a discussion of "The Direction of Contemporary Capitalism."[18] The following is a list of some of the articles this volume contains:

- The world market unbound
- Has globalization ended the rise and rise of the nation-state?
- The state of globalization: Towards a theory of state transformation
- Social movements for global capitalism: The transformational capitalist class in action
- Modernity, postmodernity or capitalism?

With globalization now filling whole issues of academic journals, the concept inevitably will be both used and exploited.[19] Some authors use their theory to illuminate aspects of global market diffusion, but just as many are probably guilty of using globalization to sell their own theories, recycle their earlier ideas, or further their academic careers.

The academic selling of globalization occurs even where it is basically unnecessary. Two of the best recent books about international political economy are *Has Globalization Gone Too Far?* by Dani Rodrik and *Globalizing Capital: A History of the International Monetary System* by Barry Eichengreen.[20] Both books are excellent and I discuss Rodrik's ideas in detail in the last chapter of this book. But neither book is especially about *globalization*. Both authors say smart things about international economic and political relations, but the *global* dimension is essentially irrelevant to what they have to say. (Globalization does not even appear in Eichengreen's index, for example.) But globalization *sells* and helps get these books sold and read, although I think that these books would be successful with any title.

Globalization is as highly marketable a product in the ivory tower as it undoubtedly is in politics, business, and the media. So useful is this concept, in fact, that if it did not exist, we might need to invent it.

GLOBALIZATION LIMITED

Globalization is hot, and it is useful—but is it real? Does the borderless world with its global markets really exist? The question sounds foolish, and many people, I suspect, think me a fool for even asking it. But I am suspicious of globalization, especially when taken to extremes.

The belief in hyperglobalization, which is the easiest kind of globalization to sell, requires a particular vision of the market. You must imagine the market to be like the ocean in the paintings of J.M.W. Turner at the Tate Gallery in London: The market is smooth and calm and seems to extend infinitely in all directions as it disappears into the mist. This kind of market seems to cover the earth. It is destiny. It is fate.

But markets are not like this, or at least not all markets all the time. When I imagine a market, especially an international financial market, I envision river rapids—turbulent cascades full of twists and turns. Financial markets do not spread out to the horizon; they flow through well-developed, relatively narrow channels. They sometimes flow smoothly, like a broad river, but they also rumble, tumble, and boil. The markets I see look like Leonardo da Vinci's hydrodynamic sketches in the *Codex Leicester.* Working as an engineer first and an artist second, Leonardo da Vinci drew currents that swirled and splashed in turbulent patterns that we now call chaotic and that we can model using the mathematics of nonlinear dynamics (like the models of international financial markets I present in Chapter 5). His sketches look like markets. They display the dynamic character of markets. But they do not look at all like Turner's globalization.

It is hard to picture globalization built on a foundation of turbulent global financial markets. In fact, this is exactly the problem with globalization.

The key to globalization in general and hyperglobalization in particular is the existence of smooth, efficient global financial markets. But there is reason to believe that global financial markets are like Leonardo's cascades—unstable and turbulent. The instability of global financial markets creates a natural limitation to globalization.

You need not look far for evidence of instability in global financial markets. During the summer of 1997, for example, currency markets in Southeast Asia erupted into chaos that distorted trade and investment patterns throughout the region and beyond. The *New York Times* of July 29, 1997, reported that

The fast-growing countries of South and Southeast Asia, regarded for years as the most economically promising of the world's developing nations, have been shaken this summer by a speculative assault that has sent their currencies tumbling.

While the crisis has reached outward to Malaysia, Indonesia, and the Philippines, its epicenter has been Thailand, where hard-willed global currency traders first sensed profit in a looming financial crisis stemming from a buildup of debt and a slowdown in growth. . . .

From small towns to meetings of top Asian leaders, the talk is of devaluation, economic stability (or instability), and the perfidy of the West. But underlying the pain and the polemics, there is a spreading concern over whether the supercharged growth of the past is ending, whether the economies of South and Southeast Asia are approaching a crossroads.

"Asia has to be prepared for much slower growth in the coming 10 years," said Nikhil Srinivasan, a vice president at Morgan Stanley in Bangkok. "These tigers are going to be roaring much less loudly."[21]

Most readers of this essay probably know that the currency rumblings we heard in the summer of 1997 were just the prelude to a much bigger explosion. As of December 1997, there is great concern that Japan and China may join a list of collapsing Asian economies that began with Thailand and now stretches to include Indonesia, Malaysia, and mighty Korea. It is said that an International Monetary Fund (IMF) stabilization fund of as much as $60 billion may be needed to keep Korean financial markets from imploding. News reports speculate that Asia may have lost a decade of economic growth in just a few weeks, that the "Asian miracle" is over, and that the United States and other industrialized countries will now also decline as dynamic Asian export markets dry up.[22] The proposition that global financial markets can be unstable and that this instability can have real and important consequences does not seem as extreme today as it did a year ago

The particular sort of market instability that was reported in Asia in 1997 is called a *currency crisis* and was due to a *speculative attack*, although there can be other causes. If you want to imagine a currency crisis, think of the famous print, "The Great Wave," by the nineteenty-century Japanese *ukiyo-e* artist Katsushika Hokusai—a beautiful scene of blues and pinks and grays. First you see the great wave rising up from left to right, powerful and beautiful. The motion of the wave leads your eye to the horizon, where a snow-crowned volcanic peak rises. Your eye follows the volcano's sides down, and you see the slender boats that are being tossed about on the waves with their rows of miserable, doomed passengers. They are about to be crushed by the Great Wave. This is what it must feel like to be in a small "global" business during a currency crisis.

Exchange rates can rise or fall by extraordinary percentages during a currency crisis, which is a very serious matter. A change in the exchange rate between two nations affects *all* the relative prices of *all* the traded goods in *all* the markets in the two countries. If prices matter, then currency crises cause *all* trade-related markets to be knocked out of kilter. (If prices do not matter, then how can we think about global markets?) It is hard to figure how globalization can be carried on the back of institutions that are as unstable as today's currency markets. It is no wonder that the future prospects of export-driven economies are so uncertain.

Worse, there is some evidence that currency markets are also subject to systematic instability in the form of chaos—that currency markets experience *exactly* the kind of unpredictable turbulence that Leonardo da Vinci saw in the chaotic hydrodynamics of the rapids on the Arno River. Even currencies that avoid crisis may be subject to chaos, which adds another layer of risk and uncertainty to international and especially global strategies and transactions.

True economic globalization is rare, or at least much less common than the conventional wisdom realizes. Globalization requires markets as smooth as a mirror pond, and not many of these markets exist.

Globalization is so useful, so easy to sell, and serves so many different interests, that it does not matter, apparently, that neither the seamless global web nor the borderless world exist. Or at least that they do not exist in the form that the conventional wisdom holds. This book tries to make sense of the whats, hows, whys, and so whats of selling globalization.

OUTLINE OF THE BOOK

Selling Globalization is divided into eight chapters. The first and last chapters can be thought of as "So what?" chapters. In this first chapter I have tried to build your interest in the subject, make its relevance clear, and give a taste of my analysis and conclusions. Hopefully you are already a little disturbed and maybe even ready to argue with me, which is the mood I'd like you in for what comes next.

The second and third chapters are "What?" chapters that examine what globalism is in theory versus what it is in practice. In Chapter 2 I work my way through what I think are the globalization myths. I try to convince you that much of what is said about globalization is exaggerated, misleading, or just plain wrong. In doing this I may be accused of building a hyperglobalized "straw man" and then knocking him down. However, I do this intentionally, since I believe that this artificial straw man is the one that globalization sellers rely on and therefore the one that must be confronted.[23] Chapter 3 presents four brief case studies of real "global" firms that reveal a good deal about what actual globalization looks like and how considerably it differs from the myth.

Chapters 4 and 5 are "How?" chapters. They explain how global financial markets experience crisis and chaos and how this limits globalization. These are the only chapters that contain anything like technical economic analysis, but case studies and real world examples make this material easy to digest. Be careful what you swallow here, however. These chapters explain but do not absolutely prove how currency market instability limits globalization. It is very hard to prove a negative, especially given the empirical difficulties of chaos analysis. So you should retain a healthy skepticism in these chapters and consider how the case made here compares with other evidence I present.

Chapters 6 and 7 are the "Why?" chapters. They ask why the myth of globalization is such a powerful force, and they find the answer in a set of political and intellectual interests that are supported by the image of an invincible, infinite global market structure. Both politicians and economists have stakes (different stakes) in the persistence of the globalization myth. It is important to understand why this trend has received so little critical examination, given its obvious importance.

Chapter 8 is the final "So what?" chapter. Here I try to make sense of the muddle we have made of understanding and misunderstanding globalization. I also discuss how we should view the dramatic changes that we see about us today. If not globalization, then what?

NOTES

1. "The G-Word" (leader), *Financial Times,* July 30, 1997.

2. I will use the term hyperglobalization when I am talking about visions of globalization that seem to me to be excessive or extreme and are, I think, more a marketing tool than an accurate description of the worldwide expansion of markets. I borrow this term from Jonathan Perraton, David Goldblatt, David Held, and Anthony McGrew, "The Globalization of Economics Activity," *New Political Economy* 2:2 (July 1997), pp. 257–277. These authors put Kenichi Ohmae and Robert Reich in the hyperglobalization school, which I think is right. You will encounter these and other hyperglobalists in Chapter 2.

3. Karen Hucks, Cynthia Flash, and Jim Szymanski, "Representatives of Oregon Sports Equipment Company Will Meet with Pierce and Thurston Officials About Possibly Building Plant for up to 5,000 Workers," *News Tribune,* August 10, 1997.

4. Christine Carson and Cynthia Flash, "Nike Studying Strategies for Long-Term Success: Physical Expansion to be Accompanied by Move into Other Product Lines," *The News Tribune,* August 10, 1997.

5. Karen Hucks and Mike Maharry, "Romancing the Swoosh, S. Sound Style: Lacey, DuPont Put Their Best Feet Forward When Nike Comes to Town," *The News Tribune,* August 20, 1997.

6. "Beaverton yields to Nike on 1 Issue," *News Tribune,* August 21, 1997.

7. This is an authentic quote that appeared in Carson and Flash, "Nike Studying Strategies for Long-Term Success," *News Tribune,* August 10, 1997.

8. "Building a Future on Global Trade" (editorial), *News Tribune,* July 23, 1997.

9. Kelso Gillenwater, "Cooperation Can Guide Region into Future," *News Tribune,* July 27, 1997.

10. Ibid.

11. Guy de Jonquières, "Boeing: Brussels Wins Fight," *Financial Times,* July 23, 1994.

12. David Sousa, "Democracy and Markets: The IPE of NAFTA," in *Introduction to International Political Economy,* ed. David N. Balaam and Michael Veseth (Upper Saddle River, NJ: Prentice Hall, 1996), p. 252.

13. Thomas L. Friedman, "The Globalutionaries," *New York Times,* July 24, 1997.

14. Patti Waldmeir, "US: Scare Stories in Washington," *Financial Times,* December 2, 1997.

15. Barry K. Gills (editor), "Globalization and the Politics of Resistance" *New Political Economy* 2:1 (special issue; March 1997).

16. John Kenneth Galbraith, "Preface," *New Political Economy* 2:1 (March 1997), p. 5.

17. Ibid.

18. Andrew Chitty (guest editor), "The Direction of Contemporary Capitalism," *Review of International Political Economy* 4:3 (special issue; autumn 1997).

19. The two journals that are mentioned in this section are not especially guilty of the criticisms that follow, which are aimed at academic journals in general.

20. Dani Rodrik, *Has Globalization Gone Too Far?* (Washington, DC: Institute for International Economics, 1997). Barry Eichengreen, *Globalizing Capital: A History of the International Monetary System* (Princeton, NJ: Princeton University Press, 1996).

21. Edwarde A. Gargan, "Speculators Shake Currencies and Poise of Asians," *New York Times,* July 29, 1997.

22. See, for example, Stephen Fidler, "Might Asia Lose a Decade?" *Financial Times,* November 27, 1997; or "The curse of contagion," *Financial Times,* November 22, 1997.

23. That is, the image of globalization that is sold to the public is different from the far more nuanced vision that the best scholars in the field perceive.

2

The End of Geography
and the Last Nation-State

Every age has its defining terms. In our day, one of those terms is "global-
ization," which conveys the widely held belief that we are living in a border-
less world. Sovereign states appear incapable of controlling transnational
flows of goods and services (much less people), and in many places the state
itself is collapsing. One can visualize globalization every night, as the Cable
News Network broadcasts its latest reports from Somalia and the former Yu-
goslavia to television viewers around the world.

—Ethan B. Kapstein[1]

Seeing is believing and Ethan Kapstein's epigraph is correct: We live in an
age of global visions, where differences in time, space, nationality, and culture seem to have melted away, leaving a vast landscape before us. The globe
stretches out at our feet. You and I can see deceptively clear images of this
global vista with our own eyes. The television news, the World Wide Web, the
Reuters quote screen: We are there, engaged in global transactions of all sorts,
with even greater ease and efficiency in this virtual world than in our real
daily lives.

In real life you've got to hunt for the newspaper in the groggy predawn
gloom, pick over produce to find the least unripe tomatoes at the supermarket,
and worry about what language the cab driver is speaking as you zoom from
the airport into uncharted territory. The actual world is local, complicated, inconvenient, incompatible, poorly lit, poorly managed, understaffed, overregu-
lated, and, well, real. Our electronic lives are much more efficient. The news
comes to us, hard-wired in, via cable connection. Shopping is a snap—just
point and click and you've bought it, whether the "it" is a book on global
businesses or shares in an emerging markets mutual fund. Language and culture differences are reduced to their least common denominators.

Seeing and experiencing all this, we can easily convince ourselves that we have entered a new age—the global age—that represents a qualitative change in how people live, how they work, and how human arrangements of all sorts are defined and conducted. Hyperbole rolls easily off the tongue as we envision ourselves the center of a well-connected universe of opportunities and experiences. The virtual world presents to us the image of a borderless globe as if it were not only real but better than real. But is it? And if it is, what are its implications?

In this chapter I explore the idea of globalization and try to put it into perspective. I think that although the *forces* or general dynamics of globalization that surround us are real, they are not so powerful or all-conquering as their video display images lead us to believe. These forces have changed human arrangements, but not to the vast extent that some people say and some people believe they see. In short, I want to deflate the global myth—not entirely, but just enough so you will be able to appreciate in later chapters what globalization really is and means and why it has turned out this way. Before I can deflate the hyperglobalization myth, however, I need to pump it up.

VISIONS OF A BORDERLESS WORLD

There is something very powerful about the image of a borderless world, where goods, services, capital, and people move about freely, with no apparent effort. This vision, once it has grabbed the imagination, drives otherwise reasonable and intelligent observers to enthusiastic extremes of overstatement. However, the reality of globalization, as important as it is, is a whole lot less than this vision and the language used to describe it. Let me give you a few examples of globalistic overkill.

Lester Thurow is one of the most sensible economists. He has made a career of saying sensible things with just enough attitude to draw attention to them. Confronting the global landscape in his 1996 *The Future of Capitalism: How Today's Economic Forces Shape Tomorrow's World*, however, he experiences visions of a qualitatively different nature. He writes that

> For the first time in human history, anything can be made anywhere and sold everywhere. In capitalistic economies, that means making each component and performing each activity in the place on the globe where it can be most cheaply done and selling the resulting products or services wherever prices and profits are highest. . . . Sentimental attachment to some geographic part of the world is not part of the system.[2]

Globalization is thus the end of geography. The world is at once a giant factory and a massive shopping mall. Businesses shop for low costs without regard for distance or national policy, and consumers shop for low prices irrespective of culture or tradition.

> A global economy creates a fundamental disconnect between national political institutions and their policies to control economic events and the international economic forces that have to be controlled. Instead of a world where national policies guide economic forces, a global economy gives rise to a world in which extranational geoeconomic forces dictate economic policies. With internationalization, national governments lose many of their traditional levers of economic control.[3]

Globalization is thus the end of the nation-state and the end of history as we have come to think of it. Global markets dictate; national governments accommodate. Anyone who thinks that states can control their fate is living a dream.

> To make the global economy work requires giving up a substantial degree of national sovereignty, but the political Left and Right are both correct when they argue that this is undemocratic. It is undemocratic rule by foreigners or, even worse, rule by international bureaucrats. It could only be democratic if there were an elected democratic world government, yet Left and Right would both be the first ones to object to any such government.[4]

Globalization is therefore the end of democracy, too. The only level of government that could regulate the global market would be a global state. But whereas an all powerful global market is easy to imagine, a democratic global state seems a foolishly naïve notion. Obviously people are too divided by culture, language, and ideology for that to occur. (I mean this statement to be ironic; it is hard to imagine a world that is both as diverse as people believe when they think with their brain's political lobe, and simultaneously as homogeneous as it appears, when considered by the brain's economic lobe.)

> Within the developed world the issue of cultural protection will be central. The American press often makes fun of French efforts to protect French culture. . . . But the only really ridiculous feature of the French argument is that France is economically the fourth largest country on the globe and is the owner of a powerful long-lasting culture that is in no real sense threatened by an Anglo-Saxon media culture. . . . Small countries if they wish to preserve their national heritage have something serious to worry about. One can legitimately argue that protecting one's culture is a matter of life and death for human societies.[5]

Finally, of course, cultural diversity is also destroyed by the powerful waves that the winds of globalization drive. The world is McDonaldized and

Disneyfied, these being the principal forms of Anglo-Saxon media culture. *Les pommes frites* cannot survive the attack of the Large Fries. It is life or death.

Of course there are good reasons why sensible people like Thurow say these things. Extreme notions of globalization's effects are in a way both necessary and useful. They are necessary implications of a particular way of thinking about markets, and they are useful stories to attract attention for policies and programs that might not otherwise attract the audience they deserve (these are points developed in detail in Chapters 6 and 7). In short, the threat of globalization—especially the threat of extreme hyperglobalization—is a useful device.[6]

I don't want to overly criticize Lester Thurow for these overstatements or to make fun of him, because he is far from the worst offender in this regard. In any case, Thurow has sensible policies and programs to sell in a political environment not overly friendly to new ideas. Extreme visions of globalization like these help create a market for his policies of educational reform and infrastructure investment. People who will not support educational reforms for good reasons may be convinced to support it as a response to the threat of globalization.

Other writers have a more direct interest in exaggerating globalization's reach. Their hyperglobal visions, by design or coincidence, help create a market for their services as global business consultants and metamanagement gurus. Kenichi Ohmae, a former senior partner of the global consulting giant McKinsey & Company, is the best known of these. I think he may have coined the image of the "borderless" world that seems so firmly to capture our imagination.

Ohmae's 1990 book *The Borderless World: Power and Strategy in the Interlinked Economy* gives a good account of his views. Although much of the basic business advice he provides is sensible and would be useful guidance to almost anyone at any time, the motivating force for his analysis is another extreme global view: "On a political map, the boundaries between countries are as clear as ever. But on a competitive map, a map showing the real flows of financial and industrial activity, these boundaries have largely disappeared."[7]

The competitive world is borderless. Markets have no national character. Borders don't matter except for political purposes, which means that they don't matter very much.

> Walk into a capital goods factory anywhere in the developed world, and you will find the same welding machines, the same robots, the same machine tools. Likewise, all trading rooms for stocks, bonds, and currency look identical to the Reuters and Telerates terminals; so much so that the traders switch companies quite liberally. When information flows with relative freedom, the old geographic barriers become irrelevant. Global needs lead to global products.[8]

The global market rules and so businesses are forced to align themselves with global needs, producing global products, which leads to global culture and the rest. Again, and not to belabor the point too much, the basic business advice that derives from this hyperglobalization is perfectly reasonable: pay attention to quality, don't assume that customers are captive, treat all your customers equally well, and so forth. But extreme visions can be contagious and mass hallucination can result. Economists, journalists, and business consultants spread hysteria to historians, political scientists, and policymakers. Here are a few short examples.

The distinguished historian Paul Kennedy featured global forces in his 1993 bestseller, *Preparing for the Twenty-First Century.* Starting with Ohmae's borderless image, Kennedy assembled a collage of financial, telecommunications, and biotechnological forces all driving business to uncontrollable extremes: "Indeed, the real 'logic' of the borderless world is that nobody is in control—except, perhaps, the managers of multinational corporations, whose responsibility is to their shareholders, who, one might argue, have become the new sovereigns, investing in whatever company gives them the highest returns."[9] In Kennedy's view, only the global corporation has the reach to begin to control global forces. The meek shareholders shall inherit the earth, although the corporate managers who read Kenichi Ohmae's books will actually run the show.

Richard Rosecrance is a respected political scientist who has written wisely about the rise of the trading state in international affairs. Infected with global vision, however, he imagines actual states evaporating and being replaced by the virtual state: "Today and for the foreseeable future, the only international civilization worthy of the name is the governing economic culture of the world market. Despite the view of some contemporary observers, the forces of globalization have successfully resisted partition into cultural camps."[10]

The economic culture of the world market has become the only international culture.

> Less-developed countries, still producing goods that are derived from land, continue to covet territory. In economies where capital, labor, and information are mobile and have risen to predominance, no land fetish remains. . . . The virtual state—a state that has downsized its territorially based production capability—is the logical consequence of this emancipation from the land.[11]

Only Third World countries think that territory still matters. The rest of us understand that life exists exclusively on the World Wide Web and the Cable News Network. States have to give up their "land fetish" and find a new role, for "the world is embarked on a progressive emancipation from land as a determinant of production and power."[12]

A more evolved institution, a *virtual state,* is needed to deal with this process. We have left the earth behind and live lives in a virtual space without dimension. (Well, that is an overstatement; but it is an overstatement of an overstatement.) To be fair, again, Rosecrance says many smart things in his writings on this theme. And at least he seems to think that states still matter, albeit in only a virtual way, whereas so many others assert that global markets make states irrelevant artifacts of a previous era. I admit that I am not really sure what the virtual state is, except that it has stopped caring about land and is focused on mobile resources. As a way of refocusing attention from one set of issues to another, the virtual state seems like a useful globalization derivative. However, as a stand-alone concept, it doesn't seem very realistic.

Robert Reich has been one of the more successful global thinkers, both as a political economist and as a high government official.[13] Reich's 1991 book *The Work of Nations: Preparing Ourselves for 21st Century Capitalism* based its analysis on the notion of a *global web* that spans the earth, connecting up people and businesses without much attention to geography, government regulation, or anything else. High-tech, knowledge-intensive connections to the global web are the source of wealth and power in Reich's world, and a sort of global class system arises that is based on access to the web, much as an industrial class system based on access to capital appeared to Karl Marx.

Access to the global web divides workers of the world into *routine production workers,* the drones of the global workshop, *in-person service providers,* who fill an intermediate role, and *symbolic analysts,* the highly trained and educated top class who surf the global web, networking with other symbolic analysts around the world. The production workers build things but suffer from the fact that most things can be built anywhere and capital is more mobile than people. So production tends to move where wages and other costs are lowest. Production workers in Ohio thus compete with production workers in Malaysia and the Philippines to see who will work for the lowest wages. This creates a global class of workers trapped in a destructive competition to attract capital by cutting costs. Anyone familiar with Marx's *proletariat* class will recognize the routine production workers.

The in-person service providers constitute the largest share of the population in the industrialized economies. Service providers are attorneys, nurses, hair dressers, and others who provide the wide range of services we all use. The economic well-being of service providers is entirely local—it depends on the fate of their client groups, whether production workers or global *webmeisters.* This is a global class, but one with distinctly local interests.

Symbolic analysts rule the web. They share no important interests with the production workers who live near them and have only a little more in common with their service providers. Their keenest affinity is to the global class of symbolic analysts with whom they interact in global web dealings.

Symbolic analysts, in Reich's global vision, represent a higher level of evolution even than the transnational corporation (TNC). Although symbolic analysts might work for TNCs, they do not tie their careers to a particular organization. Instead they contract and recontract with one another in a sort of virtual business environment. The symbolic analysts float above constraints of the routine business enterprise in the same way that Rosecrance's virtual state floats above its territorial boundaries.

Robert Reich may really see globalization's web sifting people into these three classes, but the vision of the great global web is probably more of an attention-attracting device. It is true that within nations education and training are more important and less equal than ever. As a domestic dilemma, this stratification is old news. Attach the global web, however, and the problem becomes more important, along with the sensible but otherwise unexciting policy solutions that follow.

Hirst and Thompson state, for example, "This image is so powerful that it has mesmerized analysts and captured political imaginations."[14] I could go on in this way, citing examples of sensible people making exaggerated claims for globalization. Since I first recognized this problem, I have accumulated a nice collection of excessive statements—Global Dreams inspired by Global Visions—including even some of my own work. If these broad statements exaggerate globalization, then what is globalization, anyway?

GLOBALIZATION DEFINED

There is no standard definition of globalization or even a standard model of how it works.[15] It is one of those fuzzy but familiar concepts that, to paraphrase Walter Bagehot's analysis of "nation," we understand when we are not asked about but cannot very quickly explain or define.[16]

The most important definitional issue is how a global system of political economy differs from an international one. We have had a more or less international system throughout the modern era and significant international elements, at least in important regions, for hundreds of years before that. The Italian economy was international to the extent that international trade and finance were key elements of both the political and economic structures by the fourteenth century, if not before.

Ricardo Petrella has made some progress towards a working definition of globalization.[17] Petrella considers *internationalization* to be a process in which raw materials, goods, and services are exchanged across national borders. Goods move from where they are produced to where they are consumed. *Multinationalization* is a further development in which especially capital but also some labor moves across national borders as part of the production process. Multinationalization in Petrella's analysis seems closely related to the expansion of multinational corporations. It is a system in which businesses with a specific geographic base point engage in international production and distribution.

Petrella finds globalization too vast an idea to express in a single sentence, but he tries to capture the notion in a list of seven concepts:

1. Globalization of finances and capital ownership
2. Globalization of markets and strategies, in particular competition
3. Globalization of technology and linked R&D and knowledge
4. Globalization of modes of life and consumption patterns; globalization of culture
5. Globalization of regulatory capabilities and governance
6. Globalization as the political unification of the world
7. Globalization of perception and consciousness[18]

Petrella's list is useful in that it suggests the multidimensional nature of globalization, but it suffers the obvious flaw that it defines globalization in terms of itself. Globalization writ large derives from (items 1 to 3 above) and implies (items 4 to 7) many particular types of global arrangements.

Given that I have titled this section Globalization Defined, I think I should try to define this difficult term a bit more clearly. Globalization is the process of economic, political, and social change that occurs when all agents in a system have access to a common pool of resources. The idea of the common resource pool is meant to include especially markets for capital and goods and services, but it also encompasses science, technology, and cultural goods. These resources may be available in what I call local or national pools, but the process of globalization is driven by the existence of the common resource pool.

Access to global resource pools changes the economic, social, and political dynamics of the system. Efficiency increases, but the nature of competition changes. Economically, access to the global resource pool provides efficiency advantages over those situations in which these resources are unavailable or unevenly available. The nature of competition changes because individual firms benefit to the degree that they draw from the global resource pool without bearing all its costs. This may occur, for example, if firms are able to employ labor and natural resources in a region without making long-term investments that help pay for education, training, or environmental protection. In the global market, it is possible to use up the resources in one place and then to move somewhere else in the pool. An element of the "free rider" problem is created. Firms that can draw resources without paying all their costs experience a temporary competitive advantage; the profit incentive encourages them to "exploit" the common resource pool in ways they might not exploit a local pool, where benefits and costs are more clearly linked.

The efficiency element I have just noted accounts for the widespread enthusiasm toward globalization among economists, whereas the competition aspect explains in part both the anxiety of agents in precarious competitive niches and the marketing success of global business consultants like Kenichi Ohmae, who are able to sell their books and services to these agents.

Politically, the existence of the global resource pool seems to weaken state power simply because, by definition, the state cannot control access to it and so loses a set of policy levers it might have previously employed. The assumption is that the global resource pool strips the state of its power. Logically, the main limits to access must derive from power (the state) and costs (technology). State actions and technological advances are both logically and actually the critical forces in globalization, and of these two, state actions have been the more important. The main limits to common pool access in the twentieth century have been political, not technological.

Socially, the global resource pool provides access to a wider range of cultural goods and social arrangements. Although some authors of globalization argue that the pool swamps the individual social systems it encounters, the definition of globalization I present focuses on *access* to these resources, not forced *consumption* of them. How this access conditions behavior depends on human nature and cultural norms. In general, local cultural pools are not swamped by globalization, and access to Michael Jackson recordings is not a serious threat to real cultural values. I explain my views of political and social globalization in more detail later in this chapter.

Financial markets are the element of the global resource pool imagined and, I will argue, the element that comes closest to being truly global in today's world. A global capital pool would consist of a set of capital markets capable of channeling global savings to global borrowers and investors, pretty much regardless of where in the economic geography of the system these markets access the pool. If any resource pool can be truly global, it is the capital market.

I do think that global resource pools are getting bigger and deeper, even if they are not yet truly global common property. This kind of globalization is not, however, a particularly new phenomenon. What is surprising about the current condition is not that we have become so global so fast but that by the 1990s we have achieved a degree of globalization comparable only to what the world experienced one hundred years ago, during the Golden Age of Globalization.

THE GOLDEN AGE OF GLOBALIZATION

Some measurements of the degree of financial integration in the world economy indicate that at the beginning of the twentieth century the world was more interconnected than at any subsequent time (including the 1990s, despite the trillions of dollars of daily currency movements). These measurements examine the behavior of saving and investment levels. Investment and savings were coordinated on a global level, with the result that a surplus of investment in one area or state (that is, a balance of payments current account deficit) could be smoothly financed by the export of surplus savings from another area. Even in the highly integrated 1980s and 1990s, such transfers were much more difficult and raised many more political eyebrows than in the golden age that preceded the First World War.[19]

Finance is a global resource pool now, but it was also a global resource pool then. In fact, I suspect that it was a more efficient pool in the 1890s because more stable exchange rates made the consequences of international capital flows more certain and therefore more efficient. At the end of the twentieth century, on the other hand, exchange rates exhibit extravagant forms of instability that add significant elements of risk to international capital movements. In extreme cases, these instabilities break down the global financial market. This argument is presented in detail in Chapters 4 and 5.

Globalization's rise and fall is illustrated fairly clearly by trade flow data. Table 2.1, for example, presents data on the relative importance of exports for selected years since 1890. By this measure of different economies' "openness" (i.e., how much they dipped into the export market resource pool), it took until the 1990s for western developed nations (including the United States and Europe) to achieve the degree of globalization that existed in 1913. Data for Japan tell a different story: Japan is apparently less global in the 1990s than it was in the 1970s and very much less global than in earlier periods.

Note the peculiar data for Japan. Is Japan really less global now than in the past? Certainly this is not the impression that most consumers have as they wheel their shopping carts full of Sony and Panasonic products out to

Table 2.1   Exports of Merchandise as a Percentage of Gross Domestic Product

Year	Western Developed Countries	United States	Western Europe	Japan
1890	11.7	6.7	14.9	5.1
1913	12.9	6.4	18.3	12.6
1929	9.8	5.0	14.5	13.6
1938	6.2	3.7	7.1	13.0
1950	7.8	3.8	13.4	6.8
1970	10.2	4.0	17.4	9.7
1992	14.3	7.5	21.7	8.8

Source: Paul Bairoch, "Globalization Myths and Realities: One Century of External Trade and Foreign Investment," in States Against Markets: The Limits of Globalization, Robert Boyer and Daniel Drache, ed. (London: Routledge, 1996), Table 7.4, p. 179.

their Honda station wagons. The deep market penetration of Japanese goods is perhaps one of the reasons most cited by casual empiricists for the globalization phenomenon.

One way to explain these data, however, is to consider how many of those Japanese products are no longer produced entirely in Japan. They are produced in Thailand, Indonesia, and even in the United States. Many "Japanese" goods are no longer produced in Japan because Japan's businesses are drawing on global resource pools to streamline their production. This is an indication of globalization's force and not an argument against its spread. On the other hand, part of the trend is also caused by exchange market swings and protectionist political threats against Japanese products, which run counter to the globalization trend. It is hard to know, therefore, what to make of these data on Japan.

Data are dandy, but policy economists (like me) learn early in their training that one well-told story is more powerful than a hundred econometric studies or a thousand illustrative tables. Empirical evidence of the golden age of globalization, therefore, must be supplemented by a first-hand account. The following account is from *The Economic Consequences of the Peace* (1920) by John Maynard Keynes.

> What an extraordinary episode in the economic progress of man that age was which came to an end in August, 1914. . . . The inhabitant of London could order by telephone, sipping his morning tea in bed, the various products of the whole earth, in such quantity as he might see fit, and reasonably expect their early delivery upon his doorstep; he could at the same moment and by the same means adventure his wealth in the natural resources and new enterprises of any quarter of the world, and share, without exertion or even trouble, in their prospective fruits and advantages. . . . He could secure forthwith, if he wished it, cheap and comfortable means of transit to any country or climate without passport or other formality, could dispatch his servant to the neighboring office of a bank for such supply of the precious metals as might seem convenient, and could then proceed abroad to foreign quarters, without knowledge of their religion, language, or customs, bearing coined wealth upon his person, and would consider himself most greatly aggrieved and much surprised at the least interference. But, most important of all, he regarded this state of affairs as normal, certain, and permanent.[20]

When I read this passage to my students, they first think that this is an account of the present, or perhaps the near future. There is nothing particularly Victorian about this image of Keynes, propped up in bed with his newspapers and telephone, effortlessly shifting resources around the globe like a skilled expert in cyber-finance. Trade, finance, travel, all effortlessly, or nearly so. Yes? Well, to a degree. Certainly Keynes was different from most people, with special connections and abilities and a certain grand vision of things. Certainly most people in England in 1910 could not even have imagined the *global vision* that Keynes presents. Clearly the global resource pools existed prior to World War I. The breadth of their domain was probably not so great as today, but this is a question of degree, not existence.

Most people probably perceive technology as the driving force for globalization. This is natural, since global market expansion has taken place in the last part of the twentieth century alongside great advances in telecommunications and microelectronics. But Keynes's experiences force us to ask whether these two trends (globalization and telecommunications advances) are not perhaps less closely related than is commonly assumed. Just what are the technological requirements for globalization? Pre–World War I globalization seems to have been based on the building of the Suez and Panama Canals and improvements in ship design, which reduced transportation costs, and the laying of the transoceanic telegraph lines, which made faster global communications possible. The domestic phone line that connected Keynes's bedroom to the global financial network was a convenience that he surely appreciated, but it probably was not really necessary to the global market process. The bottom line is that the golden age of globalization was a pretty low-tech affair.

The notion that globalization is based on recent technological advances takes an even greater beating if we look back in history a few more years—to the era of the early Renaissance in Europe, for example.

> The idea of a world financial system is very old—at least as old as the fact of long-distance trade. . . . In the fourteenth century, merchants in the Mediterranean developed the negotiability of foreign bills of exchange. By the sixteenth century, bills drawn on Genoese or Seville or London houses could be traded, endorsed, and discounted hundreds of miles away. . . . The result of this period of innovation was the creation of what might be termed an integrated international capital market.[21]

The global financial networks constructed especially by the Italians—the Bardi, the Peruzzi, and the Medici among them—were very low tech in terms of hardware. No fax or telegraph existed, obviously, but there was a surprisingly efficient courier system that delivered commercial news (especially price information) and financial documents, especially letters of credit, to any of the major market cities in only a matter of weeks. Goods moved much more slowly than this, and apparently that was all the speed that was necessary.

The fact that globalization is not a new or novel phenomenon helps us better understand it, but the fact is that some of these previous experiments in globalization came to bad ends. The Bardi and Peruzzi disbanded in the 1340s when the European monarchs they were backing defaulted on their "sovereign" debt. The global infrastructure investment boom of the late nineteenth century, which is mirrored by the "emerging market" investment rush (and crash?) of today, also featured episodes of default, collapse, expropriation, and national-ization. Looking back at this history, I am nearly convinced that the present enthusiasm for globalization really is the triumph of hope over experience.[22]

Summing up, globalization is not as new or as technologically driven as most of us think. The telecommunications and microelectronics revolutions have made global resource pools more widely available to people *within* particular nations by reducing the transactions costs, but most of the information that needs to move *between* and *among* nations can flow comfortably through a few transoceanic telegraph lines. Technology makes international information available to more people within each nation, and this is the key change we are experiencing today. From a technical standpoint, if these "global" pools are broader or deeper now, it is due more to changes *within* nations than *between* them.

If technology has not been the limiting factor on globalization in the recent past, then what accounts for the dramatic decline in global economic structures after World War I and the extremely slow rebuilding of global pools after World War II? In simple terms, the answers are financial instability and state power.[23] Financial instability in the 1920s and 1930s made global capital markets an unstable foundation for a more fully integrated global economy. In reaction to this fact, the architects of Bretton Woods designed a system that was more stable but that used state power to separate and insulate national capital markets. Capital controls made global finance impossible even as GATT (General Agreement on Tariffs and Trade) pursued the goal of global free trade. Global finance, and with it globalization generally, was possible only when state power over these capital controls was finally loosened.

Before we explore the nature of actual globalization today, we need to deflate even more thoroughly the great globalization myths. That is, I want to address head-on the most powerful images of globalization: globalization as the End of Geography, the End of the Nation-State, and the End of Culture. Until we have these images out of the way, I don't think we will be able to see real globalization clearly, along with the forces driving it and the factors limiting it.

THE END OF GEOGRAPHY

The popular image of globalization was captured best in the subtitle of Robert O'Brien's influential little book, *Global Financial Integration: The End of Geography*.[24] Much of what is written about globalization is based on this idea. The notion that distance and geography are outdated concepts inspired *The Economist* to ask "Does it matter where you are?" and to provide this tongue-in-cheek reply:

> The cliché of the information age is that instantaneous global telecommunications, television and computer networks will soon overthrow the ancient

tyrannies of time and space. Companies will need no headquarters, workers will toil as effectively from home, car, or beach as they could in the offices that need no longer exist, and events half a world away will be seen, heard, and felt with the same immediacy as events across the street—if indeed streets still have any point.[25]

This powerful image, inspired as it is by "gee-whiz" technology, lies at the heart of Robert Reich's notion of the global web and Kenichi Ohmae's borderless world. In the real world, however, geography still counts. As *The Economist* noted,

> Save for transport costs, it should not matter where a tradable good or service is produced. . . . The reality is otherwise. Some economists have explained this by pointing to increasing returns to scale (in labour as well as capital markets), geographically uneven patterns of demand and transport costs. The main reason is that history counts: where you are depends very much on where you started from.
>
> The new technologies will overturn some of this, but not much. . . . The weight on mankind of time and space, of physical surroundings and history—in short of geography—is bigger than any earthbound technology is ever likely to lift.[26]

Real reality, in other words, is at least as important as virtual reality. Most serious studies of the actual organization of industrial competition end up concluding that it *does* matter where you are, or at least that businesses organize themselves *as if* location matters. A 1996 study undertaken by Morgan Stanley demonstrated the unsurprising persistence of place in international business management.[27] Morgan Stanley analysts throughout the world were asked to identify companies with a "sustainable competitive edge worldwide." Of the 238 "global" companies they found, more than half (125) were based in the United States. Both the small number of global businesses and the large geographic concentration in the United States come as a surprise to those who subscribe to the End of Geography line of reasoning.

Why so few global firms? The interpretation provided by Morgan Stanley is that a sustainable global competitive edge derives from either successful product differentiation or consistently lower-cost production techniques. Apparently the ability to sustain either of these advantages on a *global* scale is an unusual condition.

In the automobile industry, for example, the three firms that Morgan Stanley identified included one successful differentiator (BMW) and two successful cost controllers (Toyota and Honda). No U.S. firms? No. General Mills and Ford sell vehicles worldwide, but the basis is neither persistently cost advantage nor product difference. The Morgan Stanley analysis concluded that these firms are not global so much as what I call *multilocal*.

Multilocal enterprises operate in several different countries but establish a distinct local presence in each and compete in each based on local, not global, advantage. They are international businesses, in a technical sense, with international and sometimes global investment and production structures. However, they compete within local markets that are not fully integrated parts of a global pool. The characteristic of their market and its customers is local, and therefore their competitive strategies are also local, with limited external application.

One of the necessary conditions for the end of geography is that many markets are really global consumption pools, where nongeographically differentiated consumers collectively draw from a market for a universal commodity. Coca-Cola and McDonald's are the most commonly mentioned global products.

These global consumption pools are probably rarer than is commonly assumed. In part, this is because globalization has not produced the end of culture, an issue that I address later in this chapter. Generally, however, local differences in incomes, relative prices, distribution networks, history, language, religion, and the rest all still matter a great deal. Because most markets are more local than global, the spread of global firms is limited.

Since Coca-Cola and McDonald's are the quintessential global businesses in most people's minds, it is useful to consider the degree to which they really remain multilocal enterprises. The value of their global trademarks cannot be denied. (Only Coke is the Real Thing.) But a trip through the Coca-Cola museum in Atlanta reveals surprising degrees of product adaptation to local market conditions. The Coca-Cola product line—its flavorings, packaging, and distribution system—are all very much tailored to local tastes and conditions. Coca-Cola is a successful global brand precisely because it is so successfully multilocal.

In the same way, McDonald's product lines adapt to local market conditions to a surprising degree. The new stores in India, for example, make their hamburgers from lamb. The "global recipe" was changed to meet the requirements of the local Hindu market pool. Similarly, the McDonald's in Munich sells draft beer. In the past, McDonald's has relied on local suppliers, a high degree of local ownership, and its ability to adapt to local consumer demands, which is a multilocal strategic arrangement. In the future the corporation hopes to create a more integrated regional supply strategy, but marketing will remain multilocal. James Cantalupo, head of McDonald's International, has said that "You don't have 2,000 stores in Japan by being seen as an American company. Look, McDonald's serves meat, bread, and potatoes. They eat meat, bread, and potatoes in most of the world. It's how you package it and the experience that you offer that counts."[28]

Really global businesses need to develop global consumption pools for their products and to draw from a global supply pool for productive inputs.

The Morgan Stanley study, along with only casual analyses of Coca-Cola and McDonald's, suggests that these actual global business conditions are not so common as many people believe. When truly global conditions don't exist, which is apparently most of the time, then the local pools create local markets and firms are international or multilocal, but not global.[29] Geography matters.

In fact, one of the most influential recent books on business management in this age of globalization—Michael Porter's 1990 business bestseller *The Competitive Advantage of Nations*—takes as its premise that local pools are the key to global competitiveness. Porter distinguishes between several different types of international competition that are useful to us here. At one end of the spectrum is what he calls the *multidomestic enterprise,* in which competition within each nation is based mainly on domestic supply and demand characteristics, regardless of whether the firms have international ownership structures. This is like the multilocal concept I have proposed. At the other end is the *global industry,* in which events in one market affect competition in other markets through the shared impacts on the global production or consumption pool.[30] In either case, however, Porter's case study analysis indicates that local factors matter considerably. Porter writes that

> Companies, not nations, are on the front line of international competition. They must increasingly compete globally. Yet globalization does not supersede the importance of the nation. We have seen how its home nation plays a central role in a firm's international success. . . . A global strategy supplements and solidifies the competitive advantage created at the home base; it is the icing, not the cake.[31]

At the heart of Porter's analysis is his discussion of four factors that—separately and through their interaction—are associated with global success. A thorough discussion of these sources of competitive advantage goes beyond our purpose here, but I do want to note that each is decidedly a local pool property. Competitive advantage derives from the combination of desirable elements:

1. *Factor conditions.* The quality and dynamic nature of local labor and resource pools contribute to the success of the firms that draw from them. The success of local firms in turn stimulates the growth and development of factor pools, giving a further advantage to local businesses. This cycle gives local firms a competitive advantage over those in regions with shallower, less dynamic factor pool conditions. The global web is a thin structure. Most productive resources exist in local pools, not global webs.
2. *Demand conditions.* If the standards and expectations of buyers in the local consumption pool are high, local firms are forced to raise their own standards of quality and innovation. The assumption here is that

local markets set standards for producers, who then take these standards into the global market. If this is true, then it is an advantage to have demanding local customers and a competitive disadvantage to aim for some global least common denominator.

3. *Related and supporting industries.* The notion here is that every business depends for its success on the quality of other firms to whom it sells and from whom it purchases goods and services. These related and supporting industries form another resource pool that is more local than global.

4. *Firm strategy, structure, and rivalry.* Finally, the nature of competition among local firms conditions their success in global markets. Essentially, Porter argues that intense local rivalries, especially when combined with desirable factor, demand, and related industry conditions, force the rival firms to achieve levels of quality, efficiency, and innovation that produce global market success.[32]

Globalization is clearly not the end of geography. No amount of electronic technology can eliminate the importance of local factors to global businesses.

THE END OF THE NATION-STATE

Globalization is a zero-sum proposition, or that at least seems to be the dominant view of those who write about expanding global markets. More market means less state. Kenichi Ohmae typically takes an extreme view of this process and its implications. Follow the logic of the argument closely.

> In today's borderless economy, the workings of the "invisible hand" have a reach and strength beyond anything Adam Smith ever could have imagined. In Smith's day, economic activity took place on a landscape largely defined—and circumscribed—by the political borders of nation-states; Ireland with its wool, Portugal with its wines. Now by contrast, economic activity is what defines the landscape on which all other institutions, including political institutions, must operate. Business and government are just beginning to live with the consequences.[33]

Here we begin with the extreme view that economics is all that matters. Economic activity defines the (borderless) landscape. *All* other institutions (all!) must deal with the consequences: "Most visibly, the nation-state itself—that artifact of the eighteenth and nineteenth centuries, has begun to crumble, battered by a pent-up storm of political resentment, ethnic prejudice, tribal hatred, and religious animosity."[34] Interesting. Now suddenly it is cultural factors that really matter. Global markets make local cultural resource pools more important. The state is attacked from above and below by these two forces. The argument seems reasonable: Global markets weaken unified states and thereby become more prone to attack by the traditional local forces of division. This fact, if it is a fact, appears to make the state more important, not less, but let us continue.

> Since nation-states were created to meet the needs of a much earlier histori-cal period, they do not have the will, the incentive, the credibility, the tools, or the political base to play an effective role in the borderless economy of to-day. By heritage and by experience, nation-states are comfortable with the market's invisible hand only when they can control and regulate it. . . . The bottom line is that they have become unnatural—even dysfunctional—as ac-tors in a global economy because they are incapable of putting global logic first in their decisions.[35]

This *is* interesting. Globalization increases the need for states to deal with local problems, which were in fact the sorts of problems that they were designed to deal with. But they cannot deal with local problems because they are unwilling to put global logic ahead of local logic. They are dysfunctional and unnatural because they insist on using local logic to deal with local prob-lems. Try to follow this line of reasoning:

> Nation-states are no longer meaningful units in which to think about eco-nomic activity. In a borderless world, they combine things at the wrong level of aggregation. . . . In a borderless economy, the units that do make sense are what I call region state . . . the natural economic zones. They may or may not fall within the boundaries of a particular nation. If they do, it is an accident of history. In practical terms, it does not really matter.[36]

So here is Ohmae's vision of the nation-state. It is meaningful only if its boundaries overlap the regional resource pools that he assumes to exist. Na-tion-states do not matter, in practical terms, except to the extent that their bor-ders are aligned with economically significant landmarks.

I find it hard to take this argument seriously. The obvious reason, from what I have quoted and written above, is that it is so badly confused and inter-nally inconsistent. The notions of states, markets, regions, and globalization seem to expand and contract to fit the needs of the rhetorical devices at hand and the metaphors that come to mind. It is hard to have much faith in a view-point that is argued in this way. This notion of globalization goes down smooth as silk and even tastes yummy, but you don't want to look closely at the nutritional analysis—these are empty calories.

There is also a practical reason for my skepticism. On December 5, 1996, U.S. Federal Reserve chairman Alan Greenspan commented during an after-dinner speech that financial markets seemed to be driven by an "irrational ex-uberance" that could not indefinitely sustain the then high stock values. The following day global stock markets lost billions, perhaps trillions of dollars in value as investors (in a fit of irrational exuberance?) dumped stocks. They feared that Greenspan's remark was a signal that he might be thinking of higher interest rates sometime in the future and wanted to prepare the markets for a soft landing.

Global markets dictate; national institutions accommodate. That's the core of the End of the Nation-State literature. Someone should tell Greenspan about this. Otherwise he might mistakenly conclude that governments and central banks still have real power over market forces.

Lowell Bryan and Diana Farrell are both more exuberant and yet more reasonable than Kenichi Ohmae in their global business book *Market Unbound: Unleashing Global Capitalism*. Their basic argument is much the same as Ohmae's, although their focus is more clearly on financial globalization rather than on global markets generally.

> We are moving toward a world where the capital markets constrain what government can do—not the other way around. . . .
> The engine behind this change is the growing power of the global capital market. Its power is coming from its overwhelming and increased scale and ability to integrate and act as a single market. Individual national financial markets are losing their separate identities as they merge into a single, overpowering marketplace. . . .
> This revolution will be sufficiently powerful to change the traditional roles of governments. The world will move from closer nationally controlled systems toward an open, global system under no one's control. At the center of this open system, a global capital market will motivate businesses to become more productive and motivate governments to dismantle restrictive regulation, cut deficits, and pursue sound monetary policy. . . .
> National governments have long been the most powerful agents on the planet and are used to exercising control over most aspects of their local economy. . . . However, the ability of a single national government to control its own financial system is being undermined by the growing power of the global capital market.[37]

Bryant and Lowell take this basic argument to a pair of extremes, and their metaphors get way ahead of them: "Like Prometheus, the global capital market is unbound. The release has taken nearly 50 years, but the global capital market has just about thrown off its bonds."[38]

The death of the nation-state is at least as oversold as is the dominance of a fully integrated global capital market. It is amazing that people seriously think the nation-state is doomed by the slow advance of globalization. To think this, it seems to me, one must be blind both to the current world, where national power persists and prevails, and to history, where the forces of globalization and nation building often have coincided.

The nation-state is a badly strained institution today, but globalization may be one of its lesser problems.[39] Population dynamics both within and among nations probably impose more constraints on national policy than does globalization. The bases for many political and economic problems that the nation-state faces today lie in birth rates, death rates, life spans, population age and momentum, and relevant differences among nations in these factors. These demographic factors, especially when combined with vastly differing economic growth rates, put all sorts of stresses and strains on the framework of national policy. Compared to these *real* social, political, economic, and cultural forces, the constraints imposed by global money markets are small change.

This doesn't mean that I think globalization does not change things for nation-states. Many regulatory aspects of national policy are certainly complicated by the expansion of global resource pools and the industries that draw from them. The state's role in this changing environment is certainly changed but is not especially lessened.

Ethan B. Kapstein's recent study of this problem, *Governing the Global Economy: International Finance and the State,* takes an especially level-headed view of the situation. Kapstein concludes that financial globalization has weakened domestic regulatory powers in three ways:[40]

1. The existence of global financial markets increases the cost of domestic stabilization policies that must attempt to offset market pressures that are transmitted through global capital and foreign exchange markets. Government's ability to regulate macroeconomic forces is reduced because the costs of regulation are increased.
2. Global financial markets increase the risk of domestic crises that are caused by the international transmission of financial problems. External sources of instability impose internal costs.
3. Increased competition exists among nation-states for global resource pools, just as greater competition exists among the global businesses themselves. This competition imposes a cost on nations that choose to deviate from global regulatory standards or that adopt more stringent regulations on commerce or finance.

Kapstein is right that all three of these factors make it more costly and difficult for nation-states to do their mainly local jobs in an increasingly global world. External forces like these do divert resources from internal priorities. But I think Kapstein understands that this makes states more important than before, not irrelevant, as some authors suggest. Weak states, or states that merely ride global waves up and down, would merely transmit global instability and crisis to local and national citizens. Strong states are needed to dampen the effect of global instability on local resource pools and to shape global forces to accommodate local needs.

Leon Grunberg has made this point in another way. In a world where global businesses are increasingly demanding of local governments and increasingly likely to attempt to exploit local resource pools, state power is even more important, especially in less developed countries. States can provide public goods and help create more competitive local factor pools, for example, and they can also serve as more effective bargaining agents for local resource owners. Increased market power creates a need for increased state power, Grunberg argues.[41]

I think the argument that strong states are needed to deal with global instability is especially important and underappreciated—at least it was until the 1997 Asian financial crisis. The state will persist because the need for the state has grown, but also because the local resource pools and socioeconomic problems on which states are based are undiminished. But what will become of culture?

THE END OF CULTURE

If you have watched the television show *Star Trek: The Next Generation*, you have probably encountered a most peculiar alien race: the Borg. The Borg are a *collective* race. They do not exist as separate individuals, except in the trivial sense that they live in separate physical bodies. They are like networked computers—individual keyboards and screens linked to a common processor and memory. Once assimilated into the Borg collective, individuals are hard-wired into a collective intelligence. They lose their ability to think or act as individuals. The only pronouns they are capable of using are plural forms: *I think* becomes *we think,* and so forth. On *Star Trek*, the Borg is (are?) the ultimate irresistible foe. "Resistance is futile," they say, "you *will* be assimilated."

The Borg collective civilization is a metaphor for the global financial markets and their impact on local cultures. Is "Borg" some sort of anagram for the global market? I say this because perhaps the most durable notion about globalization is that it assimilates local cultures and destroys them. Resistance is futile; you *will* consume Coca-Cola, eat Big Macs, watch junk television, adopt western dress and customs, listen to pop music, and generally cast off all the characteristics that differentiate societies, civilizations, and religions. Globalization is Borgization. In the end, all parts of the globe will be indistinguishable, with the same people in the same clothes, driving the same cars, listening to the same music, eating the same food. There will be just one culture: the materialist culture of the United States. *That* is the *end* of culture.

Casual empiricism confirms every bit of the Borgization hypothesis. If you want to see it, you have only to look around for signs of the End of Culture. The evidence appears mainly in the form of widespread consumption of western-type goods and services, especially brand-name items, and increasing urbanization, which seems to leave a western cultural stamp on whatever society experiences it.

Now the problem here is that you can see the End of Culture if you look for it, but you can also see different and even opposing trends, if that's what you are looking for. Cultural globalization is even harder to measure than economic or financial globalization. The evidence is all anecdotal, which means that it persuades without convincing. You can think what you want to think and see what you want to see. In other words, the End of Culture is as serious a problem as you want it to be. I think that the End of Culture is a more serious matter than the End of the Nation-State, but I do not think it is as serious a problem as is preached by the prophets of hyperglobalization.

Culture is a strong force in human societies. Whereas some people see global capitalism destroying every last shred of local culture, however, I see a world in which the persistence of local differences actually limits the expansion of multinational business on nearly every front. International business texts are filled with examples of global businesses that fail in specific markets because they cannot overcome even the most trivial cultural barriers. Language, for example, is so obvious a barrier to globalization that we all assume that smart managers successfully overcome it. But they don't.

A story of a subtle cultural business barrier is currently being passed around the Internet. Like many Internet items, it may be true or it may be urban legend. The story goes that a Japanese computer firm wanted to try to break into the U.S. market with a particular product. This firm wanted to make the product user friendly and also differentiate it from other similar items. With this in mind, they licensed the rights to Woody Woodpecker, the popular cartoon character, to use as an on-screen image. Users were instructed to "point your pecker . . ." at this or that icon to make the program work. Only at the last minute did the company learn of the slang definition of "pecker" in the United States. True or not, this story illustrates the same point documented by hundreds of business school case studies: that local language, culture, and institutions represent a significant but not impregnable barrier to foreign businesses.

Although I do not think that globalization is the End of Culture, I am not so naïve as to believe that the processes associated with globalization leave local cultures completely intact. Societies that become more open economically are also necessarily exposed to foreign social, cultural, and political influences. Some of these are presented passively, whereas others are actively sold through the various advertising media. People everywhere seem to be attracted to the image of a more sophisticated foreign culture and seek to emulate it in superficial ways. In Malaysia this may mean wearing NBA–logo clothing and eating Kentucky Fried Chicken. In Seattle it means drinking espresso and wearing Italian shoes. Neither of these attempts to replicate another culture and achieve sophistication is completely successful.

Not all the cultural implications of the process of globalization are superficial, however. Globalization is associated with the expanding sphere of the market, and the culture of the market is "rationalistic and anti-heroic," to use

Schumpeter's phrase.[42] Science replaces magic. Profits and losses replace heroes and villains. This is no small thing. It is quite the opposite, in fact, not in the least because cultural diversity is sacrificed at the margin: There are more varieties of magic than there are varieties of science. But rationalistic beliefs are not what seem to worry people who write about this issue. They are more concerned about Coca-Cola, Nike, and McDonald's and the consumption of nonindigenous cultural goods and services generally. Here is my take on this aspect of cultural globalization.

Globalization is associated with changing income distributions, especially in less-developed countries. The processes that we associate with globalization in less-developed countries tend to increase the size of the urban middle class. This growing class has *vulgar* tastes; in the original sense of that word, they are common, uneducated, unrefined. They are the sort of tastes you see in reruns of *Married with Children*. What we find offensive about cultural globalization is that the dominant tastes are vulgar middle class tastes, not quaint traditional tastes or refined elite tastes. We associate these middle class tastes with the United States because the United States is Number One in the production and consumption of vulgar goods. However, the fact that these tastes rise up and demand attention as the urban middle class expands does not mean that globalization *causes* the particular tastes we observe.[43] The United States may produce a lot of vulgar consumer goods and services, but it is simply wrong to think that, through globalization, it has caused the rise of this sort of culture everywhere.

Although global business does in some ways transform local societies as I have just described, it is much too soon to write off local culture. Culture is an effective counterforce to the process of globalization. Local culture is so strong that foreign businesses are forced to adapt and change their practices to accommodate local language, customs, and beliefs. *The Economist* has noted that

> Would-be multicultural multinationals are struggling to solve a dilemma that has bedeviled their predecessors: the clash between global standardisation and local roots. The first offers huge advantages of both scale and speed. . . . But local knowledge can help Davids slay Goliaths; and ignorance can fell Goliaths even if there are no Davids around. . . .
>
> In the end, running a company in a borderless world is about trying to resolve a number of apparent contradictions. Firms have to be responsive to national needs, yet seek to exploit knowhow on a worldwide basis, while, all the time, striving to produce and distribute goods globally as efficiently as possible. Many companies manage to achieve one, even two of these objectives. It is hard to think of any company that has yet managed to balance all three simultaneously.[44]

The challenges of being a multicultural multinational are significant. This is probably one of the most important reasons why the Morgan Stanley survey found so few truly globally competitive firms.

If the challenges are so significant, then why is it so easy to see signs of globalization's impact on culture at every turn in every part of the world? One answer is that it is easy to see global culture if you do not look too deep or too hard. *Coca-Colaization* and *Disneyfication* are pretty shallow concepts and pretty modest threats to real cultural heritage and real religious tradition, for example.

Samuel P. Huntington has argued in a series of *Foreign Affairs* articles and a book, *The Clash of Civilizations and the Remaking of World Order,* that what we think of as the End of Culture is really a different dynamic: modernization.

> Advocates of the Coca-Colaization thesis identify culture with the consumption of material goods. The heart of a culture, however, involves language, religion, values, traditions, and customs. Drinking Coca-Cola does not make Russians think like Americans more than eating sushi makes Americans think like Japanese. Throughout human history fads and material goods have spread from one society to another without significantly altering the basic culture of the recipient society.[45]

Huntington argues that there is a difference between global culture (which is often equated with *westernization*) and the broader and fundamentally different forces of modernization. Modernization, which includes especially the process of urbanization, is driven by different forces, including simple population growth. Modernization produces a structural transformation of society, to be sure, but it would do this whether globalization was present or not:

> Modern societies have much in common, but they do not necessarily merge into homogeneity. The argument that they do rests on the assumption that modern society must approximate a single type, the Western type; that modern civilization is Western civilization, and Western civilization is modern civilization. This, however is a false identification.[46]

In fact, Huntington argues, modernization actually makes the difference in local cultural pools far more important because it is the understanding of their *differences* rather than their similarities that is most important.

Barrie Axford has also stressed the durable nature of local cultural resource pools in his complex and interesting book, *The Global System: Economics, Politics, and Culture.* Fundamentally, Axford argues, it is important to appreciate the difference between material goods and cultural beliefs. Perhaps some of us have become so materialistic, or think that society has so evolved, that we fail to appreciate this important difference. But, Axford notes,

> The main objection to the idea of global culture is that spatialized communities are the 'containers' of real culture, of meaning and identity, not the 'vir-

tual' communities created by forms of electronic communication, and the networks built around flow of goods and services. . . . It is wise to be cautious . . . since it would be very easy to slip into the assumption that, because global flows constrain local production and consumption, they must also modify local cultures and identities.[47]

If globalization is really the End of Culture, if Coca-Cola equals the end of meaning and identity, then culture is not much of a loss in my view.

BORDERS IN THE BORDERLESS WORLD

This chapter has looked at extreme visions of globalization and found them to be inflated and oversold. It can be argued that in doing this I have set up an especially weak straw man in the form of hyperglobalization just so that I could knock him down. Aren't there more sophisticated visions of globalization and more considered arguments concerning globalization's effect on the state and on culture? Yes, of course, and I will come back to these arguments later. But sophisticated scholarly notions about globalization are not what concern me in this book. Public debate is framed by the ideas of hyperglobalization that I have discussed in this chapter. Before we can discuss what actual globalization looks like, we must understand that the image of hyperglobalization is wrong.

At different points in this chapter, I have briefly touched on two ideas that will be addressed in much more depth later in this book. One reason why the processes of economic, political, and cultural globalization are so incomplete is that they must be built on the foundation of financial globalization, and financial instability makes that foundation inherently unstable. Financial instability limits globalization. This issue is explored in Chapters 4 and 5.

Second, globalization remains an important issue, despite its built-in limits, because the globalization myth serves certain political and intellectual interests. I think that Hirst and Grahame got it right when they titled the first chapter of their book "Globalization—A Necessary Myth?" Some interests absolutely depend on globalization to be an unchallenged concept, an accepted force. I'll outline these arguments in Chapters 6 and 7.

Before going on to these issues, however, I think we should get a better idea of what actual globalization is, so that we can better appreciate how it differs from global dreams. I do this in the next chapter, through an analysis of the theory of multinational corporations and short case studies of four representative "global" firms.

I want to close this chapter with a story that I think illustrates vividly the myth of the borderless world. Kenichi Ohmae concludes his book *The Borderless World* with an account that reveals the fundamental poverty of the "end of geography" argument.[48] It seems that for many years the Ohmae family has spent their summer vacation in a home on Vancouver Island, Canada, which is only a few hours away via car and ferry from my home in Tacoma, Washington. It is a great place; I love it. Ohmae explains that he had heard stories from many people about a beautiful place called Campbell River located further north on the island, on the inside passage. It is a good place to fish for salmon, observe whale pods, or just watch the eagles soar. Year after year the Ohmae family was tempted by tales of Campbell River's natural beauty, but they were always held back by uncertainty. How long would it take to get there—one day or two or three? Were the roads good? Would they enjoy the drive? Would they like it once they got there? All the uncertainties of real life and its solid geometry kept them frozen in the island's main town of Victoria, which admittedly is not a bad place to be stranded.

One year they finally resolved to go up to Campbell River, no matter how long it might take and what hardships they might have to endure along the way. The trip from Victoria to Campbell River takes only a few hours to drive, over good roads, through beautiful scenery. The Ohmae family had a wonderful leisurely drive, saw all the sights, had time to catch a salmon, and were back home in Victoria by dinnertime the next day.

The conclusion that Ohmae draws from this story is that living in a borderless world requires a change in mindset. You've got to confront your anxieties and break out of old patterns of doing things. When you try to live beyond the old borders, you will experience the same pleasure and freedom as his family did when they finally drove off for Campbell River. Ohmae uses the story to illustrate how easy it is to adopt global vision.

For me, Ohmae's story has a different moral. Even a world traveler and global business consultant is still tied to the land, to the security of familiar territory, and is conditioned by the uncertainty of what lies around the next bend. Geography still counts; it really is a barrier. The gap between the borderless virtual world of our imaginations and the border-defined world of our daily experience has shrunk, but not so much as you might think.

NOTES

1. Ethan B. Kapstein, *Governing the Global Economy: International Finance and the State* (Cambridge, MA: Harvard University Press, 1994), p. 1.

2. Lester Thurow, *The Future of Capitalism: How Today's Economic Forces Shape Tomorrow's World* (New York: William Morrow, 1996), p. 114.

3. Ibid., p. 127.

4. Ibid., p. 138.

5. Ibid., p. 133.

6. Chapters 6 and 7 explore the uses of hyperglobalization for economists and policymakers.

7. Kenichi Ohmae, *The Borderless World: Power and Strategy in the Interlinked Economy* (New York: HarperPerennial, 1990), p. 18.

8. Ibid., pp. 21–22.

9. Paul Kennedy, *Preparing for the Twenty-First Century* (New York: Random House, 1993), p. 55.

10. Richard Rosecrance, "The Rise of the Virtual State," *Foreign Affairs* 75:4 (July/August 1996), p. 45.

11. Ibid., p. 46.

12. Ibid., p. 54.

13. Reich was Secretary of Labor in President Bill Clinton's first administration.

14. Paul Hirst and Grahame Thompson, *Globalization in Question* (Cambridge, UK: Polity Press, 1996), p. 1.

15. Ibid., p. 2.

16. See David N. Balaam and Michael Veseth (editors), *Introduction to International Political Economy* (Upper Saddle River, NJ: Prentice Hall, 1996), p. 20.

17. Ricardo Petrella, "Globalization and Internationalization: The Dynamics of the Emerging World Order," in *States Against Markets: The Limits of Globalization,* ed. Robert Boyer and Daniel Drache (London: Routledge: 1996), pp. 62–83.

18. See ibid., Table 2.1, p. 66.

19. Harold James, *International Monetary Cooperation Since Bretton Woods* (New York: Oxford University Press, 1996), p. 12.

20. John Maynard Keynes, *The Economic Consequences of the Peace* (New York: Penguin, 1988), pp. 10–12.

21. James, *International Monetary Cooperation,* pp. 12–13.

22. But, given how little history many people study, it might just be the triumph of ignorance over experience.

23. Financial instability and state power are offered here only as simple, tentative approaches to the answer to this large question. A fuller analysis goes beyond the boundaries of the present study.

24. Richard O'Brien, *Global Financial Integration: The End of Geography* (New York: Council on Foreign Relations, 1992).

25. "Does It Matter Where You Are?" *The Economist* (July 30, 1994), p. 13.

26. Ibid., pp. 13–14.

27. Tony Jackson, "Global Competitiveness Observed from an Unfamiliar Angle," *Financial Times,* November 21, 1996, p. 18.

28. Quoted by Thomas Friedman, "Big Mac II," *New York Times,* December 11, 1996, p. 23.

29. Thomas Friedman has coined the term *glocal* for the combination of global + local. We can only hope it is not widely adopted.

30. Michael Porter, *The Competitive Advantage of Nations* (New York: The Free Press, 1990), p. 53.

31. Ibid., p. 57.

32. Ibid., p. 71.

33. Kenichi Ohmae, "Putting Global Logic First," in *The Evolving Global Economy: Making Sense of the New World Order,* ed. K. Ohmae (Cambridge, MA: Harvard Business Review, 1995), p. 129.

34. Ibid., p. 129.

35. Ibid., p. 131.

36. Ibid., p.132.

37. Lowell Bryan and Diana Farrell, *Market Unbound: Unleashing Global Capitalism,* (New York: John Wiley, 1996), pp. 1–8.

38. Ibid., p. 17.

39. Aurora Ferrari reminded me of this fact.

40. Kapstein, *Governing the Global Economy,* pp. 6-7.

41. Leon Grunberg, "The Changing IPE of Multinational Corporations," in *Introduction to International Political Economy,* ed. Balaam and Veseth, pp. 352–354.

42. Joseph A. Schumpeter, *Capitalism, Socialism, and Democracy* (New York: Harper & Brothers, 1942), p. 127. Schumpeter's chapter, "The Civilization of Capitalism," is necessary reading for anyone who wants to understand how globalization affects social values.

43. As the urban middle class grew during the Italian renaissance, tastes changed in just this way, and what we might call "western" tastes appeared. These tastes developed into the consumer culture we associate with globalization today. An interesting analysis of the rise of consumer culture in the Italian renaissance is found in Richard Goldthwaite's *Wealth and the Demand for Art in Italy, 1300–1600.*

44. "The Discreet Charm of the Multicultural Multinational," *The Economist* (July 30, 1994), pp. 57–58.

45. Samuel P. Huntington, "The West: Unique, Not Universal," *Foreign Affairs* 75:6 (November/December 1996), pp. 28–29.

46. Ibid., p. 30.

47. Barrie Axford, *The Global System: Economics, Politics, and Culture* (New York: St. Martin's Press, 1995), p. 164.

48. The story is told in the Epilogue to Ohmae, *The Borderless World,* pp. 213–214.

3

The Center of the Universe

Throughout history, gold was the currency that drove business, even though it was bulky and hard to distribute. But today, the currency that matters is information. That's why we've designed our products to distribute information quickly and to make it accessible to the broadest group of people. And why the Internet—which can literally transfer information around the planet in seconds—makes it possible to expand that access even more.

—Microsoft Corporation[1]

The cover of Bill Gates's bestselling 1995 book, *The Road Ahead*, shows him standing alone on a country road.[2] The road begins at Gates's feet and runs arrow-straight to the horizon—and beyond for all we know. *The Road Ahead* communicates Bill Gates's vision of the future, and most people see in the cover photo what they expect to find in the book: that the microcomputing and communications revolutions have joined to form that smooth white line that runs down the center of the information superhighway. It starts at your keyboard and leads away infinitely, in all directions at once. Wherever you are, you are in touch. You stand (or sit, probably, since the computer is involved) at the center of the universe.

This is not the first time that we can imagine someone standing at the center of the universe, doing business around the globe with confidence and ease. As mentioned earlier, John Maynard Keynes wrote of a similar time in Europe before World War I. Sitting in bed reading newspapers, connected to global markets by telephone and telegraph, Keynes felt himself a master of the universe, buying and selling without regard to time and place.

Perhaps the very first businessmen to sit at the center of the universe were the Italian merchants of the middle ages, the heads of the international businesses that produced what economic historians call the *commercial revolution of the twelfth century*. Like Gates and Keynes, these global traders benefited from advanced technology. Their global reach, however, was not based on electrical (Keynes) or electronic (Gates) innovations. Their vast empires were connected by an intellectual network called *commercial arithmetic,* which was imported along with spice and silks in trade with the Middle East. We call it double-entry accounting. Before the commercial revolution, businessmen conceived of each individual transaction as a separate event, evaluated on its own. Double-entry accounting, however, provided a way of thinking about business that linked transactions together and allowed the businessman to conceive of a global network.[3]

It is easy to picture Bill Gates at the center of the universe, connected by a network that extends infinitely in all directions, the commercial heir to a legacy that runs arrow straight from Lorenzo de Medici to John Maynard Keynes to Bill Gates, and off to an infinite future. Thus we imagine the global business today.

The reality is much different, or at least Bill Gates seems to think so. While business writers and politicians imagine him at the center of the universe, he seems to see himself and his global business empire in a vastly different way.

If you look for a discussion of global business strategy in *The Road Ahead,* you will be disappointed. Globalization does not even appear in the index, although *GLOBE* (an acronym for a global learning project) and *global positioning system* do. For Bill Gates, the road ahead is pretty much a continuation of the road behind, which is really the biggest surprise in the book.[4]

The image of the future that Gates outlines in *The Road Ahead* is basically a picture of the world of the past but with reduced transactions costs. The road ahead, in other words, is pretty much the same as the road behind, but with the curves and bumps removed. Information (that's the thing he focuses on here) moves at a lower cost, which means that more people have access to it and are more efficiently able to sift through its content to find what is important. The information revolution allows business to do what it has always done, but more efficiently.

Does this make business big and global? Well, no. In fact, Gates argues that small and local businesses are better able to carve out niches because the lower transaction costs make them more efficient. One size does not fit all. Micromarkets appear.

What Gates suggests is that instead of global business, the horizon holds a world that is multilocal. Businesses have the ability (and consumers the information) to focus markets at a very small level. Basically, if global business is a mainframe, then *The Road Ahead* is the notebook personal computer or, better, the personal digital assistant.

In short, Bill Gates's vision of global business seems to have little in common with the general conception, especially the hyperglobal visions I criticized in the last chapter. This is truly unexpected, not only because most people think that Gates's business empire, the Microsoft Corporation, is a perfect example of globalization at work but also because Microsoft software lies at the heart of the technology that people imagine is driving the globalization process. You would think that Bill Gates would actively sell the idea of globalization because he appears to have a commercial interest in its popularity. Not so. Why?

I propose that we reject quickly the idea that Bill Gates might be naïve and unaware of his own economic interests in economic globalization. If Gates is not wrong, then perhaps the common image of the global business is not right—or not entirely right. This chapter intends to raise doubts about the extent of economic globalization and expose some contradictions in the globalization process through a comparison of globalization in theory with case studies of actual globalization drawn from among the most global firms in my home region, the Pacific Northwest of the United States: Nike, Boeing, the Frank Russell Company, and of course Microsoft.

THE GLOBAL BUSINESS IN THEORY AND IN PRACTICE

What would a truly global firm look like? Like so many things, true globalization is easier to recognize than to define. I propose that we think of the truly globalized firm as being a business that exhibits both demand side and supply-side globalization.

Demand-side globalization is the idea that a firm sells its product in a global consumption pool. A global business exists to satisfy a global demand for identical, or at least highly similar, goods and services. There is a lot of superficial evidence that these global markets exist. I am writing this chapter in Bologna, Italy, which is about as far away from my home in Tacoma, Washington, as you can get. Yet when I walk down the block to the Piazza Maggiore, I can see McDonald's hamburger signs, Nike shirts and caps, and assorted Chicago Bulls paraphernalia. Businessmen pause beside the Neptune fountain and yell into their cell phones, just as they do at home. When we think of global businesses, we imagine an enterprise scaled to service a global market.

Supply-side globalization is the idea that a firm's production function draws resources from global pools. Its goods and services are made wherever production is most efficient, drawing raw materials, labor, technology, and creative ideas from around the globe and shifting from source to source as competitive conditions apply. The output of the global business is the result of a global division of labor.

I propose that globalization means that a business firm both produces and sells in global pools—that it exhibits both demand-side and supply-side globalization. There is a qualitative difference between a global firm, as defined here, and a firm that produces in one place and sells everywhere (think Perrier) or has international production processes but essentially sells in distinct local markets (with distinct local character and competition). The former type of firm is multilocal and the latter is transnational. These are important and growing types of business arrangements, but they are not *global* in a meaningful sense. They are too tied to local resource pools of one kind or another.

A global firm, as defined here, is truly a creature of the markets. It floats in a virtual reality defined by its access to demand-side and supply-side resource pools—and is not encumbered by local attachments, loyalties, or obligations.[5] When globalization is sold, as either threat or opportunity, this is the kind of global firm that is conjured up.

This definition of a globalized business is not easy to satisfy. There are not many truly global firms, but some do exist. If any business is global in this sense, it is the Nike Corporation.

NIKE AND THE GLOBAL SWOOSH

Nike is the quintessential global firm. If the future is true globalization, then the future is Nike. It is worth taking a closer look at Nike for two reasons: to see what actual globalization looks like and to consider, perhaps, how rare a creature a truly global firm really is.

"Nike Corporation was born a globalized company," according to Miguel Korzeniewicz, who has studied the company with the global swoosh as an example of a "global commodity chain."[6] Nike's famous roots are, of course, very local. Most readers of this book are probably already familiar with the legend of college runner Philip Knight (now 35 percent owner of Nike) and his University of Oregon track coach, Bill Bowerman. Bowerman's invention of the running shoe "waffle" sole, which he made by putting rubber in a kitchen waffle iron, is the designated source of Nike's success, but Knight's marketing skills are probably more important overall. The first Nike shoes were made in Japan, and over the years more than 99 percent of Nike shoes have been imported through a global commodity chain that links Nike's mainly core markets with its contract producers in the semiperiphery (e.g., South Korea) and the periphery (e.g., China and Indonesia).

Throughout its history, Nike has consistently combined technical innovation and aggressive marketing. Its business still includes running shoes but now includes a wide range of other products in both footwear and sports-related markets. I have not yet seen a Nike perfume or cologne, but it would not surprise me if one exists. Nike's trademark is that well known.

Nike is everywhere. Here in Bologna, for example, both teenagers and adults wear Nike clothes and baseball caps as items of fashion. The older items say "Nike" in big letters; the newer stuff simply has the "swoosh," the exclusive trademark. The shoes for some reason are not as visible, perhaps an indication that Italian style persists. The African street merchants on Via Independenza hawk cheap but authentic-looking swooshed baseball caps from which Nike will surely never receive a license fee.

Nike is truly global by my definition because it swims in both pools. It has helped create a global consumption pool for its sports-related products, which it makes by drawing resources from the global production pool. It works hard at making both production and consumption global, reaps enormous profits, and takes a good deal of criticism in the process.

Nike does not have many employees (only about 14,000 in 1995) for a corporation with almost $5 billion in sales (1995) and a market value of nearly $10 billion (1995). The key to this high productivity is that Nike's core business employees do not make shoes: Their job is to make customers. To do this, they make images and icons. Shoes, I think, are almost an afterthought. Nike invests heavily in creating demand for its products by building its stable of celebrity endorsers and making the swoosh a symbol of their lifestyles. The well-publicized multimillion dollar signing of golf prodigy Tiger Woods in 1996 was only the most recent indication that Nike aims to associate the swoosh with success and celebrity in the global market.

Nike's success at creating a global trademark makes it vulnerable to charges of cultural imperialism by people who argue that globalization is the end of culture. But I am unconvinced that my Italian students experience any profound cultural transformation when they put on a swoosh cap or root for the local soccer team that wears swooshed shoes and shirts. It is a fact, however, that wherever I go I see swooshes sprouting on sports team uniforms and footwear. Nike competes in all the sports and all the markets and faces considerable specific competition in each, although it is clearly the leader in the industrial sector overall. A global firm requires much attention to detail and local market conditions, but the creation and cultivation of global superstars like Michael Jordan is part of the game, too.

Nike's global marketing strategy is postmodern, according to Miguel Korzeniewicz. He perceives a shift from the consumption of material goods to the consumption of symbols and signs. "In a sense, Nike represents an archetype of a firm selling to emerging postmodern consumer markets that rest on segmented, specialized, and dynamic features."[7] "Image is Everything," as the Nike ads themselves boldly assert. What Nike produces—where and how—depends most on the image Nike wants to sell—and the design, advertising, and marketing considerations that derive from that image.[8]

If we associate the spread of swooshes with the cultural effects of globalization, then we also associate the production of swooshed products with the globalized production's economic effects. Most Nike shoes and other products are made in Asia. Nike contracts with local firms to produce its products. It bargains effectively with local businesses and governments and has moved production (from South Korea to China and Indonesia, for example) when cost and labor market conditions have changed.

Nike does not own the factories that make its shoes. It typically forms partnerships with local firms or with Korean or Taiwanese investors. Nike pays wages that are usually high by local standards. In Indonesia, for example, factory wages of $2.28 per day are both legal (the national minimum wage is $2.28) and high enough to attract 120,000 workers to factory jobs making Nike shoes because so many other jobs do not pay even this legal minimum wage.[9] (The Nike-contracted factories in Indonesia therefore employ almost 100 times as many workers as Nike itself!)

The practice of mobile global capital paying workers a few dollars a day to make shoes that sell for over $100 a pair and are promoted by millionaire endorsers such as Michael Jordan and Tiger Woods naturally draws criticism. It isn't hard to figure out that the cost of Nike products is determined more by marketing expense than by production costs. The cost of creating and maintaining a global consumption pool are apparently very high. In fact, Nike's profit margins are not especially high: Income has historically been less than 10 percent of sales. It follows that Nike needs to keep production costs so low (and use the global production pool to do so) because its marketing expenses are so high.

Nike defends this arrangement vigorously. The company's view is that globalization is part of the process of economic growth that benefits the low-wage companies where its products are manufactured.

> "Whether you like Nike or don't like Nike, good corporations are the ones that lead these countries out of poverty," said Nike Chairman Philip Knight in an interview. "When we started in Japan, factory labor there was making $4 a day, which is basically what is being paid in Indonesia and being so strongly criticized today. Nobody today is saying, 'The poor old Japanese.' We watched it happen all over again in Taiwan and Korea, and now it's going on in Southeast Asia."[10]

The people who write about the end of the state, the end of culture, and the end of geography are imagining a world dominated by Nike-style corporations, controlled by a few dozen Philip Knights, who sit in their equivalents of Beaverton, Oregon, and pull the strings that command resources from global production and consumption pools. Sitting at the center of the universe, they are the rich and powerful masters of both demand-side and supply-side globalization.

Maybe they are correct in this view of the future. But I suspect that they do not appreciate how unusual Nike is and how rare is the actual global firm.

THE ECONOMICS OF THE GLOBAL BUSINESS

Nike is an example of where the process of globalization can lead, but there is good reason to think that truly global firms such as Nike might still be rare creatures. There are valid reasons why it is difficult to achieve both demand-side and supply-side globalization. In the next two chapters I introduce the idea that fundamental instabilities in the system of global finance creates a built-in limit to the globalization process. Here, however, I want to focus on four other factors that are easier to see and perhaps even more important.

First, I want to argue that states still exist and still matter. That is, the nation-state retains enormous power to shape the environment within which business operates. States can control critical aspects of individual markets. State power can be and is used to condition and shape both consumption and production resource pools. The resource pools for specific goods and services are a good deal less global than most people imagine, and state power is one reason why.

Second, local differences in language, culture, and history still matter. Local resource pools retain distinct characteristics that disappear when we look at them only at a high level of abstraction. Local markets are as different as they are alike. The international marketing textbooks are filled with studies of global strategies defeated by language, culture, or local practice.

In fact, the economic theory of the multinational corporation suggests that these factors generally put foreign firms at a decisive disadvantage relative to domestic firms with local knowledge. How, in general, can foreign managers hope to compete with local entrepreneurs who know the language, customs, laws, and practices? In general, it is argued, they cannot! An economic theory of multinational corporations has evolved to find explanations—abilities that a multinational might possess that would be sufficient to offset all the built-in disadvantages.[11] A successful multinational corporation must hold a special advantage, access to some resource not available on the market, that allows it to compete successfully with local firms. Special marketing or management skills or access to proprietary processes are possible sources of the "intangible" resources needed. In essence, the successful foreign firm must be a jump ahead of the domestic competition in some significant aspect of business, and it must have ways to keep the local competitors from catching up (such as patents, copyrights, trade secrets, etc.). The successful global firm must possess a special demand-side or supply-side resource, and it must be so potent as to overcome a world of local firms with local knowledge.[12]

Nike's special advantage is on the demand side. It brings special skills to its marketing efforts. Nike has consistently been able to associate itself with uniquely skilled athletes—Michael Jordan, Tiger Woods, Bo Jackson, and more. These associations, which Nike buys at high cost and uses with great skill, act as effective barriers to entry. There is really no way to compete with Michael Jordan when it comes to basketball or to celebrity associations. Nike makes the entry barrier all the more effective by signing unique talents in many individual and team sports. What Nike has done is to define a product based on personality as much as practical use and then exploit that market efficiently. As the Tiger Woods case makes clear, Nike must constantly find and invest in new personalities if it is to retain its intangible advantage. It is more expensive to make and keep the market (through personality investment) than it is to make the shoes and baseball caps themselves.

Nike makes good shoes (I wear them) and has also worked to achieve supply-side advantages. Its ability to manufacture products at low cost using global resources, however, is not in any way unique. Nike manages global production resources efficiently, but all competitive shoe manufacturers do this today.

Nike has used its research to improve its shoes, as with the patented "Air" insoles that cushion many of the more expensive shoes. The Air innovation is a good one, but other manufacturers have equivalent cushioning systems. Nike's special skill was exploiting the Air trademark by first linking it with Michael Jordan (Air Jordan) and then using it to distinguish its other products.

Nike is a successful global firm, therefore, for two reasons. On the supply side, it does not try to compete with local firms with local knowledge. Rather, it employs them to make its products efficiently and at low cost and switches among local producers as demand and design factors change. On the demand side, Nike invests heavily in unique intangible resources in the form of athletes and trademarks and uses these effectively as sources of local competitive advantage and barriers to global market entry.

The third reason why globalization is limited is that people still matter. Much business is still conducted face to face, especially business in which trust must be established. One reason (certainly not the only one) why Japan remains an island in some global markets is that its business culture holds personal relationships to be so important. It is not clear that e-mail and Web pages can replace face-to-face contact in some important business transactions.

Finally, I want to suggest that there are complex dynamics in doing "global" business that involve state power and policy, local market and resource environments, and personal business relationships. These seemingly small-scale factors can interact in ways that are far more important than access to global pools of consumers or workers. This idea—that local conditions can be more important than global reach—probably seems quaint and vaguely Victorian. It is a powerful idea, however, and it forms the basis of Harvard Business School professor Michael Porter's book *The Competitive Advantage of Nations.*[13]

Just a few miles down the road from here, northwest on the Via Emilia, is a small region where firms produce the best industrial ceramics in the world and dominate the international ceramics market. This was one of the industries that Michael Porter studied as he tried to understand what creates competitive advantage. He concluded that Modena's success in ceramics was based on the dynamic interaction of highly competitive local firms, highly demanding local consumers, competitive and innovative markets, and a supportive local economic environment. The locally driven dynamic interaction of public policies, demanding buyers, and innovative producers was the source of global success, Porter concluded.

Nike is a global success story. It is deceptively easy to let Nike's example lead us to believe that all successful international firms are global firms and that the globalization process is therefore moving ever closer to its logical extreme. The following brief case studies indicate how power of the state, individual relations, and local resource pools constrain global reach.

BOEING: THE SKY IS THE LIMIT

My Nikes and I flew from Seattle to London to Bologna on Rolls-Royce–powered British Airways Boeing 747 and 757 jets. Every single country that we flew over was part of Boeing's global strategy. Boeing sells its airplanes all over the world, as most of us know, but it also produces its products in a global workshop that extends from the factory floor in Renton, Washington, to village workshops in the Chinese periphery.

Consider the state of Boeing's global business. Boeing exports greater dollar value in a typical year than any other firm in the United States. Boeing's global commercial sales are so large that they alone can skew the balance of payments statistics of the rest of the U.S. economy. Boeing is almost big enough to be a nation in many respects, and a look at Boeing actually tells us something about both global business and the condition of the nation-state.

In November 1996, before its merger with McDonnell Douglas, the Boeing Company directly employed over 120,000 workers, most based in the United States.[14] This large workforce makes Boeing a completely different type of operation than Nike's more "hollow" corporate structure. Boeing's 1996 profits were more than $1 billion on revenues of more than $22 billion.[15] Both figures, but especially profits, are expected to grow exponentially in the future owing to a variety of factors, including the merger of Boeing and former rival McDonnell Douglas, the acquisition of Rockwell International's defense and space operations, and increasing production of the computer-designed 777 commercial aircraft, which is expected to generate profits far earlier than previous Boeing products. High-volume production of the redesigned 737 aircraft will also generate higher revenues and profits. Boeing is in many lines of business, but here I focus on its commercial aircraft operations.

Boeing is big, but *big* does not necessarily equal *global.* Big can be national, producing and selling mainly in one country. Big can be international, operating from one country but selling in many. Big can be even multilocal, competing separately in many local markets in different nations. A firm can grow large in many ways and still not be global. Big business is not necessarily global business.

But Boeing *is* a global business, in my book, because its operations display both demand-side and supply-side globalization. Boeing's commercial aircraft sales take place in a worldwide arena. Although only one serious competitor, Airbus, remains for the full range of commercial aircraft that Boeing sells, the two firms engage in apparently fierce competition for every sale. Boeing could not survive in its current configuration based on only the U.S. market. It is necessarily a global animal.

Boeing is almost equally global on the supply side. Although its main assembly plants are located in the United States, components and key subassemblies come from around the world, especially Europe and Japan but now also China. The pieces are brought together and assembled in the Pacific Northwest, but Boeing planes are actually produced one part at a time all around the world.

Boeing's business is global, to be sure, but I want to argue that it is not a global firm in the same sense as Nike. Nike is a creature of the market. Boeing is a creature of the state. It almost *is* a state.

Many of the most important aspects of Boeing's business are defined by state policy. The fact that Boeing operates as it does is an indication of the power that states retain in the world today—not their impotence, as the "end of the state" writers would have us believe.

No example so clearly illustrates the impact of state power on Boeing's global business as does its relationship with China. In 1996 the *Seattle Times* published a chronology of Sino-Boeing relations.[16] Here are a few items from the *Seattle Times* list that indicate how closely tied are politics and economics in the case of Boeing and China.

1972   Nixon meets Mao Tse-tung in Beijing. Boeing sells 10 707s to Chinese.
1978   Deng Xiaoping launches "four modernizations" program. China orders three Boeing 747s.
1979   Washington and Beijing establish diplomatic relations; Deng visits U.S. and tours Boeing assembly plants in Renton and Everett, Washington.
1980   From 1980–1989, China orders 34 Boeing 737s, 33 757s and 10 767s.

1981   Xian Aircraft Co. signs contract with Boeing to supply machine parts
        for the 747.

1982   Xian Aircraft signs second contract with Boeing to produce 737 for-
        ward-access doors. That leads to further contracts for 747 trailing-
        edge ribs, 737 vertical fins and horizontal stabilizers. Boeing eventu-
        ally signs supplier contracts with Shenyang Aircraft Co. to build 757
        cargo doors and with Shanghai Aircraft Co. to produce 737 compo-
        nent parts.

1990   China places one of the largest commercial-aircraft orders in Boeing
        history: 36 airplanes and 36 options for a total value of $9 billion.

1994   Clinton "delinks" human rights from debate over granting most-fa-
        vored-nation trading status to China. Xian Aircraft Co. wins contract
        to produce 100 tail sections for Boeing 737-300/500. China takes de-
        livery of its 200th Boeing airplane.

1996   U.S.-Sino relations deteriorate over trade, software piracy, human-
        rights abuses and nuclear-proliferation violations. China delays an es-
        timated $4 billion order for Boeing airplanes because of tensions in
        U.S.-Sino relations. Meanwhile, Xian Aircraft completes construc-
        tion of new $600 million factory, signs contract with Boeing in March
        to build at least 1,500 737 tail sections. Northrop-Grumman, which
        builds Boeing 757 tail sections, announces in March it will subcon-
        tract a percentage of the work to Chengdu Aircraft Manufacturing Co.
        Boeing announces in April that it plans to hire 8,200 employees
        (6,700 locally), mostly production workers, to meet growing demand
        for new airplanes fueled largely by the rapid expansion of air traffic in
        China and Asia. To date,[17] Boeing has sold 252 airplanes to China and
        employs more than 100 company employees throughout the country.

Boeing competes in a world where national governments still have the
ability to influence or determine the pattern and terms of the commercial aircraft sales. The notion that the nation-state is dead, the victim of global business power, would come as a surprise to executives at Boeing and Airbus.
State influence is even greater in the market for military hardware, but that
side of the business is not my concern here, although obviously it is Boeing's
concern. To market its products effectively, Boeing must be able to negotiate
with foreign governments effectively. The global business of commercial aircraft is equal parts economics, technology, and politics.

Boeing has several bargaining chips besides the obvious market ones of
price, quantity, and quality, which give it the power it needs in its relations
with powerful states. Boeing can negotiate with foreign governments using the
resources over which it has direct control, such as access to technology, contracts for parts and subassemblies, training, maintenance, and so forth. Boeing
can provide jobs, technology, and resources for a nation that places a large order, and, in fact, the company finds itself increasingly under pressure to do so.
These side payments and bargains are called *offsets*. More and more, powerful
states make Boeing pay for new orders with offset contracts and investment.

The *Seattle Times* investigated Boeing's increasing production in China, for example, and reported that

> All three Western aircraft builders—Boeing, McDonnell Douglas and Europe's Airbus—have concluded they must meet Chinese offset requirements to ensure their future. But critics see the export of Western aircraft production and technology to places like the Shaanxi Valley as a threat to the long-term interests of U.S. workers, their communities and even the companies themselves.
>
> Boeing officials say they must enter these offset agreements or they will lose the business to their rivals. Aerospace companies have long acceded to offsets in military and weapons sales, but only recently have been faced with countries that demand offsets in commercial aircraft sales.
>
> Boeing's chief international strategist, Lawrence Clarkson, said the company's strategy is "to do what it takes to remain the preferred supplier" for China, the world's fastest growing market. The price has been giving up some production work and technology to maintain access to the Chinese market.[18]

Offsets come in two flavors. A *direct offset* is very straightforward: In exchange for an aircraft purchase, the buyer nation receives subcontract work or access to production technology. A portion of the aircraft is produced under license from Boeing. Direct-offset deals with Japanese firms were key parts of the bargains that permitted Boeing to launch new aircrafts in the 1980s and 1990s.

Indirect offsets take many forms. In the 1970s they were *countertrade*—essentially barter arrangements in which aircraft producers helped their customers buy equipment by accepting part payment in locally produced goods unrelated to the aircraft business. These days, indirect offsets are more likely to take the form of technology transfer unrelated to the actual sale,[19] since nations are apparently more interested in acquiring advanced technology than in simply selling more of what they already have the know-how to produce.

The competition for sales to China has been particularly intense and has generated high levels of offset investment. China sales are large now and may be huge in the future. The International Air Transport Association estimates that by the year 2000 half of all air flights in the world will take off or land in Asia.[20] Bidding for the Chinese share of this business, Boeing has invested $100 million in a flight safety program for China. McDonnell Douglas, however, agreed to the coproduction of aircraft in Shanghai. Airbus invested $50 million in a flight simulator center.[21] The offset bidding continues between Airbus and Boeing.

Offsets have obvious benefits to foreign governments, and they may also have indirect benefits for Boeing. Offsets "force" Boeing to shift some production to lower-wage countries, which may make business sense in some cases anyway. Boeing's domestic unions clearly worry that foreign offset production weakens their domestic bargaining power with the firm. Offsets may also have some benefit in terms of insulating Boeing from foreign exchange risk, although this is probably not a very important factor in these decisions.

Boeing has to be very concerned, however, about offsets that involve technology transfer. Yesterday's barter customer is becoming today's subcontractor and may become tomorrow's competitor (at least in the cases of China and Japan). The story is told—and apparently is true—that one of the first Boeing 707s sold to China was disassembled and "deengineered" to serve as a guide for a China-built plane. So far behind was Chinese technology in the 1970s that their 707 clone, built of steel instead of aluminum, was effectively unflyable. Technology transfer today is far more likely to result eventually in marketplace competition.

Boeing feels driven by competition to risk long-term technological advantages to gain current sales. Clearly Boeing must maintain a rapid pace of technological advance if it wishes to maintain its position in this bargaining environment.

Boeing's second important bargaining chip is its potential ability to influence U.S. foreign policy to favor a customer-government. President Nixon went to China on Air Force One, a converted Boeing 707 (the President flies in a 747 today). And it is no accident that Boeing sales to China began almost immediately thereafter. It is probably also no accident that Henry Jackson, the influential anticommunist U.S. Senator who might have prevented the political and economic opening of Sino-U.S. relations—but didn't—represented Washington State, where Boeing's headquarters are located. "The sale of Boeing 707s to China was politically a very important, symbolic act and personally approved by President Nixon," said former Ambassador Chas Freeman, Nixon's China interpreter. "It was the Chinese who asked about Boeing aircraft."[22]

The foreign policy chip seems to be a less and less important factor in Boeing's strategy, however, although U.S. foreign policy still matters. One reason is that foreign governments are motivated more by offset jobs and investment rather than by potential foreign policy benefits, reflecting the triumph of the market over international relations. Even more important is the fact that Boeing's domestic political influence has diminished somewhat, and it is less able to deliver political goods for foreign governments.

With the end of the Cold War, Boeing's strategic importance has declined. Boeing has become one of several important U.S.–based global firms competing in international markets. Its days of being given special preference in foreign policy politics seem to be over. The number of international firms seeking to influence U.S. foreign policy has increased, and some of these firms have interests that directly conflict with Boeing's interests on specific issues. Microsoft's "get tough" line with China about intellectual property rights, for example, clashed in 1996 with Boeing's commercial interest, which was to pursue a policy of engagement and discussion with China on issues such as property rights and human rights, so as to minimize the risk of lost orders. Boeing is obviously less effective in advocating a foreign policy stance when it must compete with the likes of Microsoft than when it is unopposed by other "global" firms.

If it now sounds as though Boeing has its own foreign policy, that is because, essentially, it does. Every truly global firm has a foreign policy, I suspect, because each of them must negotiate with nation-states on the demand side, the supply side, or both. As yet, no global firm is more powerful than the nation-states with which it deals. The biggest difference between Boeing's foreign policy and that of a nation-state is that the former probably has greater internal consistency. Boeing's foreign policy is realist, taking state power and national interest into account in a direct and pragmatic way, as the previous comments on offsets indicate.

Boeing can also be used as a tool by foreign governments to influence (or attempt to influence) U.S. foreign policies. As a result, Boeing's fate (or at least the fate of some of its aircraft sales) is out of its hands. In 1996, for example, Boeing lost a large Chinese sale to Airbus, an event that it blamed on the Clinton administration's threat to impose trade sanctions on China if it did not more actively enforce its copyright agreements with the United States. (Microsoft, with much at stake, supported the hard line; Boeing obviously opposed it.) In all, Boeing estimated that it lost sales of ten 777 aircraft, five 747s, and as many as one hundred 737s—a huge blow.[23] No wonder Chinese pressure on Boeing translated into Boeing pressure on Washington.

In a revealing 1996 interview, Boeing Commerical Aircraft President Ron Woodard, frustrated at these lost orders, listed Boeing's recent efforts on China's behalf:[24]

- It lobbied for permanent most-favored-nation status for China that would end the annual controversial practice of granting China trading privileges.
- It supported China's inclusion into the World Trade Organization, which would prohibit offsets and promote market reforms, but would also give the Chinese access to international financing for industrial development.
- It transferred production and assembly operations to China.
- It created internships for nearly 2,000 Chinese pilots and maintenance people in Seattle and China.
- It invested $100 million to improve Chinese airport safety equipment.
- It donated two 737 simulators for Chinese training of air crews.
- The list now includes a planned visit in June by Boeing's board of directors to Beijing, Guangzhou, and Xian.

It is significant that the first two items were political—using Boeing's clout to promote Chinese interests with the U.S. government and the World Trade Organization. That these efforts appear on the same list (and ahead of) millions of dollars worth of offsets and other investments indicates clearly the importance of politics in Sino-Boeing affairs.

China seems to have been a particularly effective bargainer in its relationship with Boeing, but perhaps I draw this conclusion too easily. China's current market for commercial aircraft is large, its potential market huge, and the control that government has over orders is absolute. It may be more accurate to say that China has used Boeing and Boeing has used China. Japan has also bargained effectively with Boeing. Japanese airlines have been important early customers for Boeing's new aircraft models, and Japan has received large offset contracts in return.

The political economy of the commercial aircraft industry in general and the Boeing Company in particular is fascinating, and I clearly have only scratched the surface here. But I hope I have made my point about globalization. Boeing is as unlike Nike as can be imagined. Boeing is a global firm, with enormous market power. But it is effectively as much a creature of the state as it is of the market, in the sense that its most important choices are heavily conditioned by the existence of state power and how that power can be used.

THE FRANK RUSSELL COMPANY:
TACOMA AS THE CENTER OF TI IE UNIVERSE

Everyone reading this paragraph has heard of Nike, Boeing, and Microsoft, global firms with strong brand-name recognition. Only some of you, however, will know about the Frank Russell Company. Frank Russell represents a different aspect of globalization. It is the sort of firm that we imagine in the global dream: a high-tech financial firm with interests in every corner of the world. Frank Russell is the kind of company that can only exist in the world of postgeography globalization. What Frank Russell is and what it is not tell us a lot about the nature of globalization today.

The Frank Russell Company is amazing. It is the world's largest consultant to pension funds, including the pension funds of many of the largest international businesses. Frank Russell's main line of business is to advise these corporations about which investment advisors can most effectively meet their goals. The company directly manages about $26 billion of customer assets and provides advice that influences more than $600 billion in client assets.[25] Incredibly, about 1 percent of the New York Stock Exchange's daily volume is initiated by brokers at the Frank Russell world headquarters office in Tacoma, Washington.

Tacoma? Well, yes. The Frank Russell Company has offices in New York, Toronto, London, Zurich, Paris, Sydney, Auckland, and Tokyo, but the home office is indeed located a 30-minute walk from my home in Tacoma. Now don't get the wrong impression: Tacoma isn't Mayberry RFD, but it also isn't Seattle or San Francisco, or New York. Tacoma is a thriving port city on Puget Sound, with a population of 175,000, an active local culture, and the comfortable feeling of the blue-collar town it once was. Tacoma was built on trade, transportation, natural resources, and the financial services that go with them. As trade and transportation have become global, so has the local financial structure.

Tacoma is a nice place to live, especially if you enjoy the mountains and the sea. In fact, that's why the Frank Russell Company has been headquartered in Tacoma, not New York, Tokyo, or London, since it was founded in 1936. CEO George Russell and his family prefer the quality of life on Puget Sound to any other, and they have constructed a global financial enterprise with Tacoma as its center.

Frank Russell's 1,200 employees work in several areas of the investment business—investment strategy and research, and manager and capital market research, for example.[26] Investment and manager research is the company's bread and butter and the areas where its reputation was made. Russell researches investment managers and makes recommendations to clients. It essentially manages investment managers rather than managing investments. The company's site on the World Wide Web describes their core business in this way:

- *Manager and capital market research.* Russell's intensive research of investment managers, strategies, and markets spans the globe. Each year, through an integrated worldwide network of more than 50 analysts, Russell conducts detailed in-person evaluations of approximately 2,200 investment managers and more than 6,000 investment products in 15 countries. Their evaluations cover regional and multicurrency products in all major equity and fixed income markets:
- *Equities* (single country, emerging markets, global/non-US, and convertibles)
- *Fixed income* (single currency and multicurrency)
- *Global and domestic tactical asset allocation*
- *Currency strategies.* This comprehensive effort supports the implementation of Russell's investment programs—helping clients select money managers within each asset class and monitor investment strategies and performance. It also enables analysts to develop asset-class strategies designed to achieve client-specific investment objectives.
- *Applied research.* Clients around the world also look to Russell for well-researched advancements in investment strategy and technology. Russell's knowledge of performance measurement, strategic and tactical asset allocation, and risk analysis for global securities markets is applied to each client's investment objectives.[27]

Frank Russell's name is becoming better known as the company seeks to expand into related fields, where its knowledge and analytical abilities can be put to good use. Recently, for example, the company began to accept individual investment accounts of $50,000 or more, and it has quietly begun to advertise its services and try to develop greater name recognition among investment-minded individuals. One important element in this strategy has been the widely publicized Russell 1000®, Russell 2000®, and Russell 3000® stock indexes. Other indices track markets in Asia and in emerging markets. Index funds based on the Russell indexes are now an important investment vehicle in international finance. As of 1997, more than $100 billion was invested in these funds.[28]

Global financial analysis is necessarily highly quantitative. Frank Russell has developed powerful computer tools to aid in its analysis. Now some of these tools are being offered to clients as products for their own use, including PC software programs Russell Performance Universes for Windows™, Russell Performance Attribution for Windows™, and Russell Style Classification for Windows™. Russell also combines its analytical tools and expertise to support clients with strategic planning, product positioning, marketing, reporting, and organizational structure. More than 1,000 clients worldwide use Russell's analytical tools and services concerning investment performance.[29]

Because the Frank Russell Company seems like the model global financial enterprise, it is convenient to attribute to it certain qualities that we associate with such firms. In particular, it is easy to imagine that Frank Russell is able to do global business centered in Tacoma, Washington, on the basis of telecommunications and microcomputing power. These are the standard explanations of business location in the End of Geography scenario. This view is right, when applied to Frank Russell, but it is also totally wrong.

The Frank Russell Company does rely on telecommunications systems to link its international offices together and to link them to their various clients. And it does also use advanced computer-based methods of technical analysis. So it does fit the current image of global finance, and if you are looking for these qualities, you will find them. But, in fact, these are qualities found in nearly all businesses these days, global or not, for the costs of telecommunications and computing are low enough that their use is no longer limited to high-tech global businesses. The technology we associate with globalization now finds mundane use.[30] The Frank Russell Company uses advanced technology and would be uncompetitive if it didn't, but this is not the basis for its global competitive advantage.

Datamation, a specialized business publication, featured a profile of Frank Russell's telecommunications system in a 1993 issue.[31] Interestingly, the focus of the article, "Building a global network on a shoestring," was the company's early ability to establish effective telecommunications with minimal investment. Although the company's network today is state of the art, the company was able to do business effectively in 1985 with a 2,400 bits per second modem hooked up to ordinary phone lines—a communications system not far removed from the phone and telegraph lines that connected Keynes to his global investments in the pre–World War I era of globalized markets.

The Frank Russell company was a competitive global business long before advanced telecommunications became an important aspect of its operations. Neither computers nor telecommunications explain Frank Russell's place at the center of the universe. The source of its global advantage is one of the least mobile, lowest-tech, and most valuable business resources: people.

Walter Bagehot, the famous nineteenth-century political economist and editor of *The Economist*, was keenly aware of the importance of people and personal relations in international finance. In *Lombard Street,* his analysis of the City of London's financial markets, he noted that finance is a business of risk and trust. Financial risk, he wrote, is offset by personal trust. Banking will always involve risk, he thought, but would always be fundamentally sound because it would always be based on face-to-face dealings and personal bonds of trust.

Bagehot was right on many matters, but wrong on this one. As we will see in Chapter 4, international finance today is anything but personal, and risk and trust are sold in turbulent financial markets. The lack of human contact may be one reason why these markets are so unstable. But where it is really important—where much is at stake, as in the case of enormous pension funds—face-to-face contact, personal evaluation, and trust are indispensable. These "people" services are at the core of the Frank Russell global web.

Underneath the stock indexes and the computer programs, Frank Russell's core business is based on personal relationships among the firm, its clients, and the investment managers it evaluates. When talking with people associated with the firm in various ways, it is clear that personal contact matters. You of course do not invest $1 billion in employee pension funds with people you do not trust, nor do you recommend a pattern of investment of these funds among investment managers whose judgment you question. It is obvious that personal relations and judgment are the key factors in these transactions, and have been since the days of Keynes and Bagehot. But it is easy to overlook these factors in explaining global business; the example of the Frank Russell Company teaches us to avoid this mistake.

The power of people is perhaps best illustrated by an organization called the Russell 20-20 Association. It is an independent, nonprofit group of twenty major pension plan sponsors and twenty major money managers, who together represent more than $1 trillion in investable capital.[32] The 20-20 Association, organized by George Russell, the company CEO, travels as a group to emerging markets where relatively small amounts of investment capital can make a relatively large difference in local economic activity. The personal contacts that they make are apparently the key to making investment decisions in these markets. Their investments, secured by face-to-face contact and bonds of trust, are probably a good deal more secure than the faceless emerging market funds that so many individual investors now hold in their portfolios.

In a sense, then, global financial enterprises like Frank Russell are also local businesses, based on the same kinds of personal trust relationships that can be seen in the movie "It's a Wonderful Life." A firm like Frank Russell has global offices, but it also has important elements of an old-fashioned mom-and-pop operation. It succeeds globally because it knows how to do business locally, face to face.

Frank Russell's globalization is based on personal relations, showing that people still matter in global markets. Globalization, at least in finance, remains a stable enterprise as long as it does not expand too far beyond the range of face-to-face relations. Globalization *can* go further, of course, driven by technology and profit, but it ceases to be backed by trust and becomes potentially destabilizing.[33] At some point, globalization crosses the line and becomes susceptible to crisis and chaos, which are the topics of the next two chapters.

MICROSOFT AND THE GLOBAL SOFTWARE MARKET

This chapter began with Bill Gates's not-very-global vision of the business world, so it is fitting that the last case study is Gates's clearly global firm: the Microsoft Corporation. In fairness to BillG@microsoft.com, it must be said that *The Road Ahead* was written before Microsoft fully embraced the Internet and the vastly expanded communications possibilities it had made possible. In terms of its products and product development strategies, Microsoft is now as much an Internet company as it is a desktop PC company. But even in the pre-Internet days when *The Road Ahead* was being written, Microsoft was already a global company.

The unveiling of Windows 95 illustrates Microsoft's global strategy. This powerful new personal computing environment appeared all at once in late summer 1995. A simultaneous worldwide product introduction occurred, with press events and product demonstrations beamed globally via satellite and accompanied by custom-tailored local publicity efforts. You had to be pretty far from a center of capitalist civilization to avoid hearing about Windows 95.

Much can be learned about the nature of actual globalization from Windows 95 in particular and the operations of the Microsoft Corporation in general. Generally, we think that Microsoft is in the software business, producing and selling shrink-wrapped boxes that contain diskettes and CD-ROMs. Although this is true, it misses the point. Microsoft is really in the intellectual property rights business. The diskettes, CD-ROMs, and Internet download sites are simple, more or less efficient product delivery systems. Microsoft is really selling services—the use of the ideas and innovations of its designers, software engineers, and "content editors." The exact nature of these ideas is patented, copyrighted, or sometimes just kept secret so that Microsoft can earn an economic return on their use. Intellectual property rights are the legal instruments that guarantee Microsoft exclusive use of the ideas and innovations that it produces.

The problem with the services that Microsoft sells is that they are too easy to copy, a process called *pirating* in the software business. Even before Windows 95 was released, for example, it was available for purchase in many countries in pirated versions, which were usually illegal copies of the test or "beta" versions of the product available free over the Internet.

It is easy and relatively cheap to buy (or steal) one copy of Windows 95 and to produce thousands of pirated versions. In the early days of personal computing software, firms went to extravagant technological lengths to limit software pirating, but ultimately these efforts failed for both demand-side and supply-side reasons. On the demand side, customers did not much like their use of honestly purchased products limited by complicated passwords or other constraints. On the supply side, software pirates had a strong incentive to find ways around whatever barrier the software producers erected. Nothing stopped pirating. Today, software producers make few technological attempts to limit pirating of the popular software—the focus has changed to the legal system.

Microsoft's efforts to protect its core business have shifted to the realm of international diplomacy. Microsoft seeks to encourage individual governments, particularly of less-developed countries where pirating is an epidemic, to commit to stronger laws and the enforcement of intellectual property rights. Microsoft also encourages the U.S. government to use its influence in international organizations such as the World Trade Organization and the Asian-Pacific Economic Cooperation forum to gain stronger international agreements on trade-related international property rights. It is not surprising, therefore, that these issues were highlighted in the final Uruguay round of General Agreement on Tariffs and Trade (GATT) negotiations, are currently a major concern of the World Trade Organization, and are subject to intensive international negotiations.

It seems that a global firm needs a foreign policy and must influence the foreign policies of the nations in which it operates. During the North American Free Trade Agreement (NAFTA) treaty debate in the United States, for example, Bill Gates himself appeared in industry-sponsored television commercials supporting ratification of the NAFTA treaty. One reason for this active approach was the notion that stronger trade links would allow stronger trade rules, particularly with respect to intellectual property rights.

Global firms need to have global advantages, which increasingly take the form of patents, copyrights, or other intellectual property rights. As the Microsoft case illustrates, protecting and enforcing these valuable property rights is expensive and difficult and, at the margin, limits the degree of true globalization that we can expect. This problem also illustrates an unexpected paradox of the nation-state and globalization. Although the received wisdom is that globalizing firms such as Microsoft diminish state power, in fact the success of these firms requires a strong state. A strong state is needed to enforce the intellectual property rights that are the basis for profitable global trade and to negotiate the international standards and agreements that are necessary to create the global environment within which these industries can prosper.

State power and a commitment to the enforcement of intellectual property rights are one limit to Microsoft's global market expansion, but not the only one. For a global company, Microsoft is surprisingly multilocal, doing business in local production and consumption pools rather than in the global resource pools we found in the Nike case.

Microsoft's products, for example, must be carefully tailored to local markets, especially in terms of language. English is the *lingua franca* of the software business, but not of the mass markets of end users that Microsoft aims to please. To market on a global scale requires that products be customized to take into account language differences, at a bare minimum. There is, for example, a Vietnamese version of Windows 95. Even the standard "English (U.S.)" that I am using to write this paragraph includes 25 other keyboard systems in the control panel to deal with language barriers I might encounter.

Since there is no global language, global products must be tailored to local lingo, which introduces a strong multilocal aspect to marketing, help texts, telephone product support, and instruction manuals. But the problem sometimes goes well beyond just language differences. One of my favorite Microsoft products is *Encarta*, a multimedia CD-ROM encyclopedia. Like any encyclopedia, *Encarta* is full of history. Now history wouldn't seem to present any special problem for a global product, apart from the obvious problems of translating text from one language to another. But there is no history that is not someone's idea of history, and the particular way that history is told has deep political consequences. You can imagine, for example, that the Japanese occupation of Korea during World War II is told differently in Korea than it is in Japan or that details of the U.S.–China trade and human rights discussions are told differently in China than in the United States. *Encarta* must therefore be sensitive not only to language but also to politics and obviously culture, religious views, and other important factors. Microsoft has been forced several times to alter *Encarta*'s local content in response to local outrage and threats of government sanctions.

The cost of localization is a problem. Although software prices are higher in Europe and Asia than in the United States, for example, this in part reflects higher costs. The fixed costs of customizing the product are spread over a smaller number of units, reducing profits. Higher prices are necessary to preserve profit margins. But a vicious cycle is present. Higher prices encourage pirating, which further reduces the number of legal sales, increasing average cost and pushing the price even higher. This provides an additional stimulus for pirates, and the vicious cycle continues. The costs of localization therefore help drive the dynamic of software pirating, making localization a costly process indeed.

Global products, even highly technical ones like Microsoft's, cannot always be truly global. To a certain degree, each product is also a local product, modified and customized for the locality in which it is to be sold. This fact limits globalization, or at least limits the types of firms and products that can be truly global. It also creates opportunities for those local firms that better understand the local politics, customs, language, and culture. Demand-side globalization is deceptively difficult to achieve. Not even Windows 95 can truly claim to be a global product.

For an International Economics class project, one of my students, Jon Westerman, decided to find out where the code for Windows 95 was produced.[34] Jon is majoring in international political economy, but his hobby is personal computing, and he wanted to try to bring his two interests together. He expected to find that Windows 95 was a global product, produced around the world and sold around the world, like the Nike shoes he and his cross-country teammates wear. His research technique, naturally, was to search the World Wide Web. Much of what he learned confirmed his expectations, but not all of it.

A lot of the computer code that is at the heart of Windows 95 was written in India. In fact, Microsoft and other major software firms draw heavily from local labor pools of highly skilled software engineers in India. To a surprising extent, Windows 95 is an Indian product.

Jon went Net surfing, trying to discover why. What he discovered were highly technical and advanced graduate programs in Indian universities designed, apparently, to produce the skilled software designers and engineers that were needed by a dynamic and globally competitive local software industry. At one point Jon searched the Internet site of the Indian Institute of Technology (Bangalore) and found the following list of recent (December 1993) thesis titles:

V. Nirmala. Thesis: Implementation of a Distributed Shared Memory Platform Across a Network of Workstations

E. S. Padmakumar. Thesis: Evaluation of Cache Configurations for Future Single-Chip Uni- and Multiprocessors

G. Sridhar. Thesis: Process Scheduling Policies for a Heterogeneous Computing Environment

In each case, Jon's efforts to access further information—even an abstract of the thesis contents—was met with a firm refusal: "Access Denied." Jon concluded, and he may be right, that at least some of this research was being produced under contract for foreign clients like Microsoft. He was impressed with the sophistication of the scope of the research he discovered.

The software industry in India is of such growing importance, in fact, that it has become the subject of a series of reports in the *Financial Times*.[35] One article reported that over 140,000 Indians were working on projects for foreign firms, including (in order of sales) Hewlett-Packard, IBM, ACER, INTEL, Digital, Compaq, Sun, Microsoft, Apple, and Citizen.

Body shopping, the industry term for cheap labor for keyboard entry, was once the basis for the Indian software business. But this has clearly changed. Some of the most sophisticated software development in the world now takes place in specific centers in India, supported by advanced technical education programs in an environment fostered by government development projects. Another *Financial Times* study emphasized the increasing autonomy of the Indian industry.[36] Only a few years ago Indian software engineers were brought to Redmond, Washington, and other U.S. centers to provide lower-cost short-term assistance to U.S.–based development teams. Now, however, the resource pool in India has reached a critical mass. Indian software development is coordinated with related efforts elsewhere but no longer takes a back seat.

In effect, India has developed a pool of productive resources that displays some of the characteristics that Michael Porter finds necessary for global competitive advantage. Windows 95 diskettes and shrink-wrapped boxes are produced in many places around the world, but the key elements of its production are very local, indeed, and are based on local resource factors in places like Bangalore, India.

The nature of its business forces Microsoft to be surprisingly multilocal on both demand and supply sides of the market. Despite the global property rights that it seeks to protect and enforce, Microsoft turns out to be a firm that draws from a few skill-specific local resource pools and tailors its products to the demands of a great many local consumption pools. Microsoft's success is perhaps based less on global vision than on the ability to simultaneously make sound decisions in a number of local markets.

In other words, Bill Gates's vision of *The Road Ahead* is probably correct, at least for the Microsoft Corporation itself. The road ahead is probably *not* a radical change in the way that business operates as it has become globalized. Rather, the road ahead probably *is* to become much more efficient in managing the local resource and consumption pools that have been the object of business attention for centuries.

GLOBALIZATION LIMITED

This chapter has looked at four examples of actual globalization: Nike, Boeing, Frank Russell, and Microsoft. What we have found is revealing. Each of these firms is *global* in the general sense that the term is used in print these days. However, only Nike is global in the sense that I have defined this term (and even Nike's marketing strategy has a strong local emphasis in terms of specific celebrity endorsers).

Boeing shows us that state power is an important factor in economic globalization. As much as we expect markets to shape states, it is in fact sometimes the other way around. How and where Boeing airplanes are produced, and how and by whom they are used are very political matters.

The Frank Russell Company teaches us that people matter more and that technology perhaps matters less than is often suspected in global businesses. Global finance cannot be entirely divorced from the face-to-face evaluations and local knowledge that have always been important in the financial services industry. Finance is less trustworthy, and perhaps less stable, when personal relationships have been eliminated. Frank Russell makes its living, and a good one too, by producing trust. Even so, I suspect that trust is undervalued in the market today.

The Frank Russell case suggests that geography still matters, for no other reason than that the people who are the critical assets of a global firm must live somewhere. The local environment therefore matters. For the Russell family, I guess it was the natural environment of Puget Sound that caused them to establish roots there. But there are many elements of the environment, broadly defined, that logically matter to the people who make up a global firm.

Microsoft highlights several important aspects of globalization. The problem in which software pirating threatens intellectual property rights illustrates the high cost of globalization and the increasing importance of the state and state power, both in domestic market regulation and international negotiations. Windows 95 and other Microsoft global products turn out to be surprisingly local in their production and their sale. The truly global firm is rightly a rare animal, perhaps even an endangered one, with so many forces working against its infinite expansion in all directions.

Microsoft's business operation also illustrates a final point, which provides a link to the next two chapters. When we look closely at Microsoft's operations, we can see that they are multilocal in one more way: They are forced to deal with the problems of local currencies. Microsoft, as with Nike, Frank Russell, and Boeing to different degrees, earns revenues and experiences costs in dozens of currencies whose relative values change daily. The bottom line for each global firm, and the profitability of investments and operations in specific countries, therefore depends to some degree on developments in foreign exchange markets. For example, Microsoft's 1996 annual report listed the following global revenues:[37]

U.S./Canada	1996	$2.68 billion
Europe	1996	$2.02 billion
Other international	1996	$1.47 billion

with "Other international" revenues growing at the fastest rate.[38] The report
noted that

> The Company's operating results are affected by foreign exchange rates. Ap-
> proximately 40%, 37%, and 38% of the Company's revenues were collected
> in foreign currencies during 1994, 1995, and 1996. Since much of the Com-
> pany's international manufacturing costs and operating expenses are also in-
> curred in local currencies, the impact of exchange rates on net income is less
> than on revenue.[39]

Microsoft reported cash and short-term investments of $6.94 billion. In-
vestment was mostly in dollar-denominated assets but also in foreign currency positions in anticipation of continued international expansion. The
company engages in hedging and international cash management, although
the technical ability to hedge against foreign exchange risk for such large
amounts over long periods is still unavailable. Like it or not, Microsoft is also
a global financial firm, forced to deal with exchange rate risks and to engage
in costly hedging operations. The more unstable the currency markets, the
more costly it is to operate a *global* firm.

In the next two chapters I present what I think is a strong case: that these
foreign exchange markets are risky and unstable. These markets do not seek
out the "apple in a bowl" equilibrium that is the basis for our understanding of
economic market stability. Rather, they are at times subject to crises and may
be affected by systematic chaotic disturbances that make their motions fundamentally unpredictable.

This instability, I argue, is another limit to economic globalization. Unstable movements in foreign exchange markets discourage businesses from
true globalization, forcing them, on the margin at least, to operate as local,
multilocal, or international firms. This limit to globalization is important and
fundamental because the process of financial globalization that makes specific global firms such as Nike possible also contributes to global financial instability, which limits the degree of globalization in general. Globalization is
a self-limiting process. It would be wise to shift our attention from global theories, visions, dreams, and fears to a more focused study—of which this chapter is still just a hint—of actual globalization. Globalization in practice, I
think, is more Bill Gates than Kenichi Ohmae.

The case against globalization based on financial instability lies ahead in
the next two chapters. But financial instability is not the only limit to true
globalization. It is probably not even the most important one. The factors of
state power, personal relationships, and local resource and consumption pools
discussed in this chapter are probably more significant in defining the nature
of individual "global" firms.

Financial instability is, however, an important limiting factor to the process of globalization generally. Meaningful large-scale economic globalization is impossible in the unstable and turbulent financial markets of today.

NOTES

1. Microsoft Corporation, *1996 Annual Report* (Redmond, WA: Microsoft Corporation, 1996), p. 5.

2. Bill Gates with Nathan Myhrvold and Peter Rinearson, *The Road Ahead* (New York: Viking, 1995).

3. Schools of commercial arithmetic prospered in this time. Businessmen sent their sons to school, where they learned to master their account books and so master the business world. These schools also eventually taught the liberal arts and laid the foundation for the Renaissance. When the printing press came to Italy late in the fifteenth century, accounting books and bibles were among the most popular titles.

4. I am not really criticizing the book here; at the end of this chapter you will see that I think that Gates is right. I find the book to be interesting as a history of the microelectronics revolution through Gates's eyes. I focus here on the fact that, as indicated in this book, Gates views global business differently from the way people think of it and from the way, I imagine, they must think that Gates thinks of it.

5. For the record, I do not think that my overall argument about globalization depends critically on this *particular* definition of globalization. One may disagree with my definition of the global firm and still have doubts about the extent of actual globalization, which is my point here.

6. Miguel Korzeniewicz, "Commodity Chains and Marketing Strategies: Nike and the Global Athletic Footwear Industry," in *Commodity Chains and Global Capitalism* ed. Gary Gereffi and Miguel Korzeniewics (Westport, CT: Praeger, 1994), p. 261.

7. Ibid., pp. 258–259.

8. Ibid., p. 263.

9. An excellent survey of Nike's relationships with its subcontractors and with the governments of the nations in which its shoes are produced is found in the series "Nike's Asian Machine Goes on Trial," which appeared in *The Oregonian* on November 9–11, 1997.

10. Keith B. Ricburg and Anne Swardson, "Close Up: Nike's Indonesia Shoe Plant: Boon or 'Sweatshop'?" *Seattle Times,* August 28, 1996, world news section.

11. See Leon Grunberg, "The Changing IPE of the Multinational Corporation" in *Introduction to International Political Economy,* ed. David N. Balaam and Michael Veseth (Upper Saddle River, NJ: Prentice Hall, 1996), pp. 338–359.

12. Of course, it may be that the ability to manage production or distribution globally is itself a valuable intangible advantage.

13. Michael Porter, *The Competitive Advantage of Nations.* (New York: The Free Press, 1990).

14. The bigger Boeing that has resulted from its merger with McDonnell Douglas is expected to have 1997 revenues of $48 billion, backorders of $100 billion, and more than 200,000 employees. Profits are expected to increase, but it is too soon as of this writing to know for certain the impact of the merger on the bottom line.

15. "Booming Boeing," *Business Week,* September 30, 1996, p. 119.

16. "China and Boeing Chronology," *Seattle Times,* May 26, 1996, local news section.

17. Mid-1996.

18. Stanley Holmes, "How Boeing Woos China," *Seattle Times,* May 26, 1996, local section.

19. Ibid.

20. Stephen H. Dunphy, "Air War Over Asia," *Seattle Times,* June 16, 1996, business section.

21. Holmes, "How Boeing Woos China."

22. Ibid.

23. Stanley Holmes, "Politics Key to Boeing Sales in China?" *Seattle Times,* April 10, 1996, business section.

24. Holmes, "How Boeing Woos China."

25. "Overview," Frank Russell Company, Tacoma, Washington, http://www.russell.com, 1997.

26. "The Frank Russell Co.," *The Seattle Times*, August 25, 1996.

27. "Overview," Frank Russell Company.

28. "Overview," Frank Russell Company. I reproduce the ® sign here to emphasize that Russell sees its name and the names of its indexes as intangible factors to its global success and seeks to protect them, just as Nike does its swoosh.

29. "Overview," Frank Russell Company. Note the trademark protection.

30. Sitting in a restaurant in a remote village in Provence, I was surprised to find that my American Express card was read by a wireless, handheld machine that connected to the main computer and approved my lunch bill. If I had used a debit card, I could have punched in a personal identification number (PIN) and debited my bank account without leaving the terrace. This high-tech story is told not because it is unique, but because it is commonplace.

31. Dwight B. Davis, "Building a Global Network on a Shoestring," *Datamation* (May 15, 1993), p. 59.

32. "Overview," Frank Russell Company.

33. This point is made well by Matthew Valencia in "Banking in Emerging Markets: Fragile, Handle with Care," *The Economist* (special survey section; April 12, 1997). Valencia stresses the importance of effective banking regulation in the age of high-technology global finance.

34. Jonathan Westerman, "Microsoft Windows 95: A Product of India" (University of Puget Sound, Tacoma, WA, 1995, typescript).

35. Paul Taylor, "Financial Times Review of Information Technology: India's Software Industry," *Financial Times,* November 6, 1996.

36. Mark Nicholson, "India: Strong Growth for Software," *Financial Times,* January 15, 1997.

37. Microsoft Corporation, *1996 Annual Report* (Redmond, WA: Microsoft Corporation, 1996).

38. But other international revenues are also likely to experience the highest localization costs. My thanks to Aadip Desai for his work on this part of the analysis.

39. Microsoft Corporation, *1996 Annual Report*, p. 17.

4

Currency Crises

We have been totally defeated by reality.
—Gabriel García Márquez[1]

You don't often find Nobel Prize–winning novelists commenting on international economic news. Gabriel García Márquez, whose words are quoted in the above epigraph, received the 1982 Nobel Prize in Literature for his novels and short stories, which explore the dream qualities of reality and the reality of dreams. He's no economist, and yet he might understand the nature of global finance better than many of us who are trained in this discipline. *We* create dreams (theories) to describe a reality that *he* understands to be just a dream itself. Like a character in *One Hundred Years of Solitude,* we constantly mistake the imaginary for the real.

Was the peso crisis of December 1994, the object of Gabriel García Márquez's comments, reality or dream (or nightmare)? Is globalization—the process that tries to build solid economic, political, and social structures on the unsettled, crisis-plagued foundation of global finance—reality or dream?

Currency crises are no longer exceptional; they are now an accepted element of global finance. The Asian currency crisis of 1997, which infected Thailand, Indonesia, Malaysia, the Philippines, South Korea, and Japan with a contagious financial instability virus, is only the most recent in a long line of international financial plagues. Currency crises make true globalization impossible because the global integration of economic activity cannot take place in a world where currency values are subject to sudden jolts and long periods of instability, and where patterns of global capital movements are equally uncertain. You cannot build solid global businesses on so unsettled a foundation as this.

This chapter is built around short histories of two recent currency crises: Mexico in 1994 and Europe in 1992–1993. These real world case studies are wrapped around a theory core, where I survey the recent research on currency crises and speculative attacks. Both theory and experience persuade me that currency crises are a permanent part of global finance as we know it today and therefore a permanent constraint to the process of globalization.

THE PESO CRISIS OF 1994–1995

The peso crisis of 1994–1995 illustrates the unstable nature of international financial flows today. Although the collapse itself was sudden, the crisis that led to it developed slowly over several months. News articles from this period indicate that the possibility of crisis was always very clear to market participants, who knowingly entered into arrangements that ultimately collapsed.

Perhaps the peso crisis is so discouraging because there is so little mystery to it. Mexico was the center of the media world for much of 1994. From the advent of the North American Free Trade Agreement (NAFTA) on January 1 through the controversial presidential election in November, all the important developments were covered in great depth by the press. The facts of the case are as follows.

For Mexico, 1994 was a roller-coaster year. It began with a combination of triumph and turmoil. The triumph came on the first of January as Mexico officially entered NAFTA. Mexico looked forward to the economic benefits of free trade with the United States and Canada, which, it was thought, would also help consolidate a liberal political regime in Mexico. Capitalism and democracy were finally on the horizon. But the turmoil began on the very same day in Chiapas, a poor area in Mexico's south, where revolutionaries had armed and organized themselves, seizing control of a region in protest of NAFTA and the free-market policies of the president, Carlos Salinas de Gortari. The year ended with the currency crises that are the focus of this account, which erupted shortly after Ernesto Zedillo Ponce de León took office as president of the Republic of Mexico on December 1, 1994.

Mexico had a persistent current account deficit of about $20 billion per year that was seen by many as its most pressing short-term economic problem. NAFTA-driven optimism spurred imports of both consumer goods and capital equipment. These imports were financed by *hot money*—short-term portfolio capital that was typically invested in peso-denominated government obligations called *Cetes*.

In March 1994, Donaldo Colosio was assassinated. Colosio was the presidential nominee of the dominant Institutional Revolutionary Party (PRI) and therefore the effective designated successor to Salinas. The assassination shook Mexico by its political roots, with significant economic fallout. The Colosio assassination raised the political risk premium required to attract and hold hot money in the *Cetes*. The inflow of foreign capital dried up, putting pressure on the central bank to raise interest rates.

The problem of attracting short-term foreign capital was made even worse by rumors that came and went that Mexico might soon be forced to devalue the peso. Peso devaluation would obviously reduce the dollar value of Mexican assets for short-term investors and would unleash inflationary forces and higher interest rates that would also affect long-term investments. The Mexican government pledged repeatedly that they would not resort to devaluation. Their policy was to keep the peso-dollar exchange rate within a slowly expanding band around a central rate of about 3.2 pesos per dollar.[2]

The question was how to attract this foreign capital without raising interest rates in the face of rising rates in the United States, devaluation fears, and political uncertainty. The solution appeared in the form of dollar-indexed short-term government bonds called *Tesobonos*. The *Tesobonos* were insurance against devaluation, both because of their guaranteed dollar value and by simple logic: No rational government would agree to make payment in dollars and then devalue relative to the dollar. Such an action would massively increase the debt. The *Tesobonos* were therefore a symbol of the Mexican government's commitment to exchange rate stability. After March, the *Cetes* were converted into the popular *Tesobonos* at a high rate. By December, the *Tesobonos* debt totaled about $28 billion. Mexico's government was solvent—it had sufficient assets to pay its *Tesobonos* debt—but it was illiquid. It had only about $12 billion in ready reserves to cover the hard currency base of the *Tesobonos*. This was a sustainable situation, however, as long as the hot money flows were not diverted and the short-term *Tesobonos* were rolled over into new securities by their foreign holders. In other words, the reserves were adequate providing there was no run on *Tesobonos* that might test the reserve limits.[3]

In fact, devaluation to reduce the current account deficit seemed decidedly unlikely in March, when the *Tesobonos* policy was initiated. Devaluation would have imposed significant political costs on the governing PRI, which could not help but view all actions in terms of their likely impact on the presidential election. Besides, devaluation would probably have resulted in rapid inflation, which would quickly negate any competitive benefits. Higher price levels would also have pushed up interests rates. The real and symbolic impacts of a devalued peso would have divided the party that Zedillio, Colosio's replacement as presidential candidate, was trying to lead into the election.

The political and economic environment worsened in November 1994, establishing the dynamics of the panic that followed. Mexico's Attorney General Ruiz Massieu revealed that the government had blocked the investigation of his brother's assassination in September. Massieu resigned from office amid rumors about plots within the PRI that might affect the political stability of the nation. Capital flight from Mexico began in serious volume as hot money investors, fearing a serious breakdown in order and governance, sought sanctuary in dollar assets.

Just when Mexico's domestic political situation seemed to be bleakest, Mexico's economic problem also worsened owing to an external event with severe internal implications. The U.S. Federal Reserve Board raised interest rates in an effort to keep inflation from gaining momentum in the United States. The higher U.S. interest rates made it even harder for Mexico to attract the funds it needed to finance its international payments deficit. Mexico came under even greater pressure to increase domestic interest rates to stem the accelerating capital flight. Mexico's authorities were extremely reluctant to raise their interest rates because of the domestic economic and political risks that this action entailed. The political risks were obvious: Raising interest rates so close to the election risked further alienating voters and weakening support for the PRI and its candidates. No incumbent party wants to go into the final weeks of an election with higher interest rates.

However, the economic risks, if anything, were greater. Mexico's newly privatized banking system was fragile and in danger of serious trouble if higher rates caused loan repayment problems. All they needed was a banking crisis! However, Mexico's banking system was also in great jeopardy for another reason. Banamex and other banks were borrowing dollars at the lower dollar interest rate and using funds to make peso loans at higher interest rates—a practice that was sustainable only as long as the peso was kept stable, which the PRI promised to do. This excursion into currency speculation made Mexico's big banks especially vulnerable to a peso devaluation. It was clear, therefore, that the financial system was balanced on a knife edge and could collapse either if interest rates were raised to defend the peso or if the peso was devalued to prevent higher interest rates. No one who followed the situation closely could help but be worried about Mexico's banks.

At this point, anyone who could add and subtract whole numbers could see the potential for a crisis. The surge into *Tesobonos* beginning in March was matched by a flight from them in November, which drained Mexico's supply of hard currency reserves. With $28 billion of *Tesobonos* outstanding and only $12 billion of reserves, it was clear that Mexico would run out of reserves before it ran out of obligations if capital flight continued. Investors sold *Tesobonos* as well as peso-denominated short-term investments, which started a run on the peso itself. This is how *The Economist* summed up the climax of the peso crisis:

At the Summit of the Americas in early December 1994, the Mexican miracle was lauded as a paradigm of successful economic reform and an example to the rest of the region. Ten days later, on December 20th, plummeting foreign-exchange reserves forced the newly elected president of Mexico, Ernesto Zedillo, to devalue the peso. The badly handled devaluation created panic among investors. Money poured out of the country; within a month the economic miracle was teetering, for the second time in 12 years, on the edge of default.[4]

With its reserves depleted, there was no way for the Banco de Mexico to keep the peso within its dollar band and the peso was devalued on December 20, 1994. The peso fell in an instant from an exchange rate of about 3.2 pesos per dollar to more than 5 pesos per dollar, eventually stabilizing at about 7.5 pesos per dollar—a fall of more than 50 percent. The dream of economic prosperity and political stability for Mexico was defeated by reality—the reality of the hot money investors who led the flight from Mexico and the cold, hard balance of payments arithmetic that made devaluation inevitable. The best that can be said is that the crisis was delayed until after Zedillo's election, which probably reduced the risk of political insurrection.

The peso panic provides a clear example of the sort of crisis to which international financial markets seem prone. Investment flows, trade flows, prices, interest rates, and exchange rates—all distorted in ways that heighten social tensions—distort political choices and discourage business investment.

Devaluing the peso did nothing to resolve either Mexico's short-term liquidity problem or its longer-term current account deficit dilemma. Inflation increased to over 50 percent per year, wiping out any competitive gains from a cheaper currency, and interest rates rose to startling levels. In the end, Mexico suffered *both* devaluation and higher interest rates, the two things it wanted to avoid. About 1.5 million workers lost their jobs as recession and austerity struck.

Banamex, the largest bank, survived the crash, but only thanks to a $2 billion government aid package. Other major banks also sought government aid. Mexico was able to stabilize the peso only with the help of a controversial assistance package from the United States. A *Tequila effect* hung over Latin America and other "emerging market" economies for more than a year, as investors remained cautious.

What is most interesting to me about the peso crisis is the fact that the problem was so clear and that at each step the cause and effect relationships were so obvious. The current account deficit problem, which was the ultimate source of the peso crisis, was general knowledge, especially among financial investors. When *The Economist* magazine surveyed the situation in Mexico in February 1993, almost every aspect of the story just told, aside from assassinations, was readily apparent.[5] A survey by the *Financial Times* in March 1993 questioned whether Mexico was on its way to another debt crisis. The question, it said, "is not whether the deficit can be financed—because after the fact a country's current account deficit will always equal inflows of capital adjusted for changes in reserves. The question is at what level of interest rates and therefore economic growth will the equilibrium between capital inflows and current account deficit be reached."[6] The same story cautioned that "For comfort's sake, too high a proportion of the inflows into Latin America over the past few years is 'hot money'—money attempting to capture profit from interest differentials or foreign exchange market inefficiencies, and which is likely to be withdrawn as soon as the perceived risk associated with the investment increases."[7]

The threat of a crisis was even clearer in April 1994 after the Colosio assassination. A *Financial Times* survey of Mexico was headlined "The Picture Darkens":

> While financial markets proved unexpectedly resilient in the aftermath of the assassination of Mr. Colosio, the killing led to future increases in interest rates. If more violence lies ahead, the political uncertainty may force the government to choose between still higher interest rates that would choke the recovery or a faster rate of devaluation of the peso that could cause an upsurge in inflation.[8]

This is a sound analysis of the choice that had to be made in November 1994. Readers of the *Financial Times* were warned in April of the events of November and December. Yet even with these clear warning signs, the march to crisis continued.

On December 20, 1994, no one had much choice. Zedillo was forced to devalue—nothing else made sense. The investors were also forced to sell *Tesobonos.* The peso crisis seemed at that point inevitable. Yet this crisis resulted from actions that were rational, logical, and reasonable at the time and were taken with fairly complete knowledge of the risks and basic arithmetic of the situation.

This chapter's epigraph frames the peso crisis as a "defeat by reality." Gabriel García Márquez might better have said that they were betrayed by reason. How does reason create crisis and chaos? And is this condition an anomaly or is it a fundamental property of international capital markets and exchange rate systems? For the answers to these questions we must consult economic theory.

THE THEORY OF FINANCIAL CRISES

As stated in *The Economist,* "To many, Mexico was one more sign of how dangerously volatile the brave new world of free global capital flow is. . . . Yet for anyone with a sense of history, there was little new in the Mexican débâcle."[9] Indeed, crises of this sort are a common feature in the history of international financial markets.

Currency crises are so much a natural part of international markets that it is perhaps true that the only way to truly eliminate them is to eliminate currencies themselves by regressing to a barter system or to eliminate exchange rates by adopting a single world currency. Either of these options trades one sort of crisis for another, however.[10] Money and exchange rates will always be a feature of the international system, and so, therefore, will currency crises.

The best place to begin to learn about currency crises in particular and financial crises in general is in a little book by Charles P. Kindleberger, *Manias, Panics, and Crashes: A History of Financial Crises.*[11] Kindleberger synthesizes the theoretical model of Hyman P. Minsky with his own deep understanding of financial history and experience of contemporary international economics. His insights help us put the peso crisis of 1993–1994 into context.

Like Tolstoy's happy families, financial crises all resemble one another—in certain basic characteristics, at least—and like the unhappy families they are each unique in particular circumstance. Don't be concerned that this makes currency crises both happy and unhappy—this is a dream world, remember? The common features or stages in the development of a financial crisis are these:

1. Displacement
2. Expansion
3. Euphoria
4. Distress
5. Revulsion
6. Crisis
7. Contagion

Imagine for a moment a market for investments that has reached some sort of equilibrium, where investment flows are consistent with the information known to and expectations held by the market's participants. According to Minsky and Kindleberger, financial crises appear and then develop through these stages.

Displacement refers to an external shock or some "news" that fundamentally alters the economic outlook in a market, shifting expectations concerning future profits in some significant way. Displacement—in the sense of a change that affects expected profits—happens all the time, of course, and seldom leads to panic, crisis, or instability of any sort. The sorts of displacement we are concerned with create an object of speculation, some asset or financial instrument that becomes the focus of investors based on the news, creating a "boom."

Speculative objects appear and disappear with great frequency in financial markets, seldom creating panics or crises. So speculation and crisis may be related, but they are not the same phenomenon. *Expansion* is a necessary prerequisite for a financial crisis to rise out of a speculative episode. Expansion is the stage where the boom is fed by an increase in liquidity, which provides the means for the boom to grow, perhaps becoming a bubble. Although Kindleberger focused on increases in bank credit as a common source of expanding liquidity, there are many potential sources. Financial innovations, increased leverage, margin buying, and other techniques can stretch more buying power from a given monetary base.

Perhaps the most obvious form of expansion is the widening of the pool of potential investors or speculators, from a set of "insiders" to a larger group of "outsiders." Walter Bagehot, the great nineteenth-century political economist, suggested that panics form when an object of speculation attracts the greed of authors, rectors, and grandmothers. "At intervals, from causes which are not to the present purpose, the money from these people—the blind capital, as we call it, of the country—is particularly craving; it seeks for some one to devour it, and there is a 'plethora'; it finds some one, and there is 'speculation'; it is devoured, and there is 'panic.'"[12]

Expansion becomes *euphoria* when trading on the basis of price alone takes the place of investment based on fundamentals. The purpose of buying is to sell and take a capital gain as the price continually rises. The new buyer's motives are the same, and this euphoria continues as long as expectations do not change and liquidity holds out. This is the period of what Adam Smith called *overtrading* and Kindleberger termed *pure speculation*—that is, speculation on the basis of rising prices alone. A bubble (that will burst) or a mania (driven by wild-eyed investor maniacs) may here be created.

Distress is the next stage of a classic crisis. Distress is the stage between euphoria and revulsion when there is concern that the strength of the market may be fragile or that the limits of liquidity may be near. Distress is an unsettled time, and the reactions to this unsettled environment often deflate the bubble and defuse the mania. Distress can persist for lengths of time until the crisis is averted, or it can turn sharply into revulsion.

Revulsion is a sharp shift in actions and expectations caused by new information or a significant event. *Insiders* realize the importance of the news and sell first, perhaps at the top of the market, while *outside* authors and rectors are still buying. Liquidity dries up, especially bank lending, causing *discredit*. Walter Bagehot saw the rush to liquidity as the result of a loss of confidence in all but the most liquid assets. He wrote in *The Economist* that

It has not been sufficiently observed how very peculiar and technical is the sense in which we now talk of "panic." It would naturally signify a general destruction of all confidence, a universal distrust, a cessation of credit in general. But a panic is now come to mean a state in which there is confidence in the Bank of England, and in nothing but the Bank of England. There is an increased demand during a panic for Bank of England notes; at such times an enlarged trust is reposed in the Bank, but there is a much diminished confidence in everyone else. Distrust is diffused, but the Bank of England does not feel it; the use of its credit is augmented.

The reason is obvious. There is, in the ordinary working of banking in England, a refined mechanism of diffused credit which economises the use of bank notes, of visible instruments of exchange, of money in the ordinary sense of the word. . . . In a panic, this auxiliary and supplementary currency is at once in part annihilated. Its very foundation is taken away. That foundation is credit, and instead of credit there is discredit. . . .

In a panic, this currency of checks—this currency of refined credit—is much disturbed, and is in part destroyed; and, therefore, we fall back on credit of the first order—on credit of the coarser sort—upon bank notes. We require *more* bank notes, just because the *feeling*, the confidence which make *few* bank notes effectual has disappeared.[13]

In Minsky's model, revulsion and discredit lead to crisis, as outsiders join insiders in selling off. Kindleberger proposes the image created by the German term *Torschlusspanik*, gate-shut panic, to describe the rush to liquidity. The falling prices feed on themselves creating self-fulfilling prophecies. The result is a crisis, which may also be crash (collapse in price) or panic (sudden needless flight).

The crisis may be confined to a single market or it may spread, which is termed *contagion*. We are especially concerned with crises that spread from nation to nation through international linkages such as capital, currency, money, and commodity markets, trade interdependence effects, and shifting market psychology. Paul Krugman reserved the term *contagion crisis* for a financial crisis that spreads internationally to the extent that it causes a worldwide depression.[14]

What brings the crisis to an end? There are three possibilities, according to Kindleberger. The crisis may turn into a fire sale, with prices falling until buyers are eventually brought back into the market. Or trading may be halted by some authority, thereby limiting losses. Or, finally, a lender of last resort, of which we will hear more soon, may step in to provide the liquidity necessary to bring the crisis to a "soft landing."

THE PESO CRISIS IN PERSPECTIVE

Does Minsky's model of financial crisis describe the peso crisis? It is not difficult to frame the events of 1994 in terms of the seven stages of a financial crises just discussed.

Since we must begin somewhere, I choose Mexico's decision to join NAFTA as the critical displacement that created new objects of speculation in Mexico (how many of us bought Telefonos de Mexico stock on its way up?). It is more complicated than that, of course. Mexico's policies of liberalization, privatization, and openness created buoyant economic optimism (in foreign capital markets, anyway), and the NAFTA sealed the deal. Former "banana republic" Mexico seemed headed for a period of stable democracy, private enterprise, and growth. Everyone wanted to get in on the deal.

Expansion followed, driven by many factors. By the 1990s, financial markets were well-organized to mobilize the funds of authors, rectors, and grandmothers to invest in foreign countries that many would be hard-pressed to find on a map. The era of "global" and "emerging markets" mutual funds was here, creating the conditions for a classic speculative bubble. A modest recovery in economic prospects from the dismal 1980s led to large capital gains for those few investors who had been willing to put money into Third World markets. Their success led other investors to jump in, driving prices yet higher. And by 1993 or so "emerging markets funds" were being advertised on the television and the pages of some popular magazines.[15] As speculation on price alone took off, even fund managers became uncritical of their investment decisions, driven as they were to invest the huge sums coming in from authors and rectors every day. "We went into Latin America not knowing anything about the place," one of them noted after the Mexican crisis. "Now we are leaving without knowing anything about it."[16] You can see how disconnected investment became from any analysis of the realities involved.

"During the first half of the 1990s," according to Krugman, "a set of mutually reinforcing beliefs and expectations created a mood of euphoria about the prospects for the developing world. Markets poured money into developing countries, encouraged both by the capital gains they had already seen and by the belief that a wave of reform was unstoppable."[17] We have reached euphoria, in terms of Minsky's model, the condition in which rising prices draw new investors who expect capital gains when prices rise again. This was true for Mexico and for the "emerging" markets of several other countries. One reason the *tequila hangover* of the peso crisis was so severe is that it revealed the possibility of many Mexicos and many crises.

Distress can be located in March 1994, with the assassination of Donaldo Colosio, which raised significant doubts among foreign investors about the political stability of Mexico. The era of political stability and economic expansion that Carlos Salinas had engineered was suddenly threatened. Short-term foreign investment shifted away from private securities and the peso-denominated *Cetes*, focusing instead on the dollar-indexed *Tesobonos*. *Tesobonos* were investments that paid higher interest rates than other dollar investments, but without the exchange rate risk of peso securities. *Tesobonos* joined certain other Mexican assets as objects of speculation as investors shifted away from many other Mexican portfolio investments.

The critical importance of this distress is that it changed significantly the nature of Mexico's current account deficit problem. With the switch to dollar-backed *Tesobonos* as a way to finance the payments imbalance in the short term, Mexico's hard currency reserves were suddenly at risk. Mexico's $12 billion of reserves now guaranteed what became $28 billion of dollar-linked securities, with no international Federal Deposit Insurance Corporation (FDIC) insurance to prevent a run on the bank. It was at this point that the potential for crisis became clear. After March, in retrospect, the Mexican situation seems very delicate; it wouldn't take much to cause a sell-off.

The events of November 1994 caused revulsion. As an economist, I naturally look to the U.S. Federal Reserve's interest rate increase as the key factor. Insiders would have seen immediately the pressure that this put on Mexico's reserves, given their disinclination to raise interest rates to maintain foreign capital flows. It would be an error, however, to underestimate the importance of Attorney General Ruiz Massieu's resignation. A true PRI insider himself, Massieu's action was a signal of corruption and distrust inside the party and therefore the federal government. Some financial insiders might have interpreted this political crisis as an indication of the government's domestic weakness and, therefore, its eventual inability to raise interest rates once the presidential election was past.

Revulsion came, therefore, as Mexican authorities found themselves in a position of having to choose between their international financial responsibilities and their domestic political survival at a time when pressure was rising both inside and outside the country. The iron arithmetic of reserves versus dollar-indexed liabilities was suddenly a critical factor. Insiders caught the scent of a crisis and ran for the shutting gate doors.

The peso crisis was sharp and unexpected—or so the newspaper said. President Ernesto Zedillo certainly *seemed* unprepared for it. Fear of a devaluation caused the peso to drop, which put an even greater strain on Mexico's scarce reserve stock. When Zedillo abruptly canceled a television speech on the crisis, tension mounted and panic set in. When Zedillo finally did appear on December 20, he was forced to announce a very large devaluation of the peso.

Contagion occurred both within Mexico and between Mexico and other countries. The effects of peso depreciation, domestic inflation, and higher interest rates caused Mexico to experience a severe recession. Unemployment rose sharply from just 3.2 percent in December 1994 to 7.6 percent in August 1995 before falling to about 6.0 percent in 1996. Inflation, as measured by monthly changes in the National Consumer Price Index, rose from 3.8 percent per month in January 1995 to 8 percent in April, then fell back to the 2 to 3 percent per month range in 1996. Interbank interest rates soared, reaching 86.03 percent in March before falling back, although they remained above 40 percent until April 1996. It is hard to know what the final impact of capital flight from Mexico will be. Foreign capital deserted both weak and some strong investments.

Although the peso crisis recession in Mexico may turn out to be relatively short, it is also relatively deep, and its effects may be long lasting. Mexico's gross domestic product fell dramatically in 1995, effectively wiping out the short-run gains from the NAFTA boom and leaving Mexico's citizens not much better off—if at all—than in the old days before market reforms. Recovery was well under way by early 1996, but growth was highly concentrated in the export sector, which benefited from the peso's lower value. Mexico's internal economy—that part not directly affected by exports—remained deeply depressed by a combination of high interest rates, credit shortages, and general poverty.[18]

International contagion also occurred, notably to other "emerging market" nations that suffered from the tequila hangover effect. Krugman took a pessimistic view that because

> the 1990-95 euphoria about developing countries was so overdrawn, the Mexican crisis is likely to be the trigger that sets the process in reverse. That is, the rest of the decade will probably be a downward cycle of deflating expectations. . . . This new reluctance will surely be directly self-reinforcing, in that it means that the huge capital gains in emerging market equities will not continue. It will also lead to a further slowing of growth in those economies comprising much of Latin America and several outside nations, whose hesitant recovery in the 1980s was driven largely by infusions of foreign capital.[19]

International contagion was not limited to emerging markets, however. Investors who worried that the falling peso might drag the dollar down with it joined in a run on U.S. currency. The dollar fell to historic lows against the yen (trading briefly below eighty yen per dollar) and the deutschmark in early 1995. The peso crisis created a dollar crisis, which put pressures on trade and financial structures around the world.

LESSONS OF THE PESO CRISIS

What did we learn from the peso crisis? Well, I don't think we learned anything really *new*. The peso crisis and its fallout were a classic case of the sort of crisis that financial markets, and especially international financial markets, are prone to experience.

One lesson that apparently had to be relearned was the difference between direct foreign investments, which are long-term real asset purchases, and *hot money investment,* which is short-term highly sensitive portfolio investment. All capital flows are not the same: "Another problem with the capital flowing to the region was its composition. While direct foreign investment in factories, utilities, and mines was boosted by privatization and deregulation, a record-breaking portion of capital flowed in as foreign portfolio investment in stock and bonds. Portfolio investment is always volatile, and in these days of electronically linked capital markets, it can leave a country literally at the speed of light."[20]

A second lesson was that our ability to deal more effectively with domestic financial crises does not translate into a similar ability on the international level. International crises are related to domestic crises but also differ in important respects. Deposit insurance, regulatory regimes, and the existence of a domestic lender of last resort have all but eliminated the seven-year cycles of financial boom and panic observed in the nineteenth century. International crises, however, have increased in frequency. Perhaps the sense that we are better able to control domestic financial problems has prevented us from appreciating the international problems that are harder to control.

Kindleberger saw this pattern driven in part by the very communications advances that have accelerated the trend toward "global" investments. Communications lags, he argued, slow down the process of bubble building and allow more time for pressures to diffuse. Faster communications also allow bubbles to build more quickly and burst faster. As Kindleberger said, "Today's troubles travel instantaneously."[21]

I think that Kindleberger was almost right. Technological changes probably have not altered the speed of these transactions very much, or as much as we like to think, but communications improvements probably have broadened the domain of the crisis, which makes it harder to control. As I noted in Chapter 2, I think the communications and technological revolutions have done little to increase information flows between nations from Keynes's day, but they have vastly improved the spread of information within nations. There is more at stake in a currency crisis now because of this widened domain of affected parties. Expansion is not quicker now; it is just wider. Rectors and authors aren't drawn in sooner, they are drawn in more often because of the wider distribution of financial information. This tends to make the environment necessary for the development of international crises more common today than in earlier years.

A third very important lesson was that the liberal market-oriented policies that Mexico and many other "emerging market" nations adopted in the 1990s were not enough in themselves to produce stability and growth, as some apparently believed. These policies, which Paul Krugman dubbed the *Washington consensus* of desirable market reforms, exist within a larger and unaccommodating financial environment.[22] For emerging market economies, as for all economies, domestic stability is limited by the stability of the international financial markets. Mexico discovered that all its costly domestic reforms were vulnerable to a run by foreign investors. "As surprising as the dramatic swing in the perceptions of international investors about Latin America is," wrote Moisés Naím in 1995, "the region's vulnerability to such swings is even more surprising."[23]

Perhaps the last and most controversial lesson to be learned is that there is no international lender of last resort. Although the United States did eventually organize an international "bail out" of Mexico in 1995, which allowed the *Tesobonos* debt to be retired and Mexico's international reserve position to be restored, this action did nothing to calm the peso crisis at its peak and may have helped fuel the dollar crisis through errors of omission. For the most part, the peso crisis burned itself out independent of U.S. action.

The idea of a lender of last resort is usually attributed to Walter Bagehot. Bagehot argued that financial crises could be defused successfully by a lender of last resort that, in the face of a panic, would provide credit in exchange for good collateral at a high rate of discount. If a panic is a flight to liquidity in a dangerously uncertain situation, then a guarantee of liquidity would deflate the issue safely, Bagehot argued. Today, it is widely understood, although hard to prove, that a domestic lender of last resort can cut short financial crises and moderate their effects. What does remain controversial, however, is the stronger notion that the very existence of a lender of last resort causes crises to form because of the moral hazard this creates. Although the existence of a lender of last resort should prevent revulsion and crisis, it might also encourage riskier investment behavior and expand the speculative domain.

These same problems exist when we consider the notion of an international lender of last resort. Such an institution would have the resources necessary to lend reserves to nations during currency crises. If an international institution had stood ready to lend Mexico additional reserves (on good collateral, at a substantial discount, following Bagehot's dictum), would the peso crisis have happened at all? Remember that Mexico was illiquid, not insolvent; it had adequate assets, and only its ready hard currency reserve was insufficient.[24]

It can be argued, and some have argued it, that an *international* lender of last resort is unnecessary because financial crises tend to be *domestic* crises. The degree of international contagion is limited, it is argued, by the relatively low degree of true integration of the global economy.[25] Even a collapse of Mexico is unlikely to bring down the United States, Japan, and the European Union. (Although a crisis in the United States *would* have significant external effects.) A currency crisis is therefore unlikely to turn into what Krugman called a *contagion crisis*—a global depression. A crisis can do considerable damage to trade and investment flows and living standards without causing a worldwide economic catastrophe.

The idea of a lender of last resort raises all sorts of practical policy questions. What country or international institution would play this role? (This job certainly does not fall under the job descriptions of either the International Monetary Fund or the World Bank, as presently organized.) How much money would be required? Who would put up the reserves? On what terms? What sort of collateral would be accepted? At what discount? To what limit? Under *all* circumstances? And what of conditionality—shouldn't there be "strings" attached to assistance to ensure an end to the behavior that created the crisis in the first place?

Each of these questions raises important issues and so it is not surprising that although the idea of an international lender of last resort has been widely discussed ever since Bretton Woods, no consensus has been reached and no action taken. This does not mean that the question is closed. Improvements in communications technology and financial innovation make questions relating to the stability of the system of global markets *more,* not less, important.

"I do not forecast world economic collapse, because I think that our profession of economics does not know the dynamics of the system well enough to do so," Kindleberger noted. "At the same time, the international lender of last resort seems worth thinking about, if only for contingency planning."[26] The case of the peso crisis of 1994–1995 doesn't cause anyone to forecast global collapse, but it surely makes the case for "thinking about" an international lender of last resort stronger.

THE EUROPEAN CURRENCY CRISIS OF 1992

September 16, 1992, is called Black Wednesday by people who follow European currency movements. That was the date of a currency crisis distinctly different from Mexico's. Black Wednesday was no bubble or rational panic; it was a new kind of currency crisis distinctly different from anything that Walter Bagehot might have imagined. This was a *speculative attack* on the European Community's exchange rate mechanism (ERM).[27]

In 1992 the ERM was an agreement designed to limit exchange rate variation within the then twelve-member European Community (EC). The rationale for the ERM was that more stable exchange rates were needed to achieve greater regional economic integration with the EC. ERM states agreed to intervene in currency markets and to coordinate macroeconomic policies with an aim to keeping their exchange rates within (plus or minus) 2.25 percent of a central rate (a total variation of 4.5 percent was thus possible). The only exceptions to this rule were the Spanish peseta and the Portuguese escudo, which were subject to a broader band, reflecting their status as softer currencies. The ERM rules allowed for periodic revaluations of exchange rates— shifting the bands—when changing macroeconomic conditions required. In fact, however, the ERM had been stable since 1987.

The Maastricht Treaty intensified interest in the workings of the ERM. The Treaty on European Unity, which was negotiated in the Dutch town of Maastricht in October 1991, proposed tighter economic and political integration of EC members. When the treaty finally went into effect on November 1, 1993, the EC symbolically changed its name to European Union to reflect the intended closer relationship. A key element of the Maastricht Treaty was the proposal for monetary integration, with the eventual goal of a single European currency (eventually named the euro) and tight coordination of member state monetary policies.

The Maastricht Treaty proposed that the ERM was the first step in a process that would eventually lead to a single currency. As national economic policies and conditions converged, narrower exchange bands would further reduce currency variation until—voilà—a unified currency was achieved. The goal of a single currency was and, at this writing, still is very controversial because it asks nations to sacrifice one aspect of their sovereignty—self-determination of economic and especially exchange rate policies—to achieve the goal of partial exchange rate stability.[28] Because this goal was so controversial, each EC member put the Maastricht decision to its citizens in the form of referenda. The Maastricht Treaty was not ratified until October 1993, when all member states' citizens had voted approval.

The importance of economic policy autonomy was especially apparent in 1992 because a period of relative policy convergence of the main European economies was coming to an end. The unification of eastern and western Germany was very expensive and potentially highly inflationary.[29] Knowing that a tax increase to pay for unification would intensify domestic political conflicts, the German government chose to finance its actions through debt. The most important consequence for the current story was an increase in German interest rates, needed to both attract foreign capital and to contain inflationary pressures.

Germany's economic policies put them in conflict, in terms of the ERM, with those of France, Italy, and Great Britain. These countries, suffering from continued high unemployment, saw the need for lower interest rates to encourage economic expansion and job creation in their countries. This conflict of interests was a matter of concern within the ERM because higher German interest rates, if not matched by higher rates in France, Italy, and the United Kingdom (UK), would draw capital out of these countries and the resulting sell-off of their currencies would push them below the ERM floor. This is a classic case of domestic economic interests that conflict with international obligations as represented by the ERM commitment. Election cycles in these countries made their domestic interests potent, but the increased emphasis on exchange stability inherent in the Maastricht Treaty also created additional pressure to preserve the ERM relationships. Thus was created an environment conducive to a political-economic crisis.

The most important events leading up to Black Wednesday are these. On June 2, 1992, Denmark's voters unexpectedly rejected the Maastricht referendum, a vote that stunned Europe (Danish approval was gained later, in a second referendum). The Danish vote increased the doubts about the commitment of several nations to monetary unification, which also raised doubts about their commitment to defending the ERM.

These doubts grew deeper on July 16, when Germany's Bundesbank raised key interests rates in its continuing anti-inflation policy. This action was seen by many as an almost aggressive act, a statement that Germany would *not* sacrifice its domestic priorities and that other ERM states, especially France and the UK, would have to follow suit and raise their own interest rates, following the German example instead. It was not at all clear that they would do this. This set up a showdown on economic policy, with the credibility of the ERM in the balance.

"This policy conflict did not remain unnoticed by the speculators," noted Paul De Grauwe, economist and member of the Belgian parliament. "They realized that the UK and French authorities were tempted to cut their links with the deutschmark so as to be able to follow more expansionary monetary policies. Influential economists in fact openly urged the authorities to do just that. Thus speculators had good reasons to start speculating against the pound sterling and the French franc."[30]

In fact, several countries encountered great difficulty defending their ERM band commitments. Higher German interest rates pushed up the deutschmark and pushed down the other currencies. Unwilling to raise their interest rates, French, German, and Italian central bankers were forced to use their scarce reserves to defend their currencies from market forces. This was a battle they could win for only a limited time, however, because of the finite nature of their resources compared with the $1 trillion per day foreign exchange market.

On September 13, 1992, the commitment to ERM broke down. Italy devalued the lira by 7 percent but stayed in the ERM in exchange for a reduction in German interest rates. When the rate cut came the next day, it was a tiny one-quarter percent drop in the Lombard rate, clearly too small to turn around the market forces that were starting to tear the ERM apart.

France's referendum on the Maastricht Treaty was set for September 20, and this added to the pressure on the ERM. French voters, although traditionally pro-Europe, were not necessarily pro-unemployment, which is how many of them interpreted the prospect of a permanent connection to (or domination by?) the austere Germany Bundesbank. It looked like Maastricht might lose the vote in France, taking pressure off France to maintain its ERM stand. (Maastricht won, in fact, but by a slight 51 percent Yes to 49 percent No margin.)

Speculation intensified against the currencies held to have the weakest commitment to the ERM or the least reserves to defend their position. *Hedge funds* and others leveraged their assets and used them to sell short the target currencies. It was a one-way bet with enormous potential gain for someone with the resources and courage to bet really big. If the ERM held together, then the key currencies would not fall further than their floors, but they were unlikely to rise much above them, either. At worst, selling short could create a small loss. If the ERM collapsed under the speculative attack, however, short-sellers could fulfill their contracts at a much lower price and profit handsomely. Insignificant loss versus high gain. No wonder they bet against the pound and the lira.

Enormous speculative pressure was brought to bear against the pound, lira, and franc. Great Britain, facing severe reserve constraints, raised the base interest rate from 10 percent to 15 percent in two stages, but it wasn't enough.[31] Britain's actions were more than adequate to bring their "fundamentals" into line with German financial returns, but the market's driving force had shifted from investment to speculation. Britain's desperate move made further defensive action seem unlikely, strengthening the speculative attack.

The crisis came to a head finally on September 16, when speculative pressures overwhelmed Britain and Italy. Unable to muster more reserves and unwilling to raise interest rates further, Britain and Italy dropped out of the ERM and allowed their currencies to float down to market levels. The speculators covered their short contracts at the lower rate and took their profits to the bank.

The devaluations, when they came, were not nearly so large as in the Mexico crisis. The pound's value fell from its ERM floor of 2.77 deutschmarks per pound on September 16 to 2.53 deutschmarks on September 21. The devaluation of the lira was smaller, but it had already been devalued earlier in the week. France, also subject to speculative attack, successfully defended the franc in the short run, but pressure continued until it cracked, too, in 1993.

Black Wednesday and its aftermath showed clearly that currency crises were not limited to the cases of less-developed countries with current account problems. Britain and France, the largest victims in the ERM's crises, in many ways had stronger economic fundamentals than Germany, with its unification problems and costs. This did not protect them, however, from crises driven by *speculative attack.*

THE THEORY OF SPECULATIVE ATTACKS

The theory of speculative attacks, as conceived by Paul Krugman and developed by him and others, is deceptively simple.[32] Assume an exchange rate system like that of the 1980s and 1990s. Capital is highly mobile across national boundaries, so that exchange markets are *deep*—the daily flow through exchange markets, a trillion dollars a day in the mid-1990s, vastly exceeds the reserves of the central banks. Exchange rates are flexible enough so that currency speculation is an active industry. Many governments intervene in the currency markets in an attempt to keep their currencies within *target zones,* which may be formally set, as with the ERM, or informal but real, as has often been true of the yen-dollar exchange rate. A system like this, designed to provide relative stability within a regime of flexible exchange rates, contains a systematic flaw: it is prone to speculative attacks that create exchange rate crises.

This conclusion is important because it means that the exchange rate *system* just described contains inherent instabilities. It is not just that rational bubbles sometimes form and burst or that the poor policies of deficit nations can cause soft currency crises. The tendency toward instability and crisis is *built in.* The theory of speculative attacks suggests that events like the ERM crisis of 1992 are inherent risks.

Imagine a situation in which a nation, say France, has set a target zone for its currency that it will defend using only its central bank reserves or some fraction of them. When the franc is at or near the border of its target zone, the dynamics of the speculative attack come into play. Speculators attempt to force a devaluation of the franc—a realignment of the target zone—by selling short massive amounts of francs, leveraging their own assets in an attempt to gain the central bank assets and cause a currency crisis. As noted earlier, this situation can be viewed as a "one-way bet." If the franc is devalued, then speculators win, repaying the francs they have sold with cheaper francs purchased on the spot market. If the central bank succeeds in fending off the attack, the speculators lose little, since they buy back francs for roughly what they paid for them, the target zone price. If the franc appreciates, which may be viewed as unlikely, speculators lose on their short contracts—perhaps significantly—buying back francs for more than they paid for them.

One way to think of the speculative attack scenario is that when the possibility of franc devaluation appears, non-franc reserves are a scarce and valuable asset, since they gain in value when depreciation occurs. The central bank's non-franc reserves are therefore the object of the attack. Speculators want these reserves so they can sell them back after devaluation at a profit. By engaging in a speculative attack, they force the central bank to yield to them their scarce and valuable reserves.

It is the perverse logic of the target zone system that no currency is safe once it is near enough its target zone border to make a speculative attack credible. If the central bank has a relatively small amount of reserves, a single attack of short-selling will work (as with Italy in 1992). If the central bank has greater reserves, as France did in 1992–1993, for example, it is still not safe. Since speculators do not know what fraction of its reserves the central bank is willing to use in defending its currency, a series of smaller attacks occur that eventually drain reserves to the critical level where a single large attack suffices to cause devaluation. This scenario fits well the story of the French franc, which survived the 1992 ERM crisis but not the attacks of July 1993.

Speculative attacks are self-fulfilling prophecies. Because speculators believe that a currency is vulnerable to devaluation, it is. And because they think that commitment to the target zone is not credible, it isn't. The rational, profit-maximizing actions of speculators create the results they expect, which are currency crises and sharp, discontinuous changes in exchange rates. According to De Grauwe, "Some continental European observers and politicians have claimed that the speculation against the pound sterling and especially against the French franc was irrational and driven by an 'Anglo-Saxon plot' against the process of monetary unification in Europe. Such explanations based on irrational motives cannot easily be disproved. One should be suspicious about these explanations, however. In general, speculators want to make money, and do not care about the colour of the money they expect to earn."[33]

Central bank reserves are not the only tool available to squelch speculative attacks. Central bank authorities can, in theory, mobilize private capital if they are willing to alter macroeconomic policy variables as part of a defensive strategy. Great Britain, for example, raised interest rates in 1992 in just such a move. If sterling's defenders had been willing to raise interest rates high enough, eventually they would have pulled sterling back from the brink of devaluation, and speculative attacks would have ended or moved on to other targets. The problem with this strategy is that higher interest rates have domestic as well as international effects. The growth-sapping impact of higher interest rates made them an unacceptable choice in 1992.

International cooperation is another strategy that can work to defend against speculative attacks. A small increase in French interest rates combined with lower German interest rates would have the same effect on the franc-deutschmark exchange rate with fewer unpleasant side effects within France. The difficulty, apparent in the ERM crises, is that there are many circumstances in which the domestic priorities of central banks will not be so aligned as to make effective cooperation possible. Recall Germany's quarter-point cut in the Lombard rate in 1992—cooperation in technical terms but insufficient to avert a crisis. If economic policymakers give domestic concerns high priority, which they do, and the nature of macroeconomic problems and priorities differ among nations, which they do, then the strategy of cooperation is an unreliable defense from speculative attacks.

Speculative attacks are a serious matter. They can have serious effects (e.g., lost reserves, distorted macroeconomic policies, inflation, unemployment, rising interest rates) on the particular country whose currency is under attack, but the negative effects are not limited to the target country. The evidence suggests that some impacts are spread to other economies through contagion. A recent study by Barry Eichengreen, Andrew K. Rose, and Charles Wyplosz, for example, examined the factors that make currency crises contagious and therefore an even more serious systemic problem.[34] Using thirty years of panel data from twenty industrialized countries, they found evidence of contagion, which varied directly with the degree of interdependence among affected nations. "The evidence is striking," they wrote, "a variety of tests and a battery of sensitivity analyses uniformly suggest that a crisis elsewhere in the world increases the probability of a speculative attack by an economically and statistically significant amount . . . even after controlling for economic and political fundamentals in the country concerned."[35] Crisis in any single currency therefore increases the risk of crisis generally.

The problems of currency crisis seem to pass from the "affected" to the "infected" nation especially through the trade and macroeconomic policy channels. The peso crisis, for example, affected Mexico directly, but it also caused problems for nations that are closely linked to Mexico by trade ties. The greater the trade linkage, the more powerful the contagion effect. The other way that contagion occurs is through macroeconomic policy effects. When a country such as Mexico suffers a crisis, other countries in roughly similar circumstances also come into play. They find themselves under pressure to adopt preventive policies so that, for example, higher interest rates in Mexico seem to be contagious. This is at least one aspect of the *Tequila effect* that followed Mexico's peso crisis.

Because, according to this study, contagion increases with the degree of international economic integration, the problem of currency crisis and speculative attack may be directly related to economic globalization. Globalization links nations more closely together, but the closer the links the greater the risk of instability due to contagion. This situation naturally limits the extent of globalization, if an equilibrium or balance between globalization and stability occurs. But it could also lead to cycles of globalization, instability, crisis, and chaos, followed by another round of globalization. In either case, currency crises and speculative attacks seem to make the notion of true globalization more myth than reality.

What we have seen thus far is that currency crises due to speculative attacks are based on the profitability of speculating against the central bank, the finite nature of central bank reserves, conflict between domestic priorities and the need to defend the currency, and the unreliable nature of international cooperation. The effects of crisis are contagious and increase with the degree of international economic integration. The conditions for successful speculative attacks are fairly common, and the resulting currency crises have become a regular feature of foreign exchange markets. Can the exchange rate system be modified to eliminate this threat or make it a less frequent occurrence? Four types of systemic changes come to mind.

An obvious first proposal, given the earlier discussions, is an international lender of last resort, willing and able to provide liquidity to central banks facing speculative attack. Such an institution would need to have virtually infinite reserves, however, and be willing to provide them freely in emergencies. An international lender of last resort of this magnitude is not practical in either political or economic terms, and it is unclear in any case whether the establishment of such an organization would result in more stable exchange rates or just more prosperous speculators.

A worldwide tax on foreign exchange transactions has been proposed as a solution to the speculative attack problem.[36] Such a tax could conceivably alter the dynamics of the one-way bet and would tend to discourage speculation, especially highly leveraged speculation, by making it costlier than other sources of profit. Such a tax would also make all other foreign exchange transactions more costly, however, putting "sand in the wheels" of international trade and finance generally. The tax would need to be universal to be effective, and such worldwide regulatory agreement is considered unlikely.

A third solution would be monetary union, which would eliminate exchange rates through adoption of the single worldwide currency. This, too, is considered impractical at present, but it raises an important point. Once the European Union achieves monetary union, with a common monetary policy and a single currency, speculative attacks like those in 1992 and 1993 will not be possible. The goals of exchange rate stability will be achieved, presumably, by monetary union. But if the transition to monetary union must take place though a system of target zones, then the goal may never be achieved. It is the nature of speculative attacks on target zones that they produce currency crises that tear target zone structures apart. In Europe, the goal of a monetary union and the process of target zone convergence are thus inconsistent.[37]

Finally, the sharp point of speculative attacks can be blunted by target zone structures that feature broad bands, not narrow ones. Central bank intervention would tend to be less frequent under these circumstances, and so attacks of bank reserves would be less common as well. The logic of speculative attacks would remain, however, as would the problem of currency crises.

EXCHANGE MARKET MAYHEM

The exchange rate is the chink in the armour of modern-day macroeconomic policy-makers. Be it Italy and the United Kingdom in 1992, France in 1993, Mexico in 1994 or Spain in 1995, speculative pressures and the dire consequences of policy responses required to defend the exchange rate can bring a government's entire macroeconomic strategy tumbling down. . . . Even the United States, a relatively large closed economy committed to a policy of benign neglect, was forced in 1994-5 to consider sacrificing other policy goals on the altar of the exchange rate when the dollar declined precipitously against the yen. Without realizing it, many observers have derived an impossibility theorem: neither pegging like Sweden, nor occasionally realigning like Mexico and the EMS countries, nor floating like the United States is a tolerable option. Policy-makers seem to retain no acceptable international monetary alternative.[38]

How serious is the problem of currency crisis? Again, Eichengreen, Rose, and Wyplosz shed light on this question.[39] Twenty OECD (Organization for Economic Cooperation and Development) nations were studied for the period 1959–1993 using quarterly data.[40] The data included 2,516 observations of "tranquillity" (no significant change in market conditions), 61 failed speculative attacks, 81 instances of devaluation, 20 instances of revaluation (opposite of devaluation), 33 regime changes from fixed to floating exchange rates, 33 regime changes from floating to fixed, and 56 assorted nontranquil "other events."

The data on exchange crises and events are especially interesting because the theory can easily become so confusing. This chapter has focused on basic theories and case studies of currency crisis. Basically, theory suggests that currency crises should be happening all the time. The surprising event these days, from the standpoint of currency theory, is not the appearance but rather the lack of a currency crisis. The challenge for economists, therefore, is to try to figure out why some situations produce crises and speculative attacks whereas others do not. The search for answers to these questions has produced an amazing array of theoretical angles.

Some theories are based on purely *economic* problems, such as current account deficits, for example, whereas others focus on *political* problems and constraints, such as the need to create jobs, even in a surplus country, to get votes. Crises may be caused by a weak economy or a weak party or president. Some theories see currency problems as deriving from a nation's weak *external* economic position, whereas others seek their source in weak *internal* conditions. Some see currency crises as *leading* factors, which precede or anticipate a change in fundamental economic conditions, whereas other see these crises as *lagging* or following their real causes. Some theories focus on *strategic* behavior as the source of crisis, while others cite *competitive* forces. *Traders* and speculators in the private sector are the main actors in some accounts, whereas *governments* or central banks take the active role in others. Finally, some theories assume that foreign exchange markets have a *single* stable equilibrium, whereas others explore the possibility of *multiple equilibria* as the source of rapid exchange rate adjustments.[41]

Eichengreen, Rose, and Wyplosz concluded that "governments bring currency crises on themselves through the reckless pursuit of excessively expansionary policies" that create current account deficits, push the exchange rate down, and destroy the credibility of government policies.[42] If this were the whole story, then we could conclude that currency crises were the just desserts of profligate states. It isn't, however, as the ERM crisis of 1992 showed. Some states bring crises on themselves,

> But many other governments whose currencies are attacked do not clearly bring their exchange market difficulties on themselves through the reckless

pursuit of expansionary policies. Virtuous behavior, in other words, is no
guarantee of immunity from exchange market pressures. . . . Speculative attacks can occur because markets are uncertain about a government's inten-
tions and test its resolve. Alternatively, speculative attacks can be a symptom
of self-fulfilling attacks, in the sense that markets believe that the government will not resist pressure and will shift to more expansionary policies as
it abandons the exchange rate commitment in response to the attack itself.[43]

The problem of currency crisis and speculative attack seems to be an in-
tegral part of the system of national currencies. Although states sometimes
bring on these problems, it is not clear that they can entirely avoid them either. This does not mean, however, that politicians are entirely blameless. In
Mexico, Britain, and recently in Thailand, politicians seeking to protect local
interests all created or exacerbated situations in which speculators could make
a "one-way bet" against their currencies and thereby encouraged unstable
capital flows or speculative attacks.[44] The international capital markets punish
bad policies, as we have long suspected. Good policies, however, are not always rewarded.

CURRENCY CRISES AND GLOBALIZATION

Currency crises are a fact of life in today's international financial markets.
Exchange rates are subject to a variety of forces that can cause them to swing
sharply, suddenly, and by amounts that are hard to anticipate or hedge against.
Some crises, such as Mexico's 1994 collapse, are the result of bubbles, manias, or panics—logical chain reactions gone astray. Other crises are like the
ERM breakdown of 1992, the consequence of speculative attacks driven by
the iron logic of profit maximization.

It would be one thing if we could say that currency crises are a curse on
sinners, a plague on their houses for poor choices and unrealistic economic policy. But, as we have seen, currency crises are driven by their own logics, and it
is not just sinners who are punished. The studies cited here suggest that we cannot truly know the sources of currency crises, their timing, their incidence, or
their eventual total direct and contagion impacts. This is a lot to not know.

The persistence of currency crises means that exchange rates are subject
to tremors that are like earthquakes. The ground shifts suddenly, by an un-
known amount, at moments that are very hard to predict. This would matter
little if the exchange rate were an insignificant item. Currency crises would
then be like earthquakes in Antarctica—of interest only to penguins and academic researchers.

Unfortunately, the exchange rate is a price, and economists think that
prices are very important. Prices are the invisible hands that guide the market
system. They point to scarcity and to abundance, and they coordinate activi-

ties in the most efficient way. When prices are right, resource allocation is efficient. When they are wrong, the wrong signal is sent, and individuals acting in their own self-interest make mistakes. Getting prices right is therefore the most important thing that markets can do.

The exchange rate is the one price that matters most because it is the one price that most directly affects all other prices in a market system. When the U.S. dollar declines in price, for example, everything in the United States is cheaper for foreign buyers or investors, and everything in other countries is more expensive for U.S. citizens. Contagion effects from currency swings are therefore wide, if not also deep. The potential for resource misallocation is tremendous.

For globalization's advocates, the fact of currency crises creates a logical dilemma. If currency crises are unimportant, then prices are unimportant, which means that markets are unimportant. But markets are the driving force of globalization. If currency crises are important, on the other hand, then they create a risk that is associated with global or international activities and that naturally limits the extent of these activities. True globalization, in the sense of a single market operating according to the law of one price, is impossible. Global can only be international or multilocal in this context.

Currency crises are a significant barrier to globalization, but the situation is worse. Global financial markets suffer from both crisis and the potentially more serious property of *chaos,* which is the subject to which we now turn.

NOTES

1. Quoted by Moisés Naím, "Latin America the Morning After," *Foreign Affairs* 74:4 (July/August 1995), p. 45. García Márquez here is speaking to Carlos Fuentes, suggesting they dump their fiction into the sea because reality has outdone their imaginations.

2. This is a rate that Rudiger Dornbusch and others have argued made the peso overvalued. Dornbusch called for Mexico to devalue the peso as early as November 1992. It is significant that Finance Minister Pedro Aspe was a student of Dornbusch when he studied at MIT.

3. This point is made by Jeffrey Sachs, Aaron Tornell, and Andrés Valasco, "The Collapse of the Mexican Peso: What Have We Learned?" *Economic Policy* 22 (April 1996), pp. 13–64.

4. Zanny Minton-Beddoes, "A Survey of Latin American Finance," *The Economist* (December 9, 1995), p. 1.

5. Christopher Wood, "A Survey of Mexico," *The Economist* (February 13, 1993), p. 1.

6. Stephen Fidler, "Survey of Latin American Finance," *Financial Times*, March 29, 1993, p. 2.

7. Ibid., p. 3.

8. Stephen Fidler, "Survey of Latin American Finance," *Financial Times*, April 11, 1994, p. 2.

9. Zanny Minton-Beddoes, "A Survey of Latin American Finance," *The Economist* (December 9, 1995), p. 1.

10. The particular problems of a single currency are discussed in Chapter 6.

11. Charles P. Kindleberger, *Manias, Panics, and Crashes: A History of Financial Crises* (New York: Basic Books, 1978).

12. Walter Bagehot as quoted in Rudiger Dornbusch's, "International Financial Crises," in *The Risk of Economic Crisis,* ed. Martin Feldstein (Chicago: University of Chicago Press, 1991), p. 117.

13. Walter Bagehot, "What a Panic Is and How It Might Be Mitigated," *The Economist* (May 12, 1866). Reprinted in *The Collected Works of Walter Bagehot,* vol. 10, ed. Norman St. John-Stevas (London: The Economist, 1978), pp. 88–89.

14. Paul Krugman, "Financial Crises in the International Economy," in *The Risk of Economic Crisis,* ed. Martin Feldstein (Chicago: University of Chicago Press, 1991), p. 100.

15. Paul Krugman, "Dutch Tulips and Emerging Markets," *Foreign Affairs,* 74:4 (July/August 1995), pp. 36–37.

16. Quoted in Naím, "Latin America the Morning After," p. 51.

17. Krugman, "Dutch Tulips," p. 39.

18. Lesley Crawford, "Survey of Latin American Finance and Investment: Only Zedillo Optimistic," *Financial Times,* March 25, 1996, p. 4.

19. Krugman, "Dutch Tulips," p. 43.

20. Naím, "Latin America the Morning After," p. 51.

21. Kindleberger, *Manias,* p. 219.

22. Krugman, "Dutch Tulips," p. 28.

23. Naím, "Latin America the Morning After," pp. 49–50.

24. This point is driven home by the success Mexico achieved in meeting its obligations once the crisis had passed.

25. See the discussion in Krugman, "Financial Crises."

26. Kindleberger, *Manias,* p. 220.

27. This term seems to have been coined by Paul R. Krugman in his 1979 article "A Model of Balance of Payments Crises," reprinted in Paul R. Krugman, *Currencies and Crises* (Cambridge, MA: MIT Press, 1992), pp. 61–75.

28. Exchange rate stability is only partial because, even though a single currency would fix exchange rates within the European Union, the euro would still vary with respect to the dollar, yen, and other currencies.

29. The decision to exchange ostmarks, the East German currency, for deutschmarks at a rate of one to one, which was far above the market rate for the currency, had the effect of creating substantial purchasing power in eastern Germany without a commensurate rise in output (in fact, output fell). More purchasing power chasing fewer goods and services is a sure recipe for inflation.

30. Paul De Grauwe, *The Economics of Monetary Integration* (2nd ed.) (New York: Oxford University Press, 1994), p. 124.

31. Sweden, also under attack, raised overnight interest rates to 500 (five hundred!) percent.

32. See Mark P. Taylor, "The Economics of Exchange Rates," *Journal of Economic Literature* 33 (March 1995), especially pp. 37–39, for an introduction to this literature.

33. Paul De Grauwe, *The Economics of Monetary Integration*, p. 123.

34. Barry Eichengreen, Andrew K. Rose, and Charles Wyplosz, "Contagious Currency Crises," National Bureau of Economic Research Working Paper no. 5681, July 1996.

35. Ibid., p. 2.

36. This idea is discussed in Barry Eichengreen, Andrew K. Rose, and Charles Wyplosz, "Exchange Market Mayhem: The Antecedents and Aftermaths of Speculative Attacks," *Economic Policy* 21 (October 1995), especially pp. 294–296.

37. This point is made by De Grauwe in *The Economics of Monetary Integration*, Chapter 5.

38. Eichengreen et al., "Exchange Market Mayhem, pp. 251–252.

39. Ibid.

40. The authors correctly point out that quarterly data are inconvenient for this purpose, since as much exchange rate variation occurs within quarters as between them. If anything, then, the use of quarterly data is likely to diminish the measured turbulence in exchange rates. Nonetheless, these data are useful and revealing.

41. The possibility of multiple equilibria is well known in foreign exchange economics. It is possible for current demand and supply curves to bend sharply and even slope the wrong way owing to elasticity conditions for the underlying goods, services, and assets, creating a number of equilibria—some stable and others unstable.

42. Eichengreen et al., "Exchange Market Mayhem," p. 294.

43. Ibid., p. 294–295.

44. Thanks to an anonymous reviewer for this point.

5

Turbulence and Chaos

In order to master the unruly torrent of life the learned man meditates, the poet quivers, and the political hero erects the fortress of his will.
　　　　　　　　　　　　　　　　　　　　　—José Ortega y Gasset[1]

There are two ways of looking at the landscape of global finance: the perspectives of theory and of practice. As is often the case in economics, the images of theory seem to reveal a wholly different panorama from that which emerges from the viewpoint of practice. Both are true images, yet each is unique. Not surprisingly, we tend to focus on the more understandable and logical scene, which may be a serious mistake.

Exchange rates and the international flows that influence them are determined, in theory, by *fundamentals*. Fundamentals are the essential characteristics of economic systems that influence real trade and investment behavior. Logically, international flows should respond to changes in their fundamental determinants, making it possible to anticipate generally—if not to predict precisely—financial movements and exchange rate changes.

The pattern of international trade, for example, is determined in part by the prices of the goods that are bought and sold. If higher rates of price inflation in Italy make that country's goods more expensive than those from other countries on international markets, then it is logical to expect that buyers will purchase fewer Italian goods and therefore fewer Italian lira. This lack of demand tends to depress the prices of both Italian goods and Italian currency, with the process continuing until a fundamental equilibrium is restored. If inflation makes Italian goods more expensive, then the lira must fall to compensate. The fundamental logic is bulletproof.

International capital movements, by the same logic, are influenced by expected real rates of return. If Italian interest rates rise relative to those of other countries and there is no offsetting change in expected prices or risk, then capital should flow to Italy to earn the higher return, with exchange rate and domestic interest rate effects that can be anticipated. The logic is clear.

Although international finance is complicated from the perspective of theory, it is not overly complex. It is complicated because there are a number of fundamental factors that can influence trade and investment decisions, several of which may be changing at the same time. But it is not very complex because each element has its own internal logic, and it is only a matter of time until you see how the pieces add up. Even the problems of currency crisis and speculative attack discussed in Chapter 4 are simple, logical processes.

Looking at international finance from the standpoint of theory, therefore, is like listening to a Bach fugue: lots to listen for, much detail to admire, and some problems to be worked out, but scrutiny is rewarded and the puzzles are solved in the end.

Practice plays a different tune, one that is much more like, say, a Dave Brubeck jazz piece: rhythmically complex, rolling and weaving, solid but ambiguous at times.

The merchants of pure practice are called *chartists* because they base their understanding of financial movements on what actually has happened, not on what should happen according to a model or equation. The chartists plot market data and analyze the patterns they find, searching for trends, turning points, support levels, and breaking points. Their charts resemble abstract drawings at times. Although theory tells us that the processes that set these prices are logically sound, the result, when it is plotted out, looks decidedly illogical. Sometimes there are no patterns at all. At other times there are patterns, but it is hard to know what they mean. How can logical forces produce such illogical-looking results?

Chaos theory provides a means to reconcile the enormous difference between the theory of international finance and its practice—to understand how the ordered, deterministic processes of the fundamentalists lead to seemingly disordered, prediction-resistant real world patterns of the chartists. Chaos theory, in other words, helps explain how Bach becomes Brubeck.

In this chapter I present a simple introduction to chaos theory and its application to economics in general and international finance in particular. I argue that exchange rates and international capital movements are not just unstable, as we saw in the analysis of currency crises in Chapter 4, but fundamentally chaotic. This is an important observation. Currency crises and speculative attacks don't happen every day. Several months can go by without even a hint of currency collapse. During these short or long periods of relative stability, it is easy to conclude that global financial markets really are very stable and predictable or are converging toward such a stable state.[2] But even if currency crises disappeared forever, the existence of chaotic movements in foreign exchange rates would continue to condition foreign trade and investment patterns and limit the globalization process.

The existence of chaotic patterns in international finance is important in several respects. First, it renders accurate long-term forecasting impossible, limiting the essential nature of global investments. Second, it increases the risk associated with even short-term international transactions, thereby limiting and altering the nature of these flows. Third, international financial chaos can lead to the delinking of exchange rates from the real economy, making nonsense of notions of rational global decision making. Finally, and perhaps most important, the turbulence of chaotic financial patterns encourages governments to intervene in financial markets to calm or steady them, which leads to crises and speculative assaults. A vicious cycle of crisis and chaos results, which further discourages the global expansion of economic activity. Chaos in financial markets, therefore, contributes to a wider chaotic condition.

This analysis of international finance using the ideas of chaos theory is thus more than just pretty pictures and interesting images, which are what most of us expect from a study of chaos: It is actually important both as theory and in practice. If international markets exhibit elements of chaos, then the global economy works differently, in fundamental respects, than most people believe, forcing us to reexamine the causes and consequences of the global expansion of economic activity.

CHAOS THEORY: WHY YOU CANNOT STIR THINGS APART

Chaos theory is more firmly established in popular culture than it is in academic circles, which is unusual for a discipline that is based on sophisticated mathematics. The language of chaos entered the common vernacular in 1987 with James Gleick's bestselling book, *Chaos: Making a New Science*.[3] Since then several interesting books and at least one serious stage play have appeared on the subject.[4] Of the 186 books with *chaos* in the title at Collins Library at the University of Puget Sound, for example, 114 were published after 1987, in the post-Gleick era. Most are about chaos theory in the sense in which I use it here—the science of complex dynamics—although there are a few works of literature mixed in that use the term in its classical sense: chaos as the formless disorder from which life sprang in Greek mythology. Book titles include *Adventures in Chaos, The Collapse of Chaos, Chaos and Complexity, Chaos in Wonderland, Coping with Chaos,* and many more. Like Gleick's book, most chaos books have pictures of startling beauty, often in color. This distinguishes them from other books on the shelf, especially the academic books. The pictures are visual representations of computer simulations of chaotic processes.

Pictures are important in chaos theory, I think, because chaos is easier to recognize than it is to define clearly. Although there is no single standard definition of chaos, I think the important ideas are perhaps best captured in Stephen H. Kellert's description of chaos theory as "the qualitative study of unstable aperiodic behavior in deterministic nonlinear dynamical systems."[5] The essential elements of chaos as I use the concept are these:

Unstable aperiodic behavior. The outcomes of chaotic systems are not regular patterns that exhibit smooth cycles or neat equilibria. Rather, a key characteristic of chaotic systems is the seeming randomness or unpredictability of the patterns and flows generated. In a nonchaotic system, a close study of the past eventually yields insights that allow us to anticipate the future. In a chaotic system, by contrast, the future is full of surprises and does not repeat the past in any periodic or regular way. Past is *not* prologue in chaos. Alfredo Medio notes that

> For nonchaotic systems, therefore, after a certain time, listening to the 'news' becomes totally uninformative. For a chaotic system, however, no matter how long we accumulate data on the past positions of the system, we cannot accurately predict its transition from the present position to the next one (or to any of the future ones). In this case, we can only make probabilistic forecasts, if any at all. For chaotic systems, therefore, coarse-grained past, however long, does not determine uniquely and completely coarse-grained future. In other words, the 'news' will continue indefinitely to be a source of additional information to the system.[6]

Deterministic systems. The paradox—and a defining element—of chaotic systems is that they seem random, but they are not. The *causes* are rational and logical; the *effects* are seemingly random. Disorder arises from order, which may be specified by a set of equations that determine the behavior of the system. If the equations are known, behavior can be simulated or anticipated. But it is hard to "work backwards" and infer from the aperiodic observations the underlying deterministic system. Thomasina Coverly, the math prodigy in Tom Stoppard's play *Arcadia,* makes the point this way:

> If you could stop every atom in its position and direction, and if your mind could comprehend all the actions thus suspended, then if you were really, *really* good at algebra, you could write the formula for all the future; and although nobody can be so clever as to do it, the formula must exist just as if it could.[7]

Dynamical systems. The key is that the deterministic system is dynamical, not static. It is not a system of equations to be solved simultaneously for equilibrium but rather a description of a movement through time, in which each instant's condition is related to the moment before and determines the condition of the next moment. In some applications, the most important contribution of chaos theory is that it shifts the focus from static to dynamical analysis. Most economic analysis, for example, is static because this allows us to work on systems of ordinary equations that can be solved generally using what Thomasina Coverly would call "good English algebra." Dynamical systems, on the other hand, require the use of difference equations, or differential equations, which have solutions but often cannot be solved in a general sense. (Numerical analysis can be used to find solutions to specific cases.)

Nonlinear systems. Not all dynamical systems are chaotic. Chaos occurs when the systems are nonlinear, and for this reason the term *nonlinear dynamics* is often applied to what I call chaos theory. In a linear system, patterns of behavior are very regular. Actions respond to their stimuli in a constant direction at a constant rate and display the same behavior going forward and backward. Linear systems are convenient for theory because they are so well behaved. The world is generally nonlinear, however. As stimuli increase, actions increase and decrease and at varying rates of acceleration and deceleration. Nature does not always work the same going forward and backward. Thomasina discovered that "When you stir your rice pudding, Septimus, the spoonful of jam spreads itself round making red trails like the picture of a meteor in my astronomical atlas. But if you stir backward, the jam will not come together again. Indeed, the pudding does not notice and continues to turn pink just as before. . . . You cannot stir things apart."[8]

A linear system may provide a workable description of nonlinear behavior within a very local region, but the resemblance breaks down over time in a dynamical system and as the focus of attention shifts from local to global. Thus, it may be reasonable for an aeronautical engineer to test an airplane wing with a constant wind of two hundred kilometers per hour from the north to learn about certain narrow aspects of design and performance, but it would be nonsense to infer from this experiment the wing's actual behavior in the real world and complex or changing airflow patterns.[9]

Qualitative study. This is controversial. Although much analysis of chaos is quantitative in nature, my focus is really qualitative, and I have chosen my definition of chaos accordingly. In this study I am not interested in being able to make exact predictions of how international financial variables change when they are in a state of chaos, although it would be useful and potentially profitable to be able to do so![10] Rather I am concerned with understanding how fundamental relationships change over time and the consequences of these changes. This is qualitative, not quantitative, analysis. Quantitative analysis of chaotic systems is important, but for reasons that I discuss later in this chapter, I think it is of relatively limited utility in economics.

The definition of *chaos* as the qualitative study of unstable aperiodic behavior in deterministic nonlinear dynamical systems suits my purposes because it effectively describes the nature of *this* study (qualitative), the *character* of international financial markets (dynamic, deterministic, and nonlinear), and the observed *outcomes* (aperiodic behavior). Other commonly cited properties of chaos, which may also be present in international financial markets, are these:

Sensitive dependence on initial conditions. One common feature of chaotic systems is that small changes in parameters ultimately cause enormous changes in outcome or behavior, as the tiny initial differences are magnified and transformed by the nonlinear dynamical processes at work. It is not very difficult to understand how sensitive dependence works. The accumulation of compound interest is a nonlinear dynamical process. Compound interest accumulates over time (dynamical) and rises exponentially (nonlinear). It makes little difference in the short run if the interest rate on a 1-year $1 bank deposit is 7 percent or 8 percent. The difference is small in proportionate terms and insignificant in absolute amounts. If we allow interest to accumulate and compound over 100 years, however, the difference *is* significant and the outcome is very sensitive to the initial interest rate. At 8 percent, the original $1 deposit compounds and accumulates to a total of nearly $3,000, whereas at 7 percent the total is only about $1,100. The total here is sensitive to initial conditions, with the difference rising as the interval of time lengthens. In chaotic systems, sensitive dependence suggests that small differences in starting points or pathways can create both quantitative and qualitative differences. I make little use of the feature of sensitive dependence of initial conditions in this chapter, but I will have something more to say about it in Chapter 7.

Presence of strange attractors. A final property often cited is the *presence of strange attractors,* which is not a very descriptive name. It means that there is a tendency for chaotic patterns to veer suddenly from one local range of observed values (an *attractor*) to another and perhaps back again at unpredictable intervals. The property of strange attractors is related critically to the notion of *unstable* aperiodic behavior discussed earlier.

In Gleick's book, the hero is the economist Brian W. Arthur, who has applied principles of chaos theory with skill and imagination to a number of problems, including population growth and patterns of technological change. Brian Arthur did not invent chaos theory, however. The French mathematician and physicist Henri Poincaré (1854–1912) usually receives credit for the discovery of the concept of systematic chaos. Edward N. Lorenz writes that Poincaré

> raises the possibility that what we generally regard as chance, or randomness, may in many circumstances be something that has of necessity followed from some earlier condition, even though we may be unaware that it has done so. He notes that in some cases we might be completely unable to detect the relevant antecedent conditions, while in others we might observe it fairly accurately, but not perfectly. In the later case the uncertainty might amplify and eventually become dominant. Is he not describing chaotic behavior?[11]

Although Poincaré posed the problems of chaos, he lacked the technology to explore them fully. In particular, he lacked the computing abilities we take for granted today that allow us to make thousands of calculations in a moment and so to explore dynamical processes more fully. Thus chaos theory waited almost half a century for its time to come.

The U.S. meteorologist Edward N. Lorenz is one of several contemporary scientists who helped create the modern science of chaos and popularize the study of chaos theory.[12] His most famous paper is called "Predictability: Does the Flap of a Butterfly's Wings in Brazil Set Off a Tornado in Texas?"[13] In it he argued that the earth's atmosphere is a complex space and it is not unreasonable to believe that small causes can have large effects—the *butterfly effect*.

The Lorenz Attractor is a cool picture that, by coincidence, actually looks a lot like a butterfly. It shows patterns of atmospheric convection modeled by simulating the flow of fluid in a box that is heated from the bottom. This process is nonlinear and dynamical. The outcome, illustrated by the Lorenz Attractor, is unstable and aperiodic. The two strange attractors are the most obvious strange visual evidence of instability; atmospheric conditions do not stay put but instead swing about wildly. The movements between and within each attractor are aperiodic. As Poincaré said of this sort of condition, "La prédiction devient impossible. . ."[14]

The important thing to remember here is this. The world is broadly characterized by the existence of nonlinear dynamical processes. They are all around us, and we are in them. Most such systems have produced chaotic behavior at some level and in some form. Because chaotic behavior is as natural as the spread of jam in your rice pudding, it is natural to take it for granted. This can be a serious mistake. Visions of globalization that fail to take into account the chaotic behavior of global financial markets risk overstating the degree of globalization that is possible and risk understating the persistent influence of local factors in the global economy.

Chaos theory is now widely applied in many fields, with uneven results. Perhaps physicists seeking to analyze turbulent fluid dynamics flows have done the best work.[15] Inevitably, however, the thought of order flowing out of disorder reminds people of economics.[16]

ECONOMICS AND CHAOS THEORY

There is little doubt that economics and finance give us examples of chaos and unpredictable behavior (in a technical sense). But it is difficult to say more, because we do not have here the kind of carefully controlled system with which physicists like to experiment. Outside events, which economists call *shocks*, cannot be neglected. Earnest efforts have been made to analyze financial data (which are known with much better precision than economic data) in the hope of isolating a moderately complicated dynamical system. Such hopes, in my opinion, have failed. We are left therefore with the tantalizing situation that we see time evolutions similar in some sense to those of chaotic physical systems, but sufficiently different that we cannot analyze them at this time.[17]

It hasn't been easy to apply chaos theory to economics. Paul Krugman has commented that economics is hard, much harder than physics (or at least classical Newtonian physics), but not nearly so difficult as sociology. Classical physics is easy, he says, because it is just math, and math always works the same way. Sociology is hard, however, because it is just people, and people hardly ever behave the same way twice. Krugman's point is that the farther we move from deterministic systems governed by mathematical laws that can be tested by reproducible experiment and the closer we get to bunches of people milling around in the town square or trading in a currency pit, the harder it is to make precise statements and draw meaningful conclusions.[18] This observation applies with special force to the case of chaos theory.

Although the practice of economics is rich in experiences that can perhaps best be understood in terms of nonlinear dynamics, the theory of economic science is not so well developed as to provide a sound foundation for such analysis. There are reasons for this, which I discuss in Chapter 7. The Economics Research Program at the Santa Fe Institute is one of the leading centers for the application of chaos theory to economics. The following is a list of working papers produced from 1993 to June 1996[19]:

- Aggregate Fluctuations from Independent Sectoral Shocks: Self-Organized Criticality in a Model of Production and Inventory Dynamics
- Pathways to Randomness: Emergent Nonlinearity and Chaos in Economics and Finance
- The Santa Fe Art Market
- Common Knowledge
- Contrarians and Volatility Clustering
- Self-Organized Markets in a Decentralized Economy
- Inductive Reasoning, Bounded Rationality, and the Bar Problem
- Economies with Interacting Agents
- Choice and Action
- Rational Routes to Randomness
- Faster Valuation of Financial Derivatives
- A Strategic Game with Secured Lending
- Connectivity and Financial Network Shutdown
- When Optimization Isn't Optimal: Aggregations and Information Contagion
- A Comparison of Political Institutions in a Tiebout Model

- Clustered Volatility in Multiagent Dynamics
- Breeding Competitive Strategies
- Neighborhood Feedbacks, Endogenous Stratification, and Income Inequality
- Nonlinear Times Series, Complexity Theory, and Finance
- Discrete Choice with Social Interactions
- Foresight, Complexity, and Strategy
- Time and Money
- Asset Price Behavior in Complex Environments
- Identification of Anonymous Endogenous Interactions
- Evolution of Trading Structures
- How the Economy Organizes Itself in Space: A Survey of the New Economic Geography
- Population Games

What these papers have in common is their focus on dynamical processes in complex environments. Apart from this, however, they are seemingly unrelated in terms of form and content. In my reading of the literature, some of the more successful theoretical applications have used chaotic dynamics to explore economic cycles, such as inventory and business cycles. The most ambitious applications in practice are attempts to discover and understand patterns of chaotic behavior in time series of economic data.[20] The relative lack of observations and the high level of noise in these data make this task difficult, however, at least as compared with problems in the physical sciences.

Although economists seek the same sort of deep understanding of social phenomena that physicists have of natural behavior, the built-in constraints of social science limit what can be accomplished. It is unlikely, therefore, that chaos theory will be useful to economists in the same way that it is useful to a physicist studying fluid dynamics or the flow of air over a wing and seeking a more precise understanding of these phenomena. Chaos theory may turn out to be a weak *quantitative* tool in economics, but it could be a strong one to expand *qualitative* understanding. Chaos theory may also turn out to be a robust quantitative tool—it is just too soon to tell. In fact, I think it is too soon to know what specific contribution chaos theory will make to our understanding of the economy. In this regard, chaos theory today is in about the same place that game theory was a generation ago.

William J. Baumol and Jess Benhabib have argued that the most important contribution of chaos theory to economics currently is its ability to broaden our vision, "revealing sources of uncertainty, and enriching the list of recognized *possible* developments."[21] Chaos theory suggests that unstable fluctuations may be at least as common or easy to produce as other sorts of economic behavior and that the seemingly random need not, in fact, be random. This information can be used, Baumol and Benhabib suggest, to disprove certain elements of conventional wisdom in theory and practice and to provide useful *caveats* to otherwise broad generalizations and accepted practices.[22]

An example illustrates this point. Economists generally believe that free trade results in an efficient use of resources and that it therefore maximizes welfare. They generally favor programs of economic integration, such as the North American Free Trade Agreement (NAFTA) or the European Union, therefore, because of their expansion of free trade's domain. The benefits of increased efficiency, however, may be offset by unexpected stability problems: ". . . the complicated system obtained by coupling together various local economies is not unlikely to have a complicated, chaotic time evolution rather than settling down to a convenient equilibrium. . . . Legislators and government officials are thus faced with the possibility that their decisions, intended to produce a better equilibrium, will in fact lead to wild and unpredictable fluctuations."[23]

This statement does not, of course, prove that economic integration leads to chaos, or even provide conditions such that chaos appears or does not appear. What it does do—and I think this is very useful—is increase the dimension of our analytical domain and challenge us to think clearly about the complex relationships we study. Globalization *might* be chaotic, and it is a mistake to plunge headfirst into the global pool without first considering this possibility.

International financial markets have proved to be one of the most successful areas in which to apply chaos theory to economics. These financial markets serve as the nexus for complex patterns of nonlinear relationships, making them an obvious hunting ground for chaos. They generate relatively large volumes of accurate data, especially on exchange rates, making it possible to actually test for chaos in some cases.

There is strong evidence that international financial markets are chaotic in the sense discussed here. Chaos is produced by three sets of interactions, which are discussed in the next three sections. Chaos is created by the interaction of fundamental analysis with chartists, by cascades of market information or "news" over time, and by the interaction of political and economic forces in these markets.

CHAOS IN THEORY AND PRACTICE

The interdisciplinary team of Paul De Grauwe, Hans Dewachter, and Mark Embrechts has produced some of the best analysis of the chaotic behavior of international financial markets.[24] De Grauwe has found that relatively simple models of foreign exchange behavior can produce chaotic patterns of exchange rate movements under reasonable conditions. Their work suggests strongly that foreign exchange markets are chaotic, at least at times.

Suppose that there are two types of participants in foreign exchange markets: *chartists* and *fundamentalists*. Chartists base their expectations of future exchange rates on the movements of the past. They base their actions on the information contained in their charts and do not explicitly take into account information, or "news," about economic variables that affect the underlying goods, services, and asset markets that are the foundation of the nonspeculative demand and supply of foreign exchange. Chartists add an element of positive feedback into the exchange markets. Chartists who observe an upward trend in a currency's value, for example, extrapolate this movement into the future and, by purchasing the currency in hopes of gain, give the trend momentum.

The fundamentalists use a model of the equilibrium exchange rate as the basis for forming expectations and determining their market behavior. Their model reflects the *fundamental* economic variables, such as interest rates, inflation rates, and money supply data that condition exchange market behavior. Fundamental indicators are used to forecast exchange rate equilibria. If the current exchange rate is different from the forecast equilibrium rate, fundamentalists expect the actual rate to move toward the forecast rate, and they will act to profit from this movement. Thus, if the actual rate is above the expected rate, fundamentalists will expect the currency to depreciate and will sell it short. This action tends to drive down the currency value toward a new equilibrium. Fundamentalists are assumed in this model to use different specific models such that their forecasts of the equilibrium exchange rate are normally distributed around the true rate.

Fundamentalists are sensitive to news about economic conditions. When fundamental economic conditions change, their estimates of the equilibrium rate also change, perhaps radically, and they make market bets under the assumption that the exchange rate will move toward the forecast rate. Their market bets tend to drive the exchange rate toward its new fundamental equilibrium.

Chartists and fundamentalists thus present two distinct types of behavior. Chartists are backward looking in their analysis, and their behavior tends to be momentum preserving (an appreciating exchange rate continues to appreciate, given the chartist model). They may, for example, base their forecasts on moving averages of past exchange rates. One important factor that affects chartist behavior is the degree to which they look backward. That is, how many hours, days, weeks, or months of prior activity do they consider in making forecasts? If long-term trends are followed, then short-term swings in chartist activity will be few. Chartist activity is more likely to change in the short run if the time series used to guide forecasts is also relatively short.

Fundamentalists are forward-looking and base their forecasts on expectations of equilibrium exchange rates, assuming that the actual exchange rate will move over time toward the equilibrium rate. Their actions tend to preserve the equilibrium in the sense that if the exchange rate is at equilibrium, their market bets do not move it away and if the exchange rate is away from equilibrium, their market bets tend to move it toward equilibrium. The sensitivity of fundamentalists to news about economic variables means that they are a source of change in the exchange market, and perhaps a sharp one at times.

One important factor that affects fundamentalist behavior is their estimate of the speed of adjustment of the foreign exchange market. That is, if a currency is overvalued by 10 percent, how long does it take for the market exchange rate to depreciate by this amount? A day or week or month or year? If adjustment to fundamental equilibrium is thought to be fast, then fundamentalist market bets will be large because short-term profits will be large and the profit window small. If, on the other hand, the market is thought to have considerable momentum, making adjustment to the fundamental equilibrium slow, then fundamentalist actions will be more modest.

In De Grauwe's model, chartists and fundamentalists are assumed to base their actions on their own methods and not attempt to anticipate the movements of the other group; the only way the two groups interact is through the market. Chartist actions, for example, may induce fundamentalist reactions by moving the exchange rate away from the expected equilibrium rate, these reactions may feed back into chartist responses, and so on.

The simple model just described was stated mathematically by De Grauwe. Computer simulations were then performed under a variety of assumptions about the degree to which chartists look backward and the fundamentalists' expectations of market adjustment. Many different dynamical patterns were found. Simulated price movements were especially stable when the chartists' time frame was short, so that the amount of "momentum" chartists induced to the market was small relative to the stabilizing force of the fundamentalists. Under some circumstances, the exchange rate developed patterns of stable cycles or limit cycles.

Most interesting for us, however, is the fact that a chaotic pattern of exchange rate movements developed in almost half of the simulations. Chaos was most frequent when the time frame on which chartists based their action was quite long. Because chartist actions were based on long-term trends, their actions provided a strong force of momentum, which produces chaos when mixed with the behaviors of fundamentalists.

Two aspects of the De Grauwe chaos are worth noting. First, chaos is produced even in the absence of news that changes fundamentalist behavior: Under some circumstances, chaos is inherent in the dynamics of the exchange market and is not produced by shocks of changed expectations of the type discussed in Chapter 4. This fact forces us to realize that crises and chaos are two different factors in the foreign exchange markets, not the same behavior interpreted in different ways.

Second, De Grauwe points out that the type of chaotic patterns this simple model generates are not especially realistic. Chaos took the form of unpredictable variation from an apparently constant mean. This type of chaos is, literally, like noise in a circuit. It would represent a problem for international traders or investors, but a problem that could reasonably be minimized using forward rates or other hedging techniques. Real world exchange rates tend to display patterns of seemingly random cycles that appear to be embedded within longer cyclical patterns, which themselves appear unpredictable, creating a sort of fractal landscape.

The simple De Grauwe model, therefore, under certain conditions produces chaotic price movements in foreign exchange markets. But these movements are of a sort that is not typical of real world foreign exchange markets. The simple model, however, is *very* simple. De Grauwe improves the model by making the behavior of fundamentalists more realistic.[25] Following standard exchange rate modeling practice, De Grauwe introduces three equilibrium conditions that guide fundamentalist analysis.

- A money market equilibrium condition holds that adjustments in real incomes, price levels, and interest rates ensure that money supply equals money demand in each country.
- An open interest parity condition holds that interest rates and exchange rates adjust over time so as to eliminate covered interest arbitrage. Exchange rates and the forward premium or discount adjust to offset differences in interest rates among countries.
- A goods market equilibrium holds that exchange rates and price levels adjust so that the law of one price (level) holds in international trade. Exchange rates adjust to offset differences in inflation rates between two countries. This is also called the Purchasing Power Parity (PPP) condition.

Further, De Grauwe assumes some degree of "interest rate smoothing" by monetary authorities. The central bank is assumed to "lean against the wind" and expand money supplies in the face of rising interest rates, for example. With this reasonable addition, the model includes several forces that preserve market momentum, other forces that seek fundamental equilibrium, and sources of news that can alter expectations and market behavior. The resulting system is fairly complex, but De Grauwe models it and performs simulations for different parameter values.

The complex exchange rate model, including interest rate smoothing, is *never* stable in the simulations that De Grauwe reports, although stable cycles and limit cycles appear under some sets of assumptions.[26] Chaotic patterns appear even more frequently than before, however, and a qualitative change occurs. Under the assumptions of interest rate smoothing, the exchange rate takes on a realistic pattern of short- and medium-term variation embedded in similar longer-term exchange rate swings. In other words, the simulation patterns actually look like actual movements in exchange rates. This property tends to increase as the degree of interest rate smoothing or monetary intervention increases. De Grauwe finds, as well, that the complex model simulations display statistical properties consistent with actual exchange rate experience.[27]

Several properties of the complex model are interesting. Chaos tends to be a qualitative feature of the exchange rate system when it is present, for example. If fundamentalists have high confidence in their model's ability to predict equilibrium exchange rates, the degree of market variation is reduced, but the essential chaotic pattern remains. Chaos, therefore, cannot be eliminated through better estimation techniques. Indeed, the chaotic movements of exchange rates, according to De Grauwe, systematically obscure the underlying fundamental relationships, making the successful construction of models difficult.[28]

De Grauwe's complex model shows that the interaction of chartists, fundamentalists, and interest rate smoothing monetary authorities produces chaotic exchange rate patterns that are similar to actual exchange rate patterns. This is not the same as showing that actual exchange rates are in fact chaotic. For this, more evidence is needed.

INFORMATION CASCADES AND MARKET TURBULENCE

A recent study by a Swiss-German team of physicists reported in scientific journal *Nature* provided evidence of chaotic foreign exchange markets.[29] Ghashghaie, Breymann, Peinke, Talkner, and Dodge obtained access to an enormous database of exchange market information: 1,472,241 bid-ask quotes that represented all activity in the U.S. dollar–German deutschmark foreign exchange market from October 1, 1992, to September 30, 1993. This deep but narrow database allowed them to perform the sort of complex empirical analysis that social scientists rarely experience.

The physicists were interested in turbulent flows. Turbulence is one of the tough problems of natural science that drove the early inquiries into chaos theory, including Edward Lorenz's "butterfly" research. Gleick wrote that "turbulence was a problem with a pedigree. The great physicists all thought about it, formally or informally. A smooth flow breaks up into whorls and eddies. Wild patterns disrupt the boundary between fluid and solid. Energy drains rapidly from the large-scale motions to the small. Why?"[30]

The answer—not so much to why this happens, but *how*—is that as more energy is released to a nonlinear deterministic system (for example, the water tap in your bathtub or the atmosphere of the planet Earth), a pattern of bifurcation occurs, and increasing numbers of strange attractors are created. Turbulence and chaos are the result.

One of the signature characteristics of turbulence in nature is a cascading effect that breaks big flows into progressively smaller ones, releasing energy in the process:

> A flow of energy from large to small scales is one of the main characteristics of fully homogeneous isotropic turbulence in three spatial dimensions. It provides a mechanism for dissipating large amounts of energy in a viscous fluid. Energy is pumped into the system at large scales of the order of, say, metres (by a moving car or a flying aeroplane) or kilometres (by meteorological events), transferred to smaller scales through a hierarchy of eddies of decreasing sizes, and dissipated at the smallest scale—on the order of millimetres in the above examples.[31]

Ghashghaie and his colleagues analyzed data from the dollar-deutschmark market using the same statistical techniques they would have used on fluid dynamics data. They found cascading effects over *time* and exactly paralleled the cascading behavior of fluids over three-dimensional *space*. That is, foreign exchange prices displayed the same turbulent patterns of activity over time that fluid flows show in space.

Other parallels between fluid dynamics and exchange markets appeared. In particular, they found that "an important aspect of turbulent flows is their intermittent behavior, that is, the typical occurrence of laminar periods which are interrupted by turbulent bursts. In the foreign exchange markets this corresponds to clusters of high and low volatility."[32] This pattern of uneven instability was, of course, a property noted earlier by De Grauwe and is found in both turbulent fluids and foreign exchange markets.

If fluid turbulence dissipates energy, then what force drives the foreign exchange cascades? Ghashghaie and his colleagues suggested that information—news—is a source of energy and the force dissipated in foreign exchange markets. They speculated that the turbulence they observed was caused by the behaviors of long-term and short-term trades. They posited that long-term traders, who watch foreign exchange markets only from time to time, influence the behavior of short-term traders, who constantly monitor market behavior. Turbulence results as the new information that long-term traders bring to the market dissipates over time to the short-term traders. Their analysis therefore draws parallels between fluid dynamics and exchange market dynamics, as noted in Table 5.1.

One way to understand the logic of the information cascade model is to think of it in terms of De Grauwe's model of interaction between chartists and fundamentalists. Suppose that the fundamentalists are the *long-term traders* who enter foreign exchange markets only when they receive "news" or funda-

Table 5.1   Correspondence Between Fully Developed Three-Dimensional Turbulence and Foreign
            Exchange Markets

Dynamic System	Hydrodynamic Turbulence	Foreign Exchange Markets
Force	Energy	Information
Turbulent domain	Spatial distance	Time delay
Dynamic characteristics	Laminar periods interrupted by turbulent bursts (intermittency)	Clusters of high and low volatility
Cascade type	Energy cascade in space hierarchy	Information cascade in time hierarchy

Source: S. Ghashghaie, W. Breymann, J. Peinke, P. Talkner, and Y. Dodge, "Turbulent Cascades in Foreign Exchange Markets," *Nature* 381 (27 June 1996), p. 769.

mental information that causes them to alter their expectations of the true
equilibrium foreign exchange rate. As the news arrives, the actions of the fundamentalists drive information into the market through changes in market
prices. Chartists react to the changing prices directly (and do not, by assumption, pay any attention to the changing news itself, nor do they attempt to anticipate the reactions of fundamentalists).

Suppose that the chartists adopt varying strategies, some using long-term
charts, others medium-term trend analysis, and still others relying on very
short time horizons, a real characteristic of different groups of speculators.
Then the short-horizon chartists will react quickly to the fundamentalist information impulse, as their estimate of the future exchange rate trend is very sensitive to recent data. Chartists with medium- and long-term analytical horizons will react and change their expectations more slowly.

The fundamental news thus cascades through the exchange market, flowing from fundamentalists to short-horizon, medium-horizon, and long-hori-
zon chartists. Turbulence and chaos are produced as the new information is
dissipated throughout the market.

De Grauwe found that realistic chaotic patterns were most common in
the complex model with interest rate smoothing by the monetary authority.
There is no direct analog to interest rate smoothing in the *Nature* study on turbulent cascades. However, we might usefully consider interest rate smoothing
as the equivalent of friction in fluid dynamics, which inhibits flow, making
fluid viscous. Viscosity in nature increases the rate of energy dissipation and
hastens the onset of turbulence. In the same way, De Grauwe found that interest rate smoothing hastens the onset of chaos of the sort found in both foreign
exchange markets and fluid dynamics.

Understanding the problems of modeling turbulent flows, the physicists
are pessimistic about the possibility of understanding foreign exchange market turbulence in any deeply systematic way. They conclude that "it is unlikely that there is a set of a few partial differential equations (like Navier

Stokes equations in hydrodynamics) which might serve as a model of foreign exchange market dynamics."[33] But, as we have seen, De Grauwe and his team have developed a model of foreign exchange behavior that produces chaotic patterns in theory that are qualitatively similar to those experienced in practice. A precise quantitative understanding of exchange rate chaos may still be beyond the horizon, but I think we are very close to a qualitative understanding of what is going on in these markets.

The case for chaotic foreign exchange markets, therefore, seems quite strong. Economics is harder than physics, however, and the empirical analysis of chaos in foreign exchange markets requires more discussion. But I think we should first consider the part of chaos that seems to be as obvious in practice as it is invisible in the theories presented here: politics.

POLITICAL ECONOMY CHAOS

The models of foreign exchange chaos that I've presented so far have focused on finding chaos within the natural forces of the market. The market agents whose interaction produced chaos came right out of the standard economic toolbox: individuals, both self-interested and profit-seeking, taking independent action without organization or coordination. The only deviation from this pattern was the added assumption De Grauwe made in the complex model of the interest rate–damping monetary authority, whose actions made the mix viscous and introduced shocks whenever "news" broke.

It seems to me that the real world of exchange rates contains not only these elements but also others that contribute to the chaos we have observed.[34] In particular, the actions of states and the motives of politics cannot be ignored. We saw in Chapter 4 that central bank policies were a potent ingredient in the mixture that sometimes explodes in currency crises. De Grauwe's complex model showed that monetary policies that seek to reduce interest rate fluctuations also increase the chaotic domain, although they are not necessary for foreign exchange chaos to occur.

States interact with the foreign exchange markets in several ways—some are systematic, others discretionary, and some appear almost random and might be chaotic themselves. Among the many ways states get into the act are these:

- *Monetary policy.* Central banks dampen interest rates and introduce news into markets, but they can also affect foreign exchange markets in other ways. Monetary authorities may target interest rates, as De Grauwe suggested, but they can also adopt systematic policies that instead target money supplies, nominal gross domestic product, or a price level. Monetary policy can be systematic, as these would be, or it can be discretionary. The possibility of monetary policy that responds to changing political winds is important in what I have to say later in this section.

- *Fiscal policy.* Tax and spending policies can have many indirect effects of international markets. Perhaps the clearest link lies in deficits and public debt policy. The timing, amount, and type of public debt, the credibility of debt policy, and the expectations of future debt patterns can have important international effects as well as the obvious domestic ones.[35]

- *Direct intervention policy.* Monetary and fiscal policies affect foreign exchange markets indirectly, but government officials also intervene directly in exchange markets, buying and selling currency for a variety of reasons. Intervention may be coordinated, as in some cases discussed later, or unilateral. It may be guided by clear policy or a discretionary response to political needs.

- *Currency target zone policy.* Government authorities may attempt to coordinate domestic policies and international direct intervention policies to support a target zone regime. De Grauwe simulated a target zone system under the assumption that it would make fundamentalists more confident in their models' abilities to forecast equilibrium exchange rates. He found that the range over which the simulated exchange rate varied was diminished but that chaos still appeared, albeit on the smaller scale. He did not attempt to model the currency crises associated with target zones.

  Not all nations belong to a given target zone regime, however, so a multispeed system is necessarily created. The deutschmark, for example, may be very stable relative to the French franc, moderately stable relative to the Italian lira and Portuguese escudo, and freely floating relative to the U.S. dollar. The fact that nations may participate in several different overlapping currency policy groups (or have unilateral but not necessarily reciprocal policies with respect to different currencies that create such an overlapping pattern) creates a complex system.

- *Pegged exchange rate policy.* Many soft currency countries attempt to fix their exchange rates against the currency of their major trading partner nation. This again creates the possibility of interesting dynamic patterns, as the strategies of floating, pegging, and setting targets interact.

It is not difficult to imagine real world scenarios in which the policy actions of states play an important part in creating a chaotic pattern in international financial markets. In fact, when the possibilities are considered, it is a wonder that anyone would ever think that exchange markets are anything *other* than chaos! Here are some thumbnail sketches of potentially chaotic policy scenarios.

State-state dynamic interaction. De Grauwe's private sector chartists and fundamentalists may have analogs among states. The European monetary system crisis of 1992–1993 showed that states do not all have the same policy goals for political reasons, even when they may have committed to coordinating economic policies. Suppose that one nation acts like a fundamentalist or perhaps a reverse fundamentalist. Suppose it seeks to attain certain domestic policy goals that are consistent with a particular exchange rate and that it intervenes in exchange markets whenever the actual exchange rate varies significantly from the one consistent with its domestic policy goals. Japan in the mid-1990s might be an example of a reverse fundamentalist. The need to promote domestic recovery from their deep recession caused Japanese officials to intervene when the yen appreciated above the range consistent with domestic policy goals. The motives for intervention to achieve domestic goals and the motives of private sector fundamentalist speculators distinctly differ, but their market behavior is qualitatively the same. Both "intervene" to push or pull exchange rates toward the target, or forecast, rate.

Other nations may be more like the chartists. These nations may be more concerned about the stability of the exchange rate than its actual level. Content to allow the market to choose the range within which its exchange rate trades, a government may adopt a stability policy of damping the exchange rate, intervening to prevent large short-term swings in what is viewed as a market-determined path. Although the motives of such a government would be much different from those of the speculating chartists, their market actions would be qualitatively the same.

Trend-smoothing policies are not the same as pegging rates or establishing a target zone. A nation may be content with the market pattern of systematic appreciation or depreciation of its currency but may still make a habit of intervening for stability's sake whenever the exchange rate moves by more than a percent or so in a given period. The potential effect of sudden exchange rate changes on domestic financial markets is such that trend-smoothing policies could be used even by governments philosophically committed to market-based policies.

As you can now imagine, if chaos can be produced when chartists and fundamentalists interact, it can also result when reverse-fundamentalist states intervene in exchange markets along with trend-smoothing states. Chaos is probably even more likely when we put all four groups together. If this analysis holds, we are faced with the irony that nations seeking stability in domestic and international affairs could, through their dynamic interaction, add to the chaos of international financial markets.

Political business cycle dynamic effects. William Nordhaus introduced the idea of the political business cycle more than twenty years ago.[36] This idea is based on the fact that economic well-being is an important factor in elections, especially national leadership elections. A leader or party is much more likely to be returned to power if the economy is growing than if it is not. Since politicians have at least some influence or control over economic policy, it is logical to suppose that they use it to improve reelection prospects. Thus, we have the political business cycle, timed to correspond with the incumbent's term in office, "starting with relative austerity in early years and ending with the potlatch right before elections."[37]

The political business cycle, superimposed over other cycles in the economy, may tend to dampen existing economic patterns, or it may exacerbate them. Or, as Kazuyuki Sasakura has suggested, the combination could produce a chaotic domestic economic pattern.[38] Sasakura assumed that fiscal policy is influenced by pressure groups and that this pressure varies nonlinearly. First, the pre-election *potlatch* stimulus is assumed to be greater than the post-election austerity because of nonlinearities in the politics of fiscal policy. (For an elected official, it is better to give to voters than to take from them.) Second, the political pressure to stimulate the economy also varies nonlinearly. When national output is near the economy's potential output, political pressure to stimulate spending and create jobs is small. As the output gap grows, political pressure grows stronger at an exponential rate. The pressure on fiscal policy is thus nonlinear and asymmetric and interacts with the underlying business cycle of the economy, with which it is not generally fully synchronized. (The period of business cycles in the United States, for example, is not obviously the four years of the presidential election cycle.)

Sasakura modeled this system under reasonable mathematical assumptions and discovered that chaotic output movements were possible. That is, the political business cycle can interact with the underlying business cycle to form patterns that are not explosively unstable but are still unpredictably chaotic. Interestingly, his model generates simulated chaotic patterns even when the political response to pressure groups, in terms of actual fiscal action, is relatively small. Sasakura found this result interesting in the particular but fascinating in terms of what it might mean for economics in general: "Economists believe that a *stable* economic system can be analyzed only linearizing it around the equilibrium. Then, is it not astonishing that chaos may emerge from such a stable system with a *fairly small* periodic external force?"[39]

Although Sasakura is content to keep his analysis on the level of domestic economic effects, it seems reasonable to speculate that chaotic output patterns by individual nations could also create chaotic patterns in international trade and finance linkages between and among nations. This may be especially true when nations experience political cycles of different types, periods, and magnitudes.

Asynchronous political business cycles. The political election cycles of major nations are not coordinated, and pressure group influence varies considerably.

This alone might be enough to generate chaotic output patterns even if global markets were perfectly integrated, creating an underlying global business cycle. In fact, however, economic integration is incomplete, so nations experience business cycles of different types, periods, and magnitudes. These many business and political cycles flow into global markets. Here, we must seriously consider the possibility that chaos breeds chaos.

J-curve policy nonlinear feedback effects. Political economy chaos may be even more likely than Sasakura's analysis suggests because of the possibility of nonlinear J-curve feedback effects. Indeed, chaotic domestic and international economic patterns are highly likely under these circumstances. Here is one scenario.

The high levels of public debt that many industrial countries have accumulated tend to limit the extent of fiscal policy responses to domestic political pressure. Suppose, however, that exchange rate policy is used instead to address domestic political-economic needs. That is, instead of fiscal expansion, a policy of currency depreciation is adopted to boost output and create jobs in the run-up to a national election.

National output does respond in most cases to currency depreciation, since a lower foreign exchange value makes exports cheaper to foreign buyers and increases the cost of imports at home. The domestic effect transmitted through the current account, however, displays the nonlinear pattern known as the J curve. In the short run, exchange rate changes affect prices before they affect output, so that the value of net exports actually falls, temporarily depressing national income. Imports are more expensive in terms of domestic currency, for example, but the quantity of imports purchased tends to be relatively sticky in the short run for a variety of reasons, such as the existence of long-term purchase agreements, uncertainty about future price and exchange rate behavior, and the costs of searching for equally reliable domestic suppliers. In the short run, then, it is possible that even more is spent on imports when the value of a currency falls, as the increased cost of each unit imported exceeds the effects of lower import quantities.

In the long run, however, contracts do run out, uncertainty diminishes, and search costs become economic. Decreased import quantities make up for higher import prices, and net exports increase, causing output, income, and employment to also rise. This creates the J-curve effect. Depreciation causes net exports to fall in the short run and then stabilize and eventually increase over time. All else being equal, the J-curve pattern of net exports is duplicated by national income.

The nonlinearity of the J-curve effect creates a potentially chaos-causing political business cycle dynamic. Pressure groups lobby for currency depreciation (and other policies to stimulate job creation) in response to the gap between current and potential output levels. Suppose that the pressure these groups exert is asymmetric and nonlinear, as was argued earlier. Now assume a J-curve effect, so that the response to currency depreciation is also asymmetric and nonlinear, which then feeds back into the pressure group equation.

Once again, the dynamic interaction contains all the elements we normally associate with chaos. Even more, however, in this scenario the international financial markets are directly affected and then feed back into the domestic political markets. Here, too, we have the well-known J-curve effect acting as a nonlinear element, making a chaotic pattern even more likely.

Turbulent vicious cycle effects. Finally, I'd like to suggest the possibility of turbulent vicious cycles. Assume that chartists and fundamentalists interact in ways that produce chaos or some weaker form of instability in foreign exchange rates. Now suppose that the very existence of exchange rate chaos creates enough instability in international economic interactions that states make the political decision to establish target zones for currencies. These target zones, as we saw in Chapter 4, are prone to speculative attacks that produce currency crises and the resulting huge swings in exchange values. These larger swings, I would argue, tend to draw even more chartists and fundamentalists into the market by increasing the sizes of speculative gains and losses.[40] This effect in turn adds to chaos, causes greater policy efforts to stabilize, and thus produces more crises. The vicious cycle of chaos, crisis, and chaos continues, with both market actions and policy efforts increasing.

This discussion of political economy chaos has been more anecdotal than analytical. It has drawn on the qualitative properties of chaos as well as recent research to suggest that political factors affect international markets and, by their nature, tend to make chaos a more likely circumstance. But *are* foreign exchange markets chaotic? It is time to examine the evidence.

EVIDENCE OF GLOBAL FINANCIAL CHAOS

My reading of the evidence about chaos in foreign exchange markets is that direct evidence of chaotic price movements exists but tends to be relatively narrow or weak; there are some technical reasons for this lack of robust evidence, which I will explain. On the other hand, various attempts to prove that foreign exchange rates are *not* chaotic are also unsuccessful. Despite many tries, it has been impossible to clearly refute the *random walk hypothesis,* which supposes that actual exchange rate movements are unpredictable. I do not believe that this is *proof* of chaos, but I do think it is *evidence* of chaos— enough evidence for me to take the chaos hypothesis seriously.[41]

Some of the evidence for chaotic exchange rate behavior is strong but narrow. One example is the findings of Ghashghaie and his colleagues as reported in *Nature.* The temporal cascading behavior they found for the dollar-deutschmark exchange rate from 1992–1993, based on almost one and a half million observations, is remarkable. But this evidence is narrow in three important ways. First, it is based on only a single exchange rate, which may not reflect behaviors in other markets. Second, it is based on a relatively narrow time frame, which by itself means that the observed behavior may not be typical of broader market patterns. Third, this *particular* period was one that might well be regarded as atypical in any case, since it includes parts of the EMS crisis discussed in Chapter 4. If you are looking for exchange rate turbulence, you are likely to find it during a currency crisis. So it would be better if we had the same sort of massive data bank and detailed analysis from some other more "normal" time period.

Thus, although I think it is fair to say that the dollar-deutschmark market was turbulent and presumably chaotic during 1992–1993, I am unwilling to draw broader conclusions based on this study alone. Broader analysis is needed.

De Grauwe, Dewachter, and Embrechts provided such evidence, but it is weak. They obtained daily exchange rate data for the period January 4, 1971, through December 30, 1990, for the deutschmark-dollar, pound sterling–dollar, and Japanese yen–dollar rates. Their study thus has the broad scope we are looking for, but there is a catch. Although for an economist this represents a fairly deep data pool, it is still not really enough. The empirical techniques for identifying chaos that have been developed by physicists require considerable data to ensure validity, perhaps twenty thousand observations.[42] The lack of a data pool that is both broad and deep thus weakens the study, but this is a problem that is almost impossible to avoid in economics. That's one reason why economics is so hard.

De Grauwe reported that "Our results are mixed. There are some indications for the occurrence of chaos in the yen/dollar and pound/dollar markets. We did not find evidence of chaotic behaviour in the mark/dollar market. Thus, although we find some evidence for chaos, it cannot be said that it is conclusive."[43] Their conclusions are reported in Table 5.2.

De Grauwe used these data to test for the existence of nonlinearities and found them strongly indicated in the daily and weekly variations in exchange rates: "The existence of nonlinearities in the exchange rate return does not prove that chaos exists. Other nonlinear structures than chaotic ones could be driving the exchange rate. However, . . . there are some theoretical reasons to believe that exchange rates can behave in a chaotic manner."[44] Although De Grauwe's study is not "conclusive evidence" of chaos, it does give "credibility to the view that chaotic processes are important in the foreign exchange markets."[45]

Although the analysis of chaotic movements in exchange rates is still in its infancy, economists have pretty thoroughly studied foreign exchange markets in testing the PPP (purchasing power parity) theory and the efficient mar-

Table 5.2   Evidence of Chaotic Foreign Exchange Rates, 1971–1990

Currency	Period	Finding
Deutschmark-dollar	1971–1972	Inconclusive
Pound sterling–dollar	1971–1972	Speculative
Japanese yen–dollar	1971–1972	Chaotic
Deutschmark-dollar	1973–1981	Nonchaotic
Pound sterling–dollar	1973–1981	Chaotic
Japanese yen–dollar	1973–1981	Inconclusive
Deutschmark-dollar	1982–1990	Random walk
Pound sterling–dollar	1982–1990	Random walk
Japanese yen–dollar	1982–1990	Random walk
Deutschmark-dollar	1973–1990	Inconclusive
Pound sterling–dollar	1973–1990	Chaotic
Japanese yen–dollar	1973–1990	Possibly chaotic

Source: Paul De Grauwe, Hans Dewachter, and Mark Embrechts, *Exchange Rate Theory: Chaotic Models of Foreign Exchange Markets* (Oxford, UK: Blackwell Publishers, 1993), p. 217.

kets hypothesis. These studies shed some indirect light on the question of exchange rate chaos.

The PPP theory is one of the most logical "fundamental" theories. It is an application of the law of one price across international borders with different currencies. If inflation in A causes its currency to purchase fewer traded goods such as wheat at home, then the law of one price argues that A's currency should depreciate so that it also purchases less wheat abroad. If the currency fails to adjust in this way, then the price of wheat (in terms of A's currency) is different at home and abroad and arbitrage profits exist, which induces behavior that drives prices and exchange rates back to parity. This process takes time and is complicated by the fact that the world has many currencies and many goods; however, the logic still holds.

In a recent survey of the PPP literature, Kenneth Rogoff commented that "While few empirically literate economists take PPP seriously as a short-term proposition, most instinctively believe in some variant of purchasing power parity as an anchor for long-run real exchange rates. Warm, fuzzy feelings about PPP are not, of course, a substitute for hard evidence."[46] The evidence about PPP that Rogoff reported, however, does little to reinforce warm fuzzy feelings.

Recent studies have shown that major exchange rates do tend to converge to their PPP levels in the long run but that the speed of convergence is very slow, only about 15 percent per year. This finding is in fact very encouraging for PPP theorists, since most past studies failed to find any PPP component in the long pattern of exchange rate movements, which could not be distinguished statistically from a random walk! Still, this leaves a puzzle, as Rogoff noted. Only a fraction of the variation in exchange rates can be explained by PPP factors. What accounts for the rest?

Another fundamental theory of exchange rates behavior is *market efficiency* (or the efficient markets hypothesis). Mark Taylor noted that "In an efficient speculative market, prices should fully reflect information available to market participants and it should be impossible for a trader to earn excess returns to speculation. Academic interest in foreign exchange market efficiency can be traced to arguments concerning the information content of financial market prices and the implications for social efficiency."[47]

Exchange rates should adjust, therefore, to eliminate speculative profits as new information is absorbed and dissipated throughout the market. Some studies have found evidence of this tendency in the exchange rates of major currencies, but "Notwithstanding this, however, it remains true that time series for the major nominal exchange rates over the recent float are extremely hard to distinguish from random walks."[48]

There is fairly strong evidence then, broad and deep, that even if exchange rate movements are not actually chaotic, neither do they follow the logical equilibrium patterns suggested by PPP or efficient markets theories, especially in the short run. It is difficult generally to dismiss the possibility that exchange rates are following a random walk.

Finally, we have De Grauwe's simulations of the interactions of fundamentalists and chartists in a system that includes interest rate damping by monetary authorities. These simulations produce chaos under many circumstances and generate patterns of exchange rate movement that are qualitatively similar to real world conditions. These simulations, combined with the empirical evidence cited above, strengthen the case for currency chaos.

The studies that seek to find chaotic behavior in real world exchange rates are either deep but not broad or broad but not deep. In neither case can they provide proof, only indicators for further study. They do, however, add credibility to the case for periods of chaotic exchange rate movements. The simulations generate chaotic behavior that mimics actual foreign exchange movements on a qualitative, if not a quantitative, level. Thus, to reinforce this point, although proof of exchange rate chaos is illusive, I think the possibility of chaos needs to be taken seriously.

Currencies are subject to crises definitely, and to chaos probably, and they follow patterns that are at least random and perhaps turbulent. What are the consequences of these conclusions?

GLOBALIZATION AND FINANCIAL CHAOS

Markets aren't supposed to behave the way the foreign exchange markets behave. Markets are supposed to be flexible but stable. They should provide just the right foundation on which to build lasting structures in an age of rapid change.

Markets matter, economists believe, and their stability and flexibility are necessary to coordinate the actions of thousands of firms and millions of consumers. If markets are global, as is the current vogue, the stakes are higher: millions of firms, billions of workers and consumers, trillions of dollars. Our understanding of markets and their effects is fundamentally wrong if a thing so big, technologically advanced, and seemingly efficient as the foreign exchange market doesn't work as it should.

One way to understand this is to assume that the financial markets really do work properly and that the problems actually lie elsewhere. For example, when the evidence shows that the foreign exchange market responds only minimally to the basic principle of the law of one price, as expressed in the PPP principle, you can keep faith in international financial markets by pointing an accusative finger at international trade. According to Mark Taylor,

> One is left with a conclusion that would certainly make the godfather of purchasing power parity, Gustav Cassel, roll over in his grave. It is simply this: International goods markets, though becoming more integrated all the time, remain quite segmented, with large trading frictions across a broad range of goods. These frictions may be due to transportation costs, threatened tariff barriers, information costs, or lack of labor mobility. As a consequence of various adjustment costs, there is a large buffer within which exchange rates can move without producing an immediate proportional response in relative domestic prices. International goods markets are highly integrated, but not yet nearly as integrated as domestic goods markets. This is not an entirely comfortable conclusion, but for now there is no really satisfactory alternative explanation to the purchasing power parity puzzle.[49]

Taylor is right in thinking that global integration is incomplete and that tariffs and such are part of the problem. But is he correct in thinking that this is the whole problem? He sees a one-way relationship: Incomplete globalization causes exchange market errors. Isn't it also possible for the arrow of causation to point the other direction? (Or both directions?) It seems even more likely that breakdowns in the financial markets are at the root of the problem and represent a built-in barrier to globalization.

Paul Krugman, ever the iconoclast, argued that the problem lies in international financial markets themselves:

> This is a highly controversial (although of course correct) position. In questioning the reliability of international financial markets I am challenging both the cherished views of economists and the preconceptions of most lay observers. It is one thing to question the functioning of global markets for goods and services, which are not very different in appearance today from what they were in the past; however, most people imagine that—at least in the case of financial markets—borders either have disappeared or are about

to. After all, computers and satellite transmission have created financial markets that almost never sleep and that can transfer billions of dollars across the world in seconds. Surely whatever imperfectness there is in the linkages between countries lies in the dull traditional world of freighters and longshoremen, not in the glittering world of international finance.[50]

I think that Krugman's analysis is incomplete. In addition to the currency crises he sees, there is also built-in chaos, at least at times and perhaps as a persistent phenomenon. This matters greatly when we think about solutions, but not so much when the focus is on the consequences for global markets. Instability, chaotic or crisis-driven, has its own effects. Krugman argued that these effects are invisible to us because we have become used to them and because, in our thinking about global markets, we have been conditioned to ignore them. He writes that

> Over the past few years, and especially since the dollar began declining, we have imperceptibly become accustomed to living in the world in which exchange rates move by huge amounts but the changes have only small effects on anything else. . . .
>
> In fact, exchange-rate fluctuations of the size we have seen recently are possible only because they have so little effect. If changes in the relative cost of producing manufactured goods in different countries were quickly reflected in changes in the actual locations of production, large swings in the dollar would produce trade-balance changes that would themselves place limits on those swings. If exchange-rate changes were passed through rapidly into domestic prices, the kind of exchange-rate movements we have seen would either lead to massive differences in inflation . . . or would be met by non-accommodating monetary policy. . . . It is only because there seems to be some kind of delinking of exchange rates and the real economy that exchange rates can be as volatile as they have been. That is, *exchange rates can move so much precisely because they seem to matter so little.*[51]

Exchange rates matter so little because markets aren't really global, except for a few exceptions. They are increasingly *multilocal* in nature. Exchange rate instability breaks down the logic of global economic activity (except in a few cases in which other factors are at work), and erects barriers to the spread of the single global market. Paradoxically, as attempts to expand global markets increase and more weight is attached to exchange rate movements, more chaos is released into financial markets, making exchange rates even less stable and further delinking exchange rates.

The bottom line of turbulence in international financial markets, therefore, is that we must thoroughly rethink globalization as the driving force of the era. Rather, we need to think seriously about the consequences of a world in which global financial markets present natural barriers to economic integration instead of smooth channels to it.

Reconsidering globalization is necessary, but it isn't easy. The idea of globalization serves many interests that are threatened in one way or another by doubts about the efficient spread of worldwide markets. In the next two chapters I examine the intellectual and political stakes in the globalization debate.

NOTES

1. José Ortega y Gasset, *Meditations on Quixote,* "Preliminary Meditation" (1914).

2. I wrote this paragraph on December 19, 1996, during a period of such stability—or so thought the *New York Times,* which included an article on currency stability on its first business page of that date. The *Times* worried that stability would cost jobs in the parts of the finance industry that hedge against or speculate on volatile foreign exchange rates. In my view, the *Times*'s concern about stability was misplaced. Although currencies in the yen-dollar-mark groupings were relatively stable during the period in question, the Thai baht had recently experienced a major speculative attack. The rumors of the death of currency crises are premature, as the subsequent Asian currency crisis of 1997 has proved.

3. James Gleick, *Chaos: Making a New Science* (New York: Viking, 1987).

4. The play is Tom Stoppard, *Arcadia* (London: Faber and Faber, 1993).

5. Stephen H. Kellert, *In the Wake of Chaos* (Chicago: University of Chicago Press, 1993), p. 2. Italics in the original.

6. Alfredo Medio, *Chaotic Dynamics: Theory and Applications to Economics* (Cambridge, UK: Cambridge University Press, 1992), pp. 5–6.

7. Stoppard, *Arcadia,* p. 5.

8. Stoppard, *Arcadia,* pp. 4–5.

9. The need to solve problems such as airflow turbulence was partly responsible for the development of both supercomputers and the formal analysis of nonlinear dynamics.

10. Some of the funding for chaos research has come from the banking and financial industry in the hopes that chaos theory will prove able to unlock the mystery of seemingly random financial market movements and allow more profitable investment or speculation. So far, this hope has gone unfulfilled.

11. Edward N. Lorenz, *The Essence of Chaos* (Seattle: University of Washington Press, 1993), pp. 118–119.

12. Other important contributors include M. Feigenbaum, B. Mandlebrot, and D. Ruelle. (This list makes no attempt to be complete.)

13. This paper was presented at the meetings of the American Association for the Advancement of Science in 1972 and is reprinted in Lorenz, *The Essence of Chaos,* pp. 181–184.

14. "Prediction becomes impossible. . ." Quoted in Lorenz, *The Essence of Chaos,* p. 118.

15. The works of David Ruelle and Steve Smale are notable here.

16. Economics is also the only social science with mathematical and empirical frameworks adequate to even attempt the analysis of chaotic behavior.

17. David Ruelle, *Chance and Chaos* (Princeton, NJ: Princeton University Press, 1991), p. 85.

18. It seems to me that Heisenburg's uncertainty principles also apply with special force to the social sciences.

19. For a current list of working papers, send e-mail to wp@santafe.edu.

20. A good example of early work that illustrates this point is William A. Brock, "Nonlinearity and Complex Dynamics in Economics and Finance," in *The Economy as an Evolving Complex System: Santa Fe Institute Studies in the Sciences of Complexity.* Vol. 5, ed. P. W. Anderson, K. Arrow, and D. Pines (Redwood City, CA: Addison-Wesley, 1988), pp. 77–97.

21. William J. Baumol and Jess Benhabib, "Chaos: Significance, Mechanism, and Economic Analysis," *Journal of Economic Perspectives* 3:1 (winter 1989), p. 80.

22. Ibid., p. 80.

23. Ruelle, *Chance and Chaos,* pp. 84–85.

24. Paul De Grauwe, Hans Dewachter, and Mark Embrechts, *Exchange Rate Theory: Chaotic Models of Foreign Exchange Markets* (Oxford, UK: Blackwell Publishers, 1993). De Grauwe is an economics professor at Katholieke Universiteit, Belgium, and a member of Belgium's parliament. Embrechts is a professor of nuclear engineering and engineering physics. Dewachter works at the National Fund for Scientific Research Belgium at Katholieke Universitcit, Belgium. In this section, text references to De Grauwe will refer to the work of this team.

25. See De Grauwe et al., *Exchange Rate Theory,* Chapter 5.

26. Ibid., p. 138.

27. In particular, the forward exchange rate is a biased estimator of the spot rate in De Grauwe's simulations, just as it is in the real world.

28. Very short-term (one period ahead) forecasting *is* possible, however.

29. S. Ghashghaie, W. Breymann, J. Peinke, P. Talkner, and Y. Dodge, "Turbulent Cascades in Foreign Exchange Markets," *Nature* 381 (27 June 1996), pp. 767–770.

30. James Gleick, *Chaos: Making a New Science* (New York: Viking, 1987), p. 121.

31. Ghashghaie et al., "Turbulent Cascades in Foreign Exchange Markets," p. 768.

32. Ibid., p. 769.

33. Ibid., p. 769.

34. One additional element not discussed here is the presence of speculators with market power who act strategically. I am thinking of hedge fund managers, such as George Soros, who played an important role in creating currency crises (see Chapter 4).

35. See the discussion of Mexico in Chapter 4.

36. William Nordhaus, "The Political Business Cycle," *Review of Economics Studies* 43 (1975), pp. 169–190.

37. Ibid., p. 187.

38. Kazuyuki Sasakura, "Political Economics Chaos?" *Journal of Behavior and Organization* 27 (1995), pp. 213–221.

39. Ibid., p. 220.

40. This conclusion assumes that speculators weigh potential gains more heavily than potential losses in choosing to enter markets.

41. If this standard of evidence seems low, and it is, I must say it is not untypical of the standards that economists and other social scientists often must apply.

42. De Grauwe et al., *Exchange Rate Theory,* p. 216.

43. Ibid., p. 242.

44. Ibid., p. 242.

45. Ibid., p. 255.

46. Kenneth Rogoff, "The Purchasing Power Parity Puzzle," *Journal of Economic Literature* 34 (June 1996), p. 647.

47. Mark P. Taylor, "The Economics of Exchange Rates," *Journal of Economic Literature* 32 (March 1995), p. 14.

48. Ibid., p. 14

49. Rogoff, "The Purchasing Power Parity Puzzle," pp. 664–665.

50. Paul Krugman, *Exchange Rate Instability* (Cambridge, MA: MIT Press, 1989), pp. 76–77.

51. Ibid., pp. 39–40.

6

The Political Economy
of Globalization

*Imagine a wondrous new machine, strong and supple, a machine that reaps
as it destroys. It is huge and mobile, something like the machines of modern
agriculture, but vastly more complicated and powerful. Think of this awe-
some machine running over open terrain and ignoring familiar boundaries.
It plows across fields and fencerows with a fierce momentum that is exhila-
rating to behold and also frightening. As it goes, the machine throws off
enormous mows of wealth and bounty while it leaves behind great furrows
of wreckage.*

*Now imagine that there are skillful hands on board, but no one is at the
wheel. In fact, this machine has no wheel nor any internal governor to control the speed and direction. It is sustained by its own forward motion,
guided mainly by its own appetites. And it is accelerating.*

—William Greider[1]

If the process of globalization is as incomplete and self-limiting as I have suggested, then why does the idea of globalization enjoy such wide acceptance?
Why isn't it subjected to sterner logical tests, more thorough empirical analysis, and critical public debate? The answer is that there are many interests that
are served by the image of globalization or that would be threatened by its
more critical consideration. I already suggested in Chapter 2 that globalization has become a profit center for management consultants. But whereas
management theories are fads that appear and disappear, the popular idea of
globalization persists. It persists, in part, because there are larger interests
served by the image of globalization as the headless horseman of international capitalism.

Globalization is a lever that special interests can use to pry open certain
public policy doors that would otherwise be tightly shut. It provides a convenient reason for fundamental institutional change, or perhaps an excuse for it,

in a world in which fundamental institutional change is slow and painful and the policies that promote it are controversial and unpopular.

The main body of this chapter is a case study of a critically important political use of globalization: the movement toward a single currency in Europe. The conventional wisdom is that a single currency is an economic necessity if Europe is to be a competitive force in the world economy, but that solving the economic problem of globalization also solves some high politics and low politics problems in the European Union (EU). In this interpretation, a single currency is, conveniently, an uncomfortable economic necessity and a comforting political windfall. In reality, I argue, a single currency makes very little economic sense for Europe—the globalization-based economic argument is fatally flawed—but the chaos that a single currency will create will force Europe to make social and labor policy reforms that would otherwise be impossible.

The single currency will force Europe to reform its welfare state and to renegotiate the social contracts on which it is based. The threat or promise of globalization, in other words, is the lever that opens up the possibility of seemingly impossible domestic policy reforms.

Globalization has its uses. These uses require and promote exaggerated images of globalization that conflict sharply with actual globalization. The consequences of the political responses to globalization may in some cases be more revolutionary and important than the actual economic processes that motivated them.

A powerful example of the political use of globalization is found in William Greider's 1997 book *One World, Ready or Not: The Manic Logic of Global Capitalism*. Greider seeks to mobilize what we used to call *the left* to oppose the seemingly invincible forces of *the right* in this post–Cold War era. Nothing unites an otherwise uncooperative group so forcefully as a common enemy, and Greider finds in globalization just the enemy he needs: one that is amoral, apolitical, and powerful beyond imagination.

GLOBALIZATION AND THE POLITICS OF CLASS STRUGGLE

If Lenin had entered a time machine in 1907 and arrived 90 years in the future, *One World, Ready or Not* is the book that he would have written. Greider's arguments are the same ones that Lenin used in his *Imperialism: The Highest Stage of Capitalism*, although Greider's are updated and improved and stated more effectively, based on the journalist's nose for a story instead of the theorist's sharp eye for statistical evidence.

What Greider seems to want to do is nothing short of organizing a global labor movement. He wants to reverse the declining influence of labor unions in advanced industrial economies, to end the competition and squabbling among national labor groups, and to forge a global labor movement that can stand up to and resist the inhuman, runamuck global capitalist machine. You can almost hear the call, *Workers of the world, unite!*

Greider frames the issue in terms of power, a key element in any political analysis. The process of economic globalization is complicated and abstract, he says, and hard to understand. But don't worry, because it can be simplified: It is all about capital and labor.

> The multinational corporations are, collectively, the muscle and brains of this new system, the engineers who are designing the brilliant networks of new relationships. It is their success at globalization that has inevitably weakened labor and degraded the control of governments. . . . Despite their supple strengths the great multinationals are, one by one, unsure themselves. Even the most muscular industrial giants are quite vulnerable if they fail to adapt to the imperatives of reducing costs and improving rates of return. . . . Behind corporate facades, the anxiety is genuine.
>
> The Robespierre of this revolution is finance capital. Its principles are transparent and pure: maximizing the return on capital without regard for national identity or political and social consequences.[2]

The multinational corporations here play a role familiar to students of Marx. They are the bourgeoisie, the class that possesses the weapons of capitalist power. They train these weapons first on workers, but cannot stop themselves inevitably from turning them on each other. Finance capital was the villain in Lenin's *Imperialism*. Finance capital extended the battle beyond Europe to the exploitation of labor around the world. Greider states:

> The fundamental struggle, then as now, is between capital and labor. That struggle is always about control of the workplace and how the returns of the enterprise shall be divided. In both dimensions, capital is winning big over employees, just as it did in Marx's time. The inequalities of wealth and power that Marx decried are marching wider almost everywhere in the world. The imbalances of power lead today to similar excesses and social abuses.[3]

Greider writes so well and so cleverly that his open statement of the Marxian theme in no way weakens the book or even lessens its appeal among some readers who are also corporate shareholders and vote Republican. He reports true stories of human suffering and labor abuse from around the world. Labor is powerless to resist because, first, power is concentrated in the hands of finance capital and, second and more important, labor is unorganized globally and so is structurally incapable of opposing global capitalism. Finance capital plays the interests of different national unions against each other, weakening union power everywhere. In Greider's view, globalization is a powerful threat to human society. Labor must organize to oppose it, or the revolution will run its destructive path.

There is much to both admire and criticize in Greider's work, but what I appreciate the most is the great paradox of the collapse of communism that he proposes. The collapse of Soviet-style communism, which was an attempt to apply Marxist/Leninist ideas, has actually contributed to the process of economic globalization, which he tells us has unleashed the harsh competitive forces that Marx and Lenin saw so clearly a few generations ago. The collapse of communist states and the ongoing accelerating globalization create a reason for—indeed the necessity of—the emergence of a reinvigorated Marxist/Leninist program today.

THE POLITICAL USES OF THE GLOBALIZATION MYTH

The political use of globalization is especially popular today, but it is not a new phenomenon. Norman Angell in *The Great Illusion* (1911) argued that the global markets that people like Keynes also saw had become supremely powerful, much more powerful than states.[4] Economic interdependence, strengthened by technological change and scientific advances, made the nations of the world so interdependent, especially in terms of finance, that sovereignty was an obsolete concept.[5]

Angell predicted that governments would be so powerless, and market forces so pervasive, as to make war unprofitable and therefore impossible (a premature obituary for the nation-state if ever there was one, since World War I began just months later). Global market logic would be the one logic of the world, and the sooner governments became connected (or got out of the way), the better it would be for them. Angell's project was to use the promise and threat of globalization to change politics, to get governments out of the business of making war. He failed, alas, because the reality of globalization in 1911 was not as strong as the reality of international political conflict.

Peter Drucker makes a similar globalization case today, but with a different purpose. Globalization today occurs within the context of the Keynesian revolution in macroeconomic policy and what might be called the *Beveridge revolution* in social policy.[6] There is much more government to deal with now, in this age of macropolicy and the welfare state. Much of the focus of government policy has been on the development of institutions to manage domestic problems, especially problems of economic and social instability. Even during the leaner post–Reagan/Thatcher years, these domestic institutions remained strong and the persistent focus of policy.

Drucker argues that globalization has made these institutions of domestic policy irrelevant, redundant, or at least inappropriate: "For developed economies, the distinction between the domestic and international economy has ceased to be a reality, however much political, cultural, or psychological strength remains in the idea. An unambiguous lesson of the last forty years is

that increased participation in the world economy has become the key to domestic growth and prosperity."[7] Inward-focused domestic institutions miss the
point. New institutions and new policies are needed.

> The world economy has become too important for a country not to have a
> world-economy policy. . . . What is needed is a deliberate and active—in-
> deed, aggressive—policy that gives the demand, opportunities and dynamic
> of the external economy priority over the domestic policy demand and prob-
> lems. For the United States and a number of other countries, it means aban-
> doning ways of thinking that have dominated American economics, perhaps
> since 1933, and certainly since 1945. We still see the demands and opportu-
> nities of the world economy as externalities. We usually do not ask whether
> domestic decisions will hurt American competitiveness, participation and
> standing in the world economy. The reverse must become the rule: will a
> proposed domestic move advance American competitiveness and participa-
> tion in the world economy? The answer to this question determines what are
> the right domestic economic policy and business decisions. The lessons of
> the last 40 years teach us that integration is the only basis for an interna-
> tional trade policy that can work, the only way to rapidly revive a domestic
> economy in turbulence and chronic recessions.[8]

Unlike those who argue simple-mindedly that the nation-state is dead,
Drucker sees it as a strong force with a clear purpose, but shackled by old
ideas and old institutions. Globalization has rendered the institutions of the
Keynesian and Beveridge revolutions irrelevant. Globalization is the reason
nation-states must fundamentally reform their domestic institutions. Economic globalization creates the necessity of political change. It is, as I said
before, the same idea that Angell argued, but Drucker aims at domestic
change, not international conflict resolution.

Susan Strange draws somewhat the same conclusions from her analysis
of international bargaining. Diplomacy, she writes, used to be a state-to-state
matter. Globalization, however, has created new actors that must be accounted
for in international relations. Global firms, no longer firmly anchored to a particular home country market, have power comparable in some cases to that of
nation-states. "Our research suggests that the crucial difference between
states these days is not, as the political scientists used to think, between
'strong' states and 'weak' ones, but between the sleepy and the shrewd. States
today have to be alert, adaptable to external change, quick to note what other
states are up to. The name of the game, for governments just as for firms, is
competition."[9] Diplomacy is now a three-way bargain: state-to-state, firm-to-
firm, and state-to-firm.[10]

Globalization has clearly created an environment in which firms bargain
with states, states compete with states, and specific government policies
change in response to these competitive forces. The process of competition
for major new industrial plants, such as the BMW factory that eventually lo-

cated in South Carolina and the Mercedes-Benz factory that was eventually built in Alabama, epitomizes the changing nature of state-market interaction. The reality of globalization creates the politics of competition, but a type of competition that Angell would find appealing—multilevel competition to create the most appealing environment for the peaceful forces of globalized interdependence.

Drucker and Strange describe a process that Wolfgang Streek calls "international regime competition."[11] This is the idea that the process of globalization forces national macrowelfare regimes to either compete with (in Drucker's framework) or bargain with (in Strange's framework) each other. The result is that internal competition forces domestic political, social, and economic change—the sort of fundamental institutional change with which we are concerned here. This is a powerful and important political use of globalization.

THE POLITICAL AND ECONOMIC
LOGICS OF EUROPEAN INTEGRATION

Perhaps the most important current case study of international regime competition driven by the political use of globalization is in the EU. The movement toward monetary union and a single currency is likely to produce international regime competition that will make the BMW and Mercedes-Benz cases seem, in retrospect, to be small potatoes.

There is perhaps no better example of the political use of economic forces than the EU. From day one, the process of integration in Europe has relied on the strategy of using economic benefits to compensate for political costs. In what I have called the great "science project" of the second half of the twentieth century, Europe is an experiment to test the hypothesis that economic unification and prosperity can produce political unification and security.

But, as I argue later, the changing environment in which European integration is taking place has created a political crisis—a crisis that can be resolved only through international regime competition. Globalization, in the form of the need of monetary union in Europe, has become the lever by which Europe is compelled to address a set of national and supranational problems that would be politically taboo without the dead hand of Greider's destructive global machine to force the issue.

In his recent book, *An Imperfect Union: The Maastricht Treaty and the New Politics of European Integration,* Michael J. Braun writes that European relations have been conditioned by

> the two primary logics of European integration, both of which have been in operation since the late 1940s. The first of these is the logic of interdepen-

dence and economic necessity. In general terms, integration has been necessary to enable relatively small European countries to survive and compete in an increasingly interdependent world economy dominated by large-market economies such as the United States and Japan. Furthermore, integration has enhanced the joint and individual capacities of European states to manage interdependence, the consequences of which—economic instability, environmental destruction, social uncertainty—are beyond the power of even larger national governments to control. In this manner, the sacrifice of some authority and policy independence to the European institutions has enabled national governments to better perform the economic and social tasks required of democratic welfare states and has thereby actually bolstered, rather than undermined, the sovereignty and legitimacy of European nation-states.[12]

This is a classic globalization argument. By expanding individual market economies into a larger integrated economy, Braun argues, European nations have achieved greater wealth, greater stability, improved economic security, and even perhaps greater legitimacy.

The second logic is political. An economically integrated Europe is more secure from both the external threat of Cold War aggression and the threat of internal political divisions that produced two world wars in a single generation. By intensifying economic interdependence, the logic goes, integration also intensifies political interdependence.

It is probably fair to say that economic means have been easier to achieve than political ends in the process of European integration. This is true in both of the "dimensions" of integration, broadening and deepening. Broadening the membership of the EU, from the original six to the fifteen EU members of 1998, has at each stage expanded the market and stimulated the collective economy, which has compensated for the difficult political choices that were necessary and the many side deals that were struck. Market deepening, especially in the form of the 1992 single market initiative, has acted to increase economic interdependence and expand the domain of collective political choice.

The problem with this, according to many observers, is that the process of European integration seems to work more like a bicycle than a train. If it were a train, the economic benefits would produce lasting political momentum. It behaves more like a bicycle, however. When economic integration stops, there is no political momentum to draw on and the process of political integration collapses. Like riding a bicycle, when you stop pedaling, you fall over.

The economic logic of European integration through free trade has been weakened by the increase in global free trade. European nations today want their economies to be part of an integrated *global* market structure for all the same reasons they wanted to be part of an integrated *regional* trade structure before.

At the same time, however, the end of the Cold War, which produced German unification and expanded relations with formerly communist nations, has created an environment that magnifies the political divisions among EU states. The eastward broadening of the EU early in the twenty-first century will likely make this problem even worse. Eastward expansion will create greater political difficulties for the states that are already EU members as their influence in EU-wide policies is further diluted. And the political cost of lost sovereignty will not this time be offset by economic gains. Careful eastward expansion of the EU will be costly. It will not be as costly as German unification, of course, because it will not be as sudden nor will it take place on the same generous terms. And it will benefit the economies of Poland, Hungary, the Czech Republic, and the other nations that eventually join the EU. But there will be costs that the present EU members will be forced to pay.[13]

A prosperous, economically vibrant European Union could well afford to pay the costs of eastward expansion, which have been estimated at perhaps one tenth of one percent of the EU gross domestic product.[14] But these terms do not describe Europe in the 1990s. European economic growth has been notoriously slow, and its unemployment rates in 1997 scandalously high: Spain, 21.8 percent; Belgium, 13.1 percent; France, 12.8 percent; Italy, 11.9 percent; and Germany, 11.2 percent. Only Britain and the Netherlands have unemployment rates within one percentage point of the United States.[15] Under these circumstances, it is understandable that many EU nations might see costly coordinated eastward expansion as less desirable than simple individual globalization initiatives. I don't think it would take much political or economic pressure to make the wheels fall off Europe's bicycle.

It is hard to imagine what could hold Europe together in this environment, especially given that forty years of cooperation on economic and political issues seem not to have produced any sort of truly pan-European political consensus or set of common values. Europe is a single market, granted, but *only* a single *market*, not a single nation or a single people or a single idea.

However, I believe that globalization, both as threat and as an opportunity, has and will serve the purpose of European unification brilliantly. The prospect of economic globalization has produced in Europe a political environment within which it may be possible for nations to address economic issues that were previously taboo politically, and so to enact the fundamental institutional changes that are now necessary. Just as Greider uses globalization to promote the political agenda of a global labor movement, the EU is using globalization to create a political environment in which labor market reform can occur.

GLOBALIZATION, EUROPE, AND MONETARY UNION

It is necessary at this point to consider how monetary union fits into Europe's dual logics. This section presents the conventional wisdom, which I consider to be incomplete. It holds that the Maastricht Treaty and the general framework of monetary union in Europe is driven by a combination of high politics and low politics and, as in the past, uses economic tools to achieve its goals.

High politics is thought to be the most important. The post–Cold War era has produced a reincarnated German Problem. Reunited Germany is the five-hundred-pound gorilla in Europe, with tremendous power and strong will. The German Problem is how to keep Germany part of Europe without dominating Europe and, hence, how to keep Europe peaceful and secure.

Monetary union accomplishes this goal, the argument goes, because these policies represent a German commitment to Europe. Germany agrees to cede sovereignty, showing its good faith, and, further, binds itself to Europe irrevocably through its adoption of a single European currency. But what is to keep Germany from dominating Europe under these circumstances? The high-politics answer is France. Using a single currency to bind Germany to Europe also binds Germany to France. A unified Europe, centered on a Franco-Germany alliance, is seen as the solution to the new German Problem. Monetary union, which leads directly or indirectly to political union, is the economic key that makes the solution possible.

According to the conventional wisdom, resolving the high politics of the German Problem has the further benefit of dealing effectively with the dangers of globalization. The global expansion of economic activity poses a high-politics threat in the form of either powerful trade blocs (Japan and Asia; the United States and the Americas), powerful multinational corporations, or international market forces that endanger Europe's security. One way or another, globalization creates economics risks and is therefore a threat to national security against which individual nations are powerless. A regionally integrated economic union, with a single currency and therefore a single economic policy, however, can more effectively confront this threat. Monetary union is the economic equivalent of NATO (the North Atlantic Treaty Organization); it is the best collective defense against globalization's economic risks.

Low politics is money politics—the politics of how to cut the pie. In Europe it is especially the politics of budget deficits, inflation rates, and the special interests that are aligned on the different sides of these issues and that must be balanced through them. European governments have uneven track records in the low politics of balancing the public's interest in balanced budgets and price stability with special interests, whose actions tend to destroy budgets and produce inflation. The solution to this low-politics problem, some believe, is a sort of binding agreement that would, for example, prevent France from acting as France has in the past and force it to act more like Germany. That is, France and Italy and other European nations need an external constraint that would prevent them from caving in to domestic special interests on matters like this and would therefore force them to honor the broader public interest.

According to the conventional wisdom, monetary union accomplishes this goal in two stages. First, to qualify for monetary union, nations must bring inflation rates, budget deficits, and public debts down to a specified level. This is intended to force national governments to deal with special interests. In fact, the external constraints of the Maastricht criteria have been remarkably successful in changing the dynamics of budget making in Europe, even if the actual numerical targets have not been met in many cases.

Second, a single currency, the euro, replaces national currencies, taking money creation choices out of the hands of national governments. Money and inflation would be the responsibility of the European central bank, modeled on and influenced by the German Bundesbank. Monetary union thus solves the low-politics problems of inflation in the long run.

High politics is the strongest motivation for monetary union among the richer nations, according to the standard interpretation of the Maastricht negotiations, whereas low politics dominates the interests of the poorer nations.[16] In simple terms, Germany is bound to France in matters of high politics, and Spain, Italy, and others are bound to Germany on the low side.

As I noted earlier, the conventional economic argument for monetary union is basically a globalization argument. National currencies and the instability of their rates, the argument goes, create transaction costs and foreign exchange risks that reduce the efficiency of expanding global markets and discourage investment in Europe. Europe must enter into monetary union if it wants to participate fully in the globalization process. Its participation is necessary, as well, to have any hope of controlling or influencing global market forces.

Without monetary union, Europe would risk globalization sweeping over it (the issue of control) or perhaps bypassing it (the stability argument). With a single currency, Europe would be in a position to both participate in economic globalization and control or influence its path. Monetary union is thus a version of the argument that "We didn't really want to have to do this (i.e., give up national currencies, monetary autonomy, and fiscal independence), but the devil (globalization) made us do it."

The economic argument for monetary union is actually better than it seems and better than its proponents suppose. True globalization is unlikely, and as long as financial instability and exchange rate chaos persist, national markets will remain delinked in important ways. The one clear way to eliminate this instability, however, is precisely to eliminate exchange rates by eliminating national currencies. The pooling of reserves that would accompany the creation of a European central bank would also reduce exchange rate instability by discouraging speculative attacks.

Although the threat of globalization is an accepted reason for the invention of a single currency, in fact the single currency is probably necessary for the "globalization" of Europe (to use this term in an awkward way). Thus globalization is not only the proclaimed reason for monetary union but also its possible incomplete effect.[17]

THE ECONOMIC ILLOGIC OF MONETARY UNION

Using the threat of globalization to drive monetary union makes some economic sense, as we have just seen, and is very useful in producing certain
high and low political outcomes. But the dirty little secret of monetary union
is that its most important economic and political effects are seldom part of the
public debate. Standard economic theory predicts that monetary union will
actually exacerbate Europe's main economic problem—structural unemployment—while it removes many of the tools that nations currently rely on to reduce unemployment's negative effects. Monetary union, I argue, will create
an environment in which it will be absolutely necessary for European governments to reform their previously untouchable welfare and labor market policies. In this line of argument, then, monetary union is the use of globalization
to force social reforms and labor market liberalization in nations with strong
political interests opposing these actions. This argument is based on what is
called the *economic theory of the optimal currency area.* This theory ad-
dresses the obviously relevant question of the conditions under which it
makes sense for different nations or regions to have the same currency versus
the situations under which separate currencies are more efficient.[18]

The role of exchange rates in this analytical framework is to help regions
or nations deal with the adjustment problems that come from asymmetrical
shocks or uneven growth rates. When economic activity is uneven, creating
pockets of unemployment and persistent payments problems, adjustments can
occur either through external exchange rate changes or through internal effects such as wage and price changes. The depressed region might, for example, experience a currency depreciation that would make its products more
competitive and help resolve its payments problems. Or it could experience
wage and price deflation that would also improve its international competitiveness, albeit at potentially severe social costs.

Generally, if exchange rates are flexible, internal adjustments are less important and need be less severe. If exchange rates are rigid, then internal adjustment must bear more of the burden. Two extreme cases illustrate the important concepts of the optimal currency area model.

First, consider the case of a set of countries or regions that *can* operate
efficiently with one currency. Assume that two nations have the following
properties: They generally experience the same sorts of macroeconomic
"shocks" that create unemployment cycles and similar rates of economic
growth; they have flexible labor markets, with high degrees of labor mobility
and flexible wage mechanisms; and they have strong systems of fiscal equalization, to transfer funds from expanding regions to those that suffer recession. Under these circumstances, the theory argues, a single currency makes
sense. Asymmetrical shocks will be uncommon, and when they occur, internal market forces and fiscal transfers will efficiently dampen them.

If an unemployment shock were to hit one region harder than the other, for example, the combination of labor mobility between regions, wage flexibility, and fiscal transfers would tend to moderate the impact and prevent serious internal dislocations. In short, the costs of internal adjustment through wages, prices, and fiscal transfers would be small relative to the benefits. This would be an "optimal" single currency area. It is argued that the United States looks something (but not exactly) like the case just described, so that the costs of a single national currency (versus a number of regional currency units) are less than the benefits of a dollar zone.

Now suppose an opposite extreme. Imagine two countries that are affected differently by macroeconomic shocks. Asymmetrical shocks or uneven rates of economic growth leave unemployment persistently high in one region and low in the other and create long-term payment imbalances between them. Suppose that labor mobility is low, wages are inflexible, and the system of fiscal transfers is not well developed. Under these circumstances, a single currency system produces persistent unemployment in hard-hit regions and persistent payments problems between regions. Under a flexible exchange rate system, these problems would not exist (or would not exist in the same persistent and serious way), since the hard-hit nation's currency would fall in value, stimulating its net exports and thus moderating both the unemployment and the payments problems.

With a single currency (or permanently fixed exchange rates, which is the same thing), the adjustment costs will be very high and will take a long time. Without flexible exchange rates to absorb the asymmetrical shocks, the adjustment must take place the hard way—through the deflationary effects of long recession and persistent unemployment. The only alternative, within the context of a single currency, is a program of radical internal changes in labor markets, social programs, and fiscal institution. Wage flexibility, labor mobility, and inter-regional fiscal transfers are required to replace exchange rates as tools to balance payments.

The point of this analysis is, of course, that the EU nations are not very good candidates for a single currency in terms of the logic of optimal currency areas. The economic structures of the different nations of Europe are different enough to make perfectly symmetrical macroeconomic shocks unlikely. Unemployment shocks are more likely to be strongly asymmetrical, therefore producing significant payments and unemployment imbalances. European labor markets, with exceptions to be noted later, are notoriously rigid, with high wages and long-term unemployment supported by generous and expensive welfare state systems. The system of regional transfers within the EU is inadequate to deal with these adjustment problems.[19]

No one would seriously propose a single European currency on the basis of the economic logic of the optimal currency area theory. The much-touted

Maastricht *convergence criteria* actually exacerbate the adjustment problem. To qualify automatically for monetary union, nations are required to satisfy the following conditions:

1. A level of inflation within 1.5 percent of the average of the three lowest countries
2. A level of interest rates with 2.0 percent of the average of the three lowest countries
3. A budget deficit less than 3.0 percent of the gross domestic product
4. A public debt of less than 60 percent of gross domestic product
5. No devaluation of the national currency within the exchange rate mechanism (ERM) for the previous two years

In addition, nations must essentially commit themselves to maintaining these economic margins in the long run.

As viewed by the conventional analysis, these Maastricht convergence criteria make monetary union with low inflation possible, thus achieving the low politics goal of the exercise. Viewed from the perspective on the optimal currency area analysis, however, the Maastricht criteria actually disable the monetary and fiscal policy levers that an individual nation might otherwise use to deal with unemployment and growth problems in the usual "Keynesian" way. Under a single currency, with exchange rates fixed and monetary and fiscal policies inflexible, the only way to address growth and unemployment problems is to attack the national policies that prevent them from being solved through wage, price, and resource movements.

In other words, the only way to solve the problems that are sure to grow worse in the post-Maastricht environment is to break the European social contract with labor and liberalize the welfare state. Thus monetary union is the road to a great political confrontation. As Eichengreen and Frieden have written,

> If it is true that shocks to European countries are more asymmetrically distributed than shocks to U.S. regions, while both labor mobility and real wage flexibility are lower in Europe, then the costs of monetary union will be higher than in the U.S. . . .
>
> Uncertainty about the empirical magnitude of every one of these benefits and costs suggests the absence of a clear economic case in favor of EMU [European monetary unification]. Given the risks and uncertainties that pervade the process, there would have to be a clear margin of benefits over costs for economic considerations, narrowly defined, to provide a justification for such radical departure in policy. The absence of such a margin implies that the momentum for monetary union must therefore derive from other, primarily political, factors.[20]

It is to these political factors that we now turn.

THE POLITICAL USES OF MONETARY UNIFICATION

The conventional interpretations and public discussion of monetary union seem to miss the link between a single currency and labor market problems. For example, the usually astute Martin Wolf of the *Financial Times* reported in the run-up to the French elections of 1997 that "European political leaders have repeatedly stated how important they think [monetary union] is; they have all, including the French, already imposed almost all the sacrifices necessary to fulfill the Maastricht treaty's economic convergence criteria; and the pain consequent upon that austerity lies largely in the past."[21]

This comment entirely misses the point that some very significant costs will follow monetary union. If it was necessary to eliminate inflation *before* a single currency, it will surely be necessary to eliminate the most important labor market rigidities *after* it. Of the two problems—inflation and labor market rigidities—the labor market probably presents the greater political challenge, because these issues cut so deeply into the social contract on which many European political systems are based.

My interpretation of EMU is that it will create an economic environment in which labor market reform *must* take place as well as a political environment in which reform is *possible* because of the powerful imagery of globalization. Whatever Europe does to free its labor markets, and however unpopular those policies are, these actions will always be considered better than the alternative—the headless demons of unrestrained global capitalism. This threatening image of globalization is useful politically and is, I think, also *necessary*, since labor market rigidities have created for Europe an economic problem that seems to defy normal political solutions for many of the countries involved.

Wolfgang Streek argues that the forces of globalization, in the form of the problems of monetary union, create a competitive environment for national policies, and that this competition results in labor market and social policy reforms. He writes that the effect of international regime competition in this case will be "diverse and subtle":

- Short of causing an instant decline in social protection and industrial citizenship rights, regime competition may *put a chill on initiatives to raise national levels of provision.* . . .
- Political demands to *roll back* national social policies will be supported in an integrated market by the presumed competitive advantages enjoyed by firms under less costly regimes . . .
- Regime competition may *preclude* certain ways of closing gaps in social protection at the national level. . . .
- Regime competition is further likely to *result in a shift of power* inside national regimes in favor of potentially outwardly mobile production factors, above all capital. Such a shift may be caused by the mere *threat of exit,* and indeed may make exit dispensable. . . .

- As regime competition limits the capacity of national governments to impose obligations on potentially migrant capital, national social policy may increasingly turn into *generation of investment incentives for business* and of *production obligations for labor.*[22]

Streek's interpretation of the competitive political effects of monetary union is persuasive. This competitive model assumes that there is no consensus on pan-European social policy that could help the EU resist what labor leaders must surely consider to be "destructive" competition.

Indeed, attempts to create EU social policy have not been notably successful. Although supranational social policy has always been on the European agenda, it has seldom been considered seriously. The practice has generally been to leave social policy issues to national governments. Early attempts at a European social policy resulted in only relatively weak statements of labor rights. Jacques Delors in 1988 proposed the addition of "social dimension" to the single market, but without success. Streek writes that

Devoid of potent political allies and swimming against the current of the neoliberal *Zeitgeist*, the Delors Commission counted on the process of market integration itself to give rise to tensions and conflicts that would demonstrate to national governments that successful completion of the process required a rebuilding of Community institutions and policies from a regime geared to market making into one capable of market correction.[23]

So Delors thought that the *fear* of globalization would allow Europe to *strengthen* its labor policies and welfare states. Tensions and conflicts surely have appeared, but ironically, according to Streek, they may be resolved through competition that "unbuilds" rigid social institutions in response to globalization's promises and threats.

European nations also are likely to face considerable external pressure to adopt reforms that make domestic labor market adjustments both possible and efficient. Absent these internal reforms, the EU and the euro will be like a bull in a china shop: powerful, but unpredictable. The single currency could represent a danger to the international financial system. Toyoo Gyohten, for example, has written on Japan's concerns about this matter. On one hand, he argues, the single currency will create opportunities for Japanese firms that do business with and in Europe because of lower transactions costs and increased efficiency. But

There will be no central fiscal authority with a substantial role in taxing or spending—so no member country can receive a fiscal transfer in a recession to stimulate a slack economy. Member countries are also required to cut government deficits under the growth and stability pact.

Some Japanese business executives argue there is a danger that economic or political instability will emerge, and that the single currency may not work well in practice.

Theoretically, the movement of labour and wage flexibility across borders will eventually solve economic disequilibrium between members of the monetary union. However, there is as yet little movement of labour, as people are discouraged to shift between countries by language and cultural barriers.

Although there is no doubt the euro can be introduced given the strong political will among EU leaders, it is not clear that monetary union can be maintained with stability.[24]

Toyoo Gyohten has written that he is confident that Europe can resolve these problems. I think this confidence is well placed. International regime competition within the EU will be supplemented by international pressures from the United States, Japan, and other nations that have much to lose if the single currency experiment becomes dangerously unstable. And there is a third force to consider—the force of domestic politics. The single currency will magnify domestic problems for some countries, and I think that these states are still powerful enough, despite what globalization theorists say, to be able to take effective action to reduce these problems. Since they will be unable to fight high unemployment and economic stagnation problems with international exchange rate tools or domestic macroeconomics tools, they will use the domestic microeconomic tools that remain.

Monetary union will put the domestic politics of European nations under stress that will be most severe for those nations with the highest unemployment. They will find themselves with only one option—labor market and social welfare reforms—to solve what are likely to become increasingly disruptive social problems. Even without international regime competition, I believe, these reforms *will* occur.

This conclusion is based on a famous result of international monetary economics called the *Mundell-Fleming theorem*.[25] Mundell-Fleming considers that national governments have three main international economic objectives: exchange rate stability, capital mobility, and monetary policy autonomy. But these objectives are mutually inconsistent. It is impossible, according to Mundell-Fleming, to have all three at once. A nation can have fixed exchange rates and monetary policy autonomy, but this requires capital controls, which limit capital mobility (an aspect of the Bretton Woods system). Or a nation can have monetary policy autonomy and capital mobility, as the United States did, especially during the 1980s, but will have to live with unstable exchange rates.

Or, to come to the point, nations can make the European monetary union bargain, which is also a bit of a trap. They can have fixed exchange rates (single currency) under a regime of capital mobility (provided by the Maastricht

Treaty), but they will have to give up their ability to use monetary policy to address domestic economic issues such as unemployment. The European nations, by agreeing to tight budget standards, also have effectively given up the right to use fiscal policy. In effect, I argue, there are no macroeconomic tools left with which national governments can address unemployment problems. The only tools that remain are microeconomic ones—labor market policies.

The Economist does not entirely agree with this analysis. They see the Mundell-Fleming trap but doubt that either internal social distress or external competitive forces will be sufficient to change Europe's political course in the short run. They write that

> Largely because of the political difficulties, the chances are that Europe's chronic unemployment will drift on for some time, further damaging the lives of the continent's least fortunate citizens. How long this continues depends partly upon whether monetary union happens, and what its effects will be. The single currency would change Europe's labour markets because it would make it harder for governments to adjust macroeconomic policies to suit circumstances in their own economies. Instead, most of the burden of adjustment would fall on the labour market. So, when change comes, if it comes, it may not be gentle at all. And if Europe's labour market comes crashing down, the ideal of consensus will probably topple with it.[26]

Policy reforms that make European labor markets less rigid and that increase the prospects of labor mobility solve the optimal currency area problem and also provide an escape from the Mundell-Fleming trap. I think that the single currency nations will have no choice in this matter, with or without international regime competition and pressures from the United States and Japan, although competitive forces and external pressures would make national adjustment more imperative and thus speed up the process.

THE POLITICAL ECONOMY OF LABOR MARKET REFORMS

Like all good European policies, monetary union moves ahead not because it appeals to any common European spirit but because it serves different political and economic interests for different nations and national leaders. In France, for example, monetary union provides a reason or an excuse (or an imperative) to reverse a long-standing bias against market forces—a bias that goes back at least as far as Colbert.

Even in the postwar era, France has tried to steer a middle road, with more "organization" and high-level bargaining than many other countries. This reflects a fundamental distrust of the market as much, I think, as an elevated opinion of technocracy. Former prime minister Edouard Balladur ex-

pressed this as "What is the market? It is the law of the jungle, the law of nature. And what is civilization? It is the struggle against nature."[27] *The Economist* stated that

> Whatever politicians promise publicly about unemployment, to do away
> with such legislation would endanger their chances of re-election. The un-
> employed are (thankfully) in a minority and are poorly organized. Those in
> work are more numerous and they are often organized in unions, which have
> a powerful voice in the political debate. Politicians know that the voters
> whose voices will carry the most weight are precisely those who stand to
> lose from any reform.[28]

Recent policies of deregulation and market liberalization in France have
pointedly bypassed labor market institutions. A recent study of economic
growth in France during the postwar era concluded that

> Despite several waves of liberalization, most active after the creation of the
> EEC and the return of the franc to convertibility, both in 1958, and then in
> the 1980s, France still appears to be struggling with lingering powerful
> rigidities. This is most evident when one considers the rate of unemploy-
> ment, which has remained stuck at very high levels for a decade. In our
> view, labor market institutions and the process of human capital accumula-
> tion play an important role in these rigidities and may be a source of slower
> growth, much as protection and inefficient productive capital accumulation
> were in the 1950s.[29]

For France, the road to monetary union is necessarily the road to labor
market reform. The French governments and the French people have become
accustomed to adopting otherwise unpalatable policies for the good of "Europe," and monetary union will be another case in which this kind of sacrifice
will be made. A single currency is the way to tie Germany to France and to
Europe in a globalizing economy, the logic goes, and to keep Germany from
dominating the scene. But the French will find that their labor market rigidities threaten to tear the single currency to bits. They will have little choice but
to accept market liberalization in this political environment.

Ironically, France's special mission to "civilize" both the market and European relations will force it to embrace the "law of the jungle" for labor relations.

Germany's political interest in monetary union is different from
France's, of course. Prior to unification, Germany might have been seen as
clearly benefiting from a single currency. In the *optimal currency area* scenario, Germany's economy might have been the one less hard hit by asymmetrical shocks. With flexible exchange rates, an asymmetrical shock would
cause, say, the franc to depreciate and the deutschmark to appreciate, spreading a bit of France's recession to German workers. With a single currency,
however, France's recession would be France's alone, assuming that wages,

prices, and labor mobility are unchanged, and German prosperity would be preserved.

This happy situation ended abruptly with unification. Suddenly, Germany itself was a "currency area" with problems of its own. It can be argued that, at least for now, unified Germany itself does not meet the requirements for a common currency—that the conversion of ostmarks to deutschmarks was as economically unwise as it was politically necessary. Given the vast differences between the eastern and western economies, a flexible exchange rate would have been desirable, at least for a period, to ease the transition problems that are otherwise exacerbated by labor immobility, inflexible wages, and incomplete systems of fiscal equalization.

Suddenly, Germany needed an excuse to revise its domestic labor market organization. This system worked well enough before unification, but created severe problems afterward:

> Germany is characterized by a dense network of unions, work councils, employers and other business associations which is embedded within a framework that promotes the continuity of economic structures and relationships. . . . It has been suggested that, in a set of core industries in Germany, this structure has proved responsive to the demands of increased competition in the product market. For other industries, the model fails to generate rapid adaptation because of a stalemate between the stakeholders as to the appropriate strategy. An effective form of government intervention to promote adjustment has not been developed. . . .
>
> Germany's institutional rigidities of employment protection, highly structured wage setting and compulsory consultation by management with the workforce ruled out adaptation through cost-cutting strategies, and forced companies to move into high-value-added products and processes.
>
> . . . The regions of East Germany are obliged to operate under the labour market and other forms of regulation transferred from West Germany and will not have the option of being a low-wage economy (cf. the Czech Republic). If they are to develop an indigenous economic base and enterprises are not to remain as the "extended workbenches" of West German companies, then the institutional structure must be created in which the long-term relationships that seem essential to West Germany's high-wage economy can be built up. . . . Without these features of a coordinated market economy, East Germany will have little chance of succeeding in the kinds of market that successful West German firms moved into in the 1980s. The danger for East Germany is of having only the constraints entailed by German labour and corporate law, and few of the positive externalities associated with that system in the West.[30]

The right reason to undertake these reforms is to deal with the extended costs of unification, which are worsened and prolonged by labor market policies. But, as *The Economist* notes, this is a politically unacceptable package in Germany, where those in the West already feel that they have paid too much for unification:

Faced with the highest unemployment for decades, Chancellor Kohl's coalition has retreated down blind alleys that raise costs rather than lower them: unemployment can be dealt with, it has suggested, by job-sharing, limits on the working week, even by restricting overtime. It has been a pitifully inadequate response. But it reflects government's priorities. Rulers have invested so much political capital in the unpopular fiscal measures required for Europe's single currency that they have had nothing left over for jobs.[31]

But monetary union is a different matter. It is external rather than internal and can be sold as being distinctly in Germany's long-term economic interests. If labor market restructuring is the price of monetary union, then perhaps Germans can bear it.

When monetary union comes into effect, it will mean that local economic slow-downs can no longer be dealt with by local monetary policies and only in a limited way by local fiscal measures. The brunt will be borne by the labour market—which, if it is not flexible enough, will mean by unemployment. If governments are to avoid the potentially disastrous consequences of that, they need to start their reforms now—when the social model still stands a chance of being preserved.[32]

Monetary union, made necessary by the threat of globalization and possible by the high and low political logics discussed earlier, will thus crack tough political nuts for both France and Germany, who therefore support it wholeheartedly. Globalization, in the form of the necessity for monetary union, creates an external need for the internal reforms that both France and Germany desperately need. This is the political use of globalization as high art.

But this version of the political economy of globalization and monetary union does not favor all interests. I think Britain's reluctance to enter into monetary union (and into other aspects of the Maastricht agreements, including especially the social chapter) reflects misunderstandings over what the single currency really means.

The conventional wisdom, as noted a few pages back, is that Britain's reluctance to commit itself wholeheartedly to Europe reflects deep concerns about autonomy and national sovereignty. "Eurosceptics" do not wish to give up the right of self-determination, especially on economic and social policies, to a less disciplined Europe.

My own interpretation of the interests involved goes a good deal beyond this. Of all the countries in Europe, Great Britain has gone the farthest in market liberalization and has therefore already borne the political costs that await other European nations. Britain's old system of industrial and union relations was one, although not the only, cause of that nation's dismal economic performance for much of the postwar era. The Thatcher revolution removed many of the structural rigidities:

During the 1980s, there was a substantial shakeout of inefficiencies in the British economy and, by now, the UK was no longer an economy with relatively low scope for catch-up. . . . Our own results . . . suggest (1) that the structure of industrial relations in the UK, with its unfortunate emphasis on fragmented bargaining and multiple unionism, operated to reduce TFP [total factor productivity] growth prior to the 1980s, and (2) that the changed industrial relations scene of the recent past has not only allowed a once-and-for-all productivity gain, but also improved future growth potential.[33]

Britain has begun to experience the economic benefits of reforms, in terms of both reduced unemployment and increased prospects for low-inflation growth. But it has also borne the social costs of the policies that were sharply divisive: "The one large European country where unemployment has fallen substantially—Britain—has junked any attempt at consensus: successive Conservative governments have stripped away the powers of trade unions, while managers' performance is measured by the stockmarket not by the smoothness of negotiations with workers or politicians. Britain has the lowest jobless rate among big European countries."[34]

Because these social and political costs have already been paid and the economic benefits are already being received, within the analytical framework I am using here, Britain does not have much to gain from monetary union. For France and Germany, monetary union is the way to make Thatcherite domestic policies economically necessary and politically possible. Britain, already having experienced the Thatcher revolution, risks losing ground on labor market policies as part of a single currency area. The risk, to be clear, is that it might be forced to weaken its reforms in order to "harmonize" its policies with those of France, Germany, and the other countries in the currency area.

In an article titled, provocatively, "Thatcherites in Brussels (Really)," *The Economist* noted accurately that monetary unification would force Europe to be more like Britain:

Sir Leon Brittan, the external trade commissioner, is clear about the impact of EMU (which, amongst other things is designed to complete the single market). "European monetary union," he says, "is forcing European countries to adopt Thatcherite policies." Governments that for years had shied away from attacking bloated public sectors are at last doing so in order to meet the Maastricht criteria for low budget deficits and debt levels. Subsidies are being slashed, not because governments dislike them but because under Maastricht they can no longer afford them.[35]

A single currency will force Europe to be more like Britain, in certain ways. Britain's reluctance to risk its hard-won reforms makes sense in this context—much more sense, I think, than as flag-draped xenophobia. As *The Econ-*

omist has noted, "In a sense it is Britain, not the continent, that may now be more in tune with the European project—the ultimate irony for Eurosceptics."[36]

The location of the economic solution to Europe's economic problems has been known for some time. Writing in the late 1980s in "Europe in the Economic Crisis of Our Time," Harold Van Buren Cleaveland noted that

> The solution of the European problem of excessive labor costs depends critically on the attitudes that shape wage bargaining. If collective bargaining remains, as it was in the 1970s, an arena of struggle over distributive shares, and if the consequences for investment, productivity, and employment are left out of consideration, the European crisis will be with us indefinitely. . . .
>
> If hypocrisy is the tribute that vice must pay to virtue, it is a big change that virtue has switched sides. . . . There are respected economists on the left side of the political spectrum, such as Alain Minc in France, who have suggested that an across-the-board cut in real wages and salaries would be the most direct way out of the employment crisis.
>
> So radical a program is unlikely to attract much support—or to work if perchance it were attempted. The negative effects on demand and on social peace would no doubt cancel the positive effects. A gradualist alternative has more to recommend it.[37]

But gradualism did not solve the problem in Europe during the 1990s. The threat of globalization and the defense of monetary union, however, may provide the means for the radical reforms that have long been necessary.

UNSETTLED POLITICAL FOUNDATIONS

Globalization is a powerful force—probably more potent in politics than it is in economics. It is also a dangerous force. The promises and threats of globalization can be used to motivate and justify many kinds of political actions. When political agendas conflict, globalization can produce a crisis. The examples that I have used in this chapter illustrate this potential.

William Greider uses the threat of globalization to call for the formation of a global labor union to represent the global class interests of alienated workers. In Europe and elsewhere, however, the threat of globalization is used to promote domestic policies that would weaken unions and make labor markets more competitive. Greider imagines a showdown between the class interests of global labor and global capital. But I don't think global capital will fight. The force that will oppose labor is the state, which will be compelled to fight unemployment and economic stagnation with the only tools it has left—labor market reforms that directly conflict with the established interests of organized labor.

In other words, the welfare state (a government organized to promote economic stability, equality, and growth) may be driven by globalization and by the constraints it seems to impose to dismantle the policies of the welfare state. The political crisis of globalization is contained in the internal illogic of this situation—or at least that seems to be true in Europe.

The economics of globalization will not produce a crisis of class conflict because actual globalization is not that strong a force. But as Greider's neo-Leninist polemic and my own analysis of monetary union in Europe suggest, the actions that are taken *because of* globalization (or a fear of globalization) just might.

NOTES

1. William Greider, *One World, Ready or Not: The Manic Logic of Global Capitalism* (New York: Simon & Schuster, 1997), p. 11.

2. Ibid., p. 25.

3. Ibid., p. 39.

4. Norman Angell, *The Great Illusion* (New York: G. P. Putnam's Sons, 1911).

5. Robert Wade, "Globalization and Its Limits: Reports of the Death of the National Economy are Greatly Exaggerated," in *National Diversity and Global Capitalism,* ed. Suzanne Berger and Ronald Dore (Ithaca, NY: Cornell University Press, 1996), p. 60.

6. The Beveridge Report of 1946 (after Lord William Beveridge, director of the London School of Economics) proposed a "welfare state" to provide economic security as an alternative to Hitler's "warfare state."

7. Peter F. Drucker, "Trade Lessons from the World Economy," in *Readings in International Political Economy,* ed. David N. Balaam and Michael Veseth (Upper Saddle River, NJ: Prentice-Hall, 1996), p. 93.

8. Ibid., p. 96.

9. Susan Strange, "States, Firms, and Diplomacy," in *International Political Economy: Perspectives on Global Power and Wealth* (3rd ed.), ed. Jeffry A. Frieden and David A. Lake (New York: St. Martin's Press, 1995), p. 67.

10. The cases of Boeing and Microsoft in Chapter 2 generally support Strange's views of the changing nature of foreign policy (that firms have foreign policies now, just like nation-states, and that bargaining between firms and states is now common), if not her broader conclusions about economic policy.

11. Wolfgang Streek, "From Market Making to State Building? Reflections on the Political Economy of European Social Policy," in *European Social Policy: Between Fragmentation and Integration,* ed. Stephan Leibfried and Paul Pierson (Washington, DC: The Brookings Institution, 1995), pp. 389–431.

12. Michael J. Braun, *An Imperfect Union: The Maastricht Treaty and the New Politics of European Integration* (Boulder, CO: Westview Press, 1996), pp. 159–160.

13. I do not think that the EU has any choice about eventual eastward expansion. An economically and politically divided Europe is fundamentally unstable. To refuse further integration would be to forget all the lessons of 50 years of successful economic and political diplomacy in Europe.

14. This is the estimate of Richard Baldwin, Joseph Francois, and Richard Portes, as reported by *The Economist* (April 12, 1997), p. 84.

15. All figures given are reported by *The Economist* (April 26, 1997), p. 120. The United States reported a 5.6 percent unemployment rate.

16. Michael J. Braun, *An Imperfect Union*, pp. 60–61.

17. The incomplete nature of these regional arrangements requires further comment. Although monetary union would end exchange rate instability within the domain of the single currency, thus removing an important barrier to economic integration, it would not guarantee stability with respect to other currencies, especially the dollar and the yen. In fact, I think it is likely that speculation would intensify in the euro-dollar, euro-yen, and yen-dollar markets, leading to even more chaotic currency movements and possibly even more severe currency crises between the regional arrangements than within them. Perhaps a European central bank will have sufficient reserves to discourage speculative attacks on the euro, but the systematic behavior that creates currency chaos would remain. Instability is shifted to a new and higher level in this scenario. Regional integration may come at the cost of even less complete global integration.

18. This discussion is based on Paul De Grauwe, *The Economics of Monetary Integration* (2nd ed.) (New York: Oxford University Press, 1994).

19. I would argue, in fact, that the regional assistance programs are more political than economic in their motivation and effect. It is not clear that they have made any significant difference in regional income disparities, but they have provided funds for politicians from poorer regions.

20. Barry Eichengreen and Jeffry A. Frieden, "The Political Economy of Monetary Unification," in *International Political Economy* (3rd ed.), ed. Jeffry A. Frieden and David A. Lake (New York: St. Martin's Press, 1995), pp. 273–274.

21. Martin Wolf, "This Emu Can Surely Fly," *Financial Times,* April 29, 1997.

22. Wolfgang Streek, "From Market Making to State Building?," pp. 420–421.

23. Ibid., p. 402.

24. Toyoo Gyohten, "Strong Yen for the Euro," *Financial Times,* May 14, 1997.

25. Named for Robert Mundell and J. Marcus Fleming.

26. "The Politics of Unemployment: Europe Hits a Brick Wall," *The Economist* (April 25, 1997), p. 25.

27. "Thatcherites in Brussels (Really)," *The Economist* (March 15, 1997), p. 23.

28. "The Politics of Unemployment," p. 25.

29. Pierre Ssicsic and Charles Wyplosz, "France, 1945–92," in *Economic Growth in Europe Since 1945,* ed. N.F.R. Crafts and Gianni Toniolo (Cambridge, UK: Cambridge University Press, 1996), p. 236.

30. Wendy Carlin, "West German Growth and Institutions, 1945–90," in *Economic Growth in Europe Since 1945,* ed. Crafts and Toniolo, pp. 460, 490–491.

31. "Europe Isn't Working," *The Economist* (April 5, 1997), p. 13.

32. Ibid., p. 13.

33. Charles Bean and Nicholas Crafts, "British Economic Growth Since 1945: Relative Economic Decline . . . and Renaissance?" in *Economic Growth in Europe Since 1945,* ed. Crafts and Toniolo, p. 161.

34. "Europe Isn't Working," p. 13.

35. "Thatcherites in Brussels (Really)," p. 25.

36. "Thatcherites in Brussels (Really)," p. 23.

37. Harold Van Buren Cleaveland, "Europe in the Economic Crisis of Our Time: Macroeconomic Policies and Microeconomic Constraints," *Recasting Europe's Economies: National Strategies in the 1980s,* ed. David P. Calleo and Claudia Morgenstern (Lanham, MD: The Washington Foundation for European Studies, 1990), pp. 197–198.

7

Unsettled Foundations

In the absence of equilibrium, the contention that free markets lead to the op-
timum allocation of resources loses its justification. The supposedly scientific
theory that has been used to validate it turns out to be an axiomatic structure
whose conclusions are contained in its assumptions and are not necessarily
supported by the empirical evidence. The resemblance to Marxism, which
also claimed scientific status for its tenets, is too close for comfort.
— George Soros[1]

If the extravagant images of globalization that condition conventional wisdom
are more political rhetoric than economic reality, why haven't economists
spoken up? Why hasn't the concept of globalization been exposed to greater
critical scrutiny? Why does the idea of a seamless global economic web persist virtually unchallenged?

The lack of a persuasive economic critique of the globalization myth is
caused by a number of factors that I discuss in this chapter. There are practical, philosophical, and institutional factors that explain why economists have
failed to critique globalization and in some cases actually have promoted the
globalization myth themselves.

Economists generally favor policies that reduce government interference
in free markets, and for some of them globalization is a convenient reason to
advance these policies. Economists, like politicians, sell globalization so they
can sell their favorite economic and social policies.

Some economists have tried to draw attention to the myth of globalization and the particular policy focus it creates, but they have failed because no
one can understand them. Clear-thinking economists sometimes don't know
how to talk to noneconomist "civilians" who do not speak their technical
lingo. They fail to communicate and they fail to persuade. Paul Krugman has
made this point in a series of essays collected under the title *Pop Internation-*
alism.[2] My discussion of this point draws heavily on Krugman's excellent
analysis of this condition.

This lack of communication and critique is exacerbated by a flaw in the fundamental nature of twentieth-century economics, which makes it difficult for economists to expose globalization to the same critical analysis as other sorts of issues. Globalization is all about markets, and the values and methods of economics are conditioned to consider markets in a very particular way. The built-in problems of global markets that I have pointed out in previous chapters challenge the values and methods of mainstream economics. It is not true, however, that economists for the most part consider and reject these criticisms of global markets. Rather, the *idea* of an economic critique of globalization is in some respects anti-economics or noneconomics and so in general never enters the economics discussion. This philosophical bias to economics makes possible the endless selling of globalization that we observe today.

Finally, I explain in this chapter why the lack of a persuasive economic critique of globalization matters. This discussion lays the groundwork for a concluding essay in the chapter that follows.

GARBAGE CAN POLICY ECONOMICS

The first reason why some economists have failed to critique hyperglobalization and may, in fact, have contributed to its wide acceptance as an inevitable force falls under what my political science colleague David Sousa calls "garbage can" politics.[3] The idea of garbage can politics (and economics) is that the process of public policy isn't very coherent. Problems and solutions are generated separately and tossed as scraps into the policy garbage can. Once in the can, problems and solutions stick to each other in sometimes unexpected ways. The solution to problem A may find itself stuck to seemingly unrelated problem B if problem B is hot and problem A is not. The trick is to get your solution stuck to the hottest possible problem. In politics, it seems, dumpster-diving is an art.

I don't have to look very far to find examples of garbage can policy economics in action. Many of us in the education business, for example, favor increased national attention to higher education. When the problem is growth, educational solutions are offered. When the problem is inequality, the solution is education. When the problem is the trade deficit, the solution is education. In an earlier book called *Mountains of Debt,* I even proposed education as part of the solution to the problem of the national debt.[4] I think that it is fair to say that people who believe sincerely that education reform is of the utmost importance will try to attach this solution to whatever problem is at hand— sometimes cynically, but most often in the honest belief that it would contribute at least to reducing whatever the problem may be.

Enter globalization. Sousa writes that "the 'global economy' is an enormously attractive problem. It can be linked with ease to other problems (wage stagnation and inequality, excessive regulation, welfare spending) and is amenable to solutions that meet the needs of domestic actors across the political spectrum."[5] As a result, the global economy is a very attractive problem to which to stick whatever solution is at hand. We saw this in the first chapter. Economists are no better and no worse than others in sticking their pet projects to globalization.

Economists tend for a variety of reasons to favor "solutions" that reduce the role of government in the economy. Deregulation, free-trade, market-based foreign exchange rate systems, labor market flexibility, and low taxes are among the "market friendly" policies that mainstream economists typically support. Even *I* think that these are good things, all else being equal, which it seldom is.

Economists as a group would favor this solution set as an effective response to many problems: growth, inflation, unemployment, inequality, and—this is my point—as the appropriate reaction to economic globalization. Globalization is, after all, the notion of creating worldwide markets, markets so broad and deep as to make government regulation obviously unwise and ineffective. The "problem" of globalization, therefore, leads directly to the sorts of solutions that mainstream economists are predisposed to favor.

Garbage can economics is, of course, simply a variation on the political use of globalization that was the main focus of the last chapter. Economics, because it is technically complex and quantitatively sophisticated but still of profound practical importance, is especially ripe for this kind of political exploitation, according to Paul Krugman. He writes that

> If economics were a subject of purely intellectual interest like astronomy it would be regarded as a quietly progressive field, one in which there has been a steady accumulation of knowledge over the past two centuries.
>
> But economics is not astronomy, because its conclusions have a direct impact on government policies that affect almost everyone. In an ideal world this would mean that large numbers of people would care about economics enough to study it closely. In our imperfect world people care about economics only enough to know what they *want* to believe.
>
> Politicization is, of course, not unique to economics or even to social science. . . . while there is a steady accumulation of knowledge in economics, there is also a constant market for doctrines that play to popular prejudices, whether they make sense or not. In times of economic distress, the search for politically useful economic ideas—which often means ideas that are demonstrably wrong, but that appeal to those impatient with hard thinking—takes on a special intensity.[6]

Economic ideas like global markets are exploited by both politicians, as Krugman notes, and economists who have a policy axe to grind. My first argument—and not the strongest one I will present—is that economists therefore view globalization uncritically because the "problem" of globalization so nicely matches up with the "solutions" they typically favor.

ECONSPEAK: WHAT ECONOMISTS SAY DOESN'T MATTER

A search of the *EconLit* American Economic Association CD-ROM database of economics articles from 1982 to March 1997 shows a growing interest in issues of globalization.[7] Over this roughly 15-year period, a total of 452 books, articles, and working papers that dealt in some way with globalization appeared in sources that were indexed by the *Journal of Economic Literature*. Of this number, however, only 64 appeared before 1990; the vast majority (392) were published since 1990, with 148 appearing between 1995 and March 1997. By comparison, 15,621 references are found for "equilibrium or equilibria" out of a total stock of about 150,000 scholarly publications. Some economists write about globalization, but not many, compared with those who write about other things, and their analysis seems to have little impact.

Why are the economists who do write critically about globalization not more effective? Why do their studies have so little impact on public debate and public policy? One part of the answer is that what economists write and say doesn't seem to be a very important part of the public discussion of *any* important issue. It is easy to understand why. First, economists as a species agree on hardly anything, so there are few opportunities to report that "economists favor" or "economists oppose" tax cuts, welfare increases, or anything else of substance. This lack of consensus on critical issues weakens the influence of economists on policy issues generally.

Even where economists do agree, however, their views frequently fail to persuade. Free trade, for example, is one of the few policy issues on which there is general agreement among professional economists. About 90 percent of working economists support the notion of free trade as a general economic policy. If economists ruled the world, it would be one giant free trade area. Yet the views of economists are seldom taken very seriously in trade policy discussions. The serene logic of the theory of comparative advantage is enormously less influential than the practical matters of jobs and votes.

Economic ideas underachieve because of what economists write (generally about models, especially mathematical ones, not about people), how they write it (in an almost impenetrably abstract style), and where it appears (usually in a scholarly journal or a book published by a specialist academic press). If you were to set out to hide your bright light under a bushel basket, it would be hard to concoct a more effective strategy than this.

Alfred Marshall, the great early neoclassical economist, apparently advised his students that economic theory should proceed in the following way. The process begins with a mathematical model of some important aspect of business. When you have solved the math, draw a graph of the model to help simplify and clarify the logic. Next, find a practical problem that can be addressed by the model's findings. Write up an explanation of the practical problem in clear and simple language that can be understood by anyone generally familiar with business. Finally, tear up the math and the graphs, because you do not need them: It is the problem that counts. However, if you can do the math and the graphs but cannot use the model to solve any problem, then tear it all up, Marshall advised, because it doesn't matter.

It seems as though many economists today spend too much of their time building models and too little of their time solving practical problems in a form that intelligent and informed citizens can understand. Although economic knowledge accumulates through this process, the influence of economists on real world problems is not advanced.

The influence of those few economists who write effectively for the public—who are public intellectuals more than footnote scholars—has long been noted. John Kenneth Galbraith, for example, has had much more influence over the economy (through the impact of his ideas on public policymakers) than he has ever had on professional economists. The same is true of Lester Thurow. When they are right, and especially when they are wrong, these wordsmith economists wield important influence.

But, right or wrong, the readable economists are vastly outnumbered by readable "civilians" (noneconomists) who write about economics from a more or less informed and unbiased perspective, sometimes reaching into the garbage can to find the problems they need to sell the solutions they champion.

Paul Krugman, an economist who sincerely wants to have influence, has noted this problem:

> In other words, all of the things that have been painfully learned through a couple of centuries of hard thinking about and careful study of the international economy—that tradition that reaches back to David Hume's essay "On the balance of trade"—have been swept out of public discourse. Their place has been taken by a glib rhetoric that appeals to those who want to sound sophisticated without engaging in hard thinking; and this rhetoric has come to dominate popular discussion so completely that someone who wanted to learn about trade without reading a textbook would probably never realize that there is anything better.[8]

Krugman, for his part, has resolved to try to reduce the influence of bad economic ideas by writing in a style and publishing in places that are more accessible to decision makers in particular and the informed public in general. He has become a regular contributor to the journal *Foreign Affairs*, for example, and writes a popular column for *Slate*, the Microsoft on-line magazine.[9]

The specific issue that provoked Krugman to take action is worth noting because it is really a globalization issue: competitiveness. Krugman has argued consistently that although international (global?) trade is important for individuals and for the nations of the world collectively, the main determinants of domestic economic well-being remain surprisingly, well, domestic. National saving, efficient investment, effective education—these are the factors that make nations rich or make them poor. Nations with high savings rates, high investment rates, and high-quality education systems naturally grow faster than other nations lacking these qualities. International trade makes a difference at the margin—and all nations benefit from an open trading system—but the fundamental factors of importance are domestic.[10]

Believing this, Krugman has been publicly frustrated with the focus of national economic policy on international competitiveness, not sound domestic policy. Krugman's sound but boring message to save, invest, and learn—to eat your spinach, it's good for you—has been less persuasive than the "competitiveness" message. In today's cutthroat global market, the key to economic success is to stop the (Japanese/Germans/Chinese/etc.) from (taking over our markets/closing their markets to us/beating us in other markets/etc.), so we must (make them back down/make our markets as closed as theirs/subsidize domestic firms/etc.). He rightly calls this focus on competitiveness a "Dangerous Obsession" because it leads in the direction of bad policies aimed at winning the globalization race and also diverts attention from the sorts of national policies that might make a difference in the long run.

What needs to be done, according to Krugman, is to find a way to reach thinking citizens and educate them about basic economic principles such as comparative advantage so that they are less susceptible to proposals that use bad economic logic to back wrong-headed policy prescriptions. This means, as noted before, changing how, where, and to whom economists communicate.

Krugman has the right idea, but he cannot reform economics writing and economics thinking all alone. For every Krugman writing about "serious economics," there must be a dozen civilians like Robert Reich, George Guilder, or William Greider writing for the general public. The serious economic case against exaggerated globalization, when it is presented, generally appears in places and in forms that cannot possibly make much of a dent in the conventional wisdom.

My second argument, therefore, is that Krugman is right. Some economists do think and write critically about globalization and its consequences, but no one (including the thinking public) can understand them, so no one pays any attention to them. They might as well be mute.

Most economists, however, are not just *effectively* silent on the issue of globalization; they are *actually* silent. They are silent, I argue here, because the idea of global market expansion is uncontroversial to them. The thought that this phenomenon should be subjected to critical analysis simply does not come up. Their attitudes toward globalization are not dictated by scientific analysis but rather by the very notion of what economics is. The discipline of economics has unexpectedly evolved in such a way as to make it difficult, if not impossible, for a person to question the properties of global markets and still remain an economist.

GREED, RATIONALITY, EQUILIBRIUM

Everyone knows that economics is all about money. Economics textbooks define economics, however, somewhat vaguely as the study of how society chooses to produce and distribute scarce resources.[11] The purpose of this awkward and complicated definition is to get students to think about the fact that the problems of scarcity and choice, which are inherent and obvious with money, are not limited to money. Scarcity and choice are facts of life, and we should try to think about them in a systematic and rigorous way. It is a good way to begin an economics course.

However, this is not generally the way that actual economists typically think about what they do. Economists, as noted above, work within the framework of models of behavior, not actual or observed behavior. They tend to define themselves by the nature of the models they work with—as macroeconomists or microeconomists, or as labor, development, monetary, or general equilibrium theory economists, depending on the properties of their models. An economist who is an expert in her model and yet knows virtually nothing about "the economy" can still be respected as a good economist by her peers. Indeed, knowing anything about the real economy can sometimes be a disadvantage.

That economics should have developed in this way would come as a surprise to Alfred Marshall and often comes as a surprise to "civilians" who pick up economics books expecting to learn about the real economy.

Since the box in which economists work is defined by their models, the set of problems that they find before them (and the larger set of problems that lie outside the box) depends on the qualitative nature of economic models. George Ackerlof has written that "economic theorists, like French chefs in regard to food, have developed stylized models whose ingredients are limited by some unwritten rules. Just as traditional French cooking does not use seaweed or raw fish, so neoclassical models do not make assumptions derived from psychology, anthropology, or sociology."[12]

A few generations ago, this set of ingredients, to use Ackerlof's metaphor, was very broad and not at all inconsistent with the everyday notion of what economists study. Johns Stuart Mill, for example, defined the scope of economics this way:

> There is, for example, one large class of social phenomena in which the immediate determining causes are principally those which act through the de-

sire of wealth, and in which the psychological law mainly concerned is the familiar one that a greater gain is preferred to a smaller one. . . . By reasoning outwards from that one law of human nature . . . we may be enabled to explain and predict this portion of the phenomena of society, so far as they depend on that class of circumstances only, overlooking the influence of any other circumstances of society. . . . A department of science may thus be constructed, which has received the name of Political Economy.[13]

Economics in the nineteenth century, according to Mill, looked at problems using models of greed and confined itself to activities and behaviors in which the desire of wealth was the principal but not necessarily the only motive. This class of behaviors being quite large, the domain of political economy was broad.[14]

Without much notice, however, this domain has narrowed considerably in the twentieth century. It has narrowed in a way that places a critical examination of globalization out of the economist's box.

In the winter 1997 issue of *Daedalus* (the journal of the American Academy of Science), three economists were asked to assess the status quo of the discipline of economics. David M. Kreps insightfully noted the critical change in method:

In the fifty-odd years since World War II, economics has undergone a substantial transformation. Before the war the discipline was defined by the subject matter it encompassed, i.e., things connected with prices and markets. But the tools and theories used to study, say, international trade bore only scant resemblance to those used to study labor markets. In the two decades that followed the war, this largely changed. Mathematical modeling rose to preeminence in economics, and a sparse set of canonical hypotheses—Robert Solow has characterized them as *greed, rationality, and equilibrium*—became the maintained hypotheses in almost all branches of the subject.[15]

Economic models assume greed, rationality, and equilibrium—or, as Kreps prefers to state, far-sighted rationality, purposeful behavior, and processes that tend toward a stable equilibrium. Economists cook with these ingredients and tend to ignore recipes that deviate from them. For the most part, economists see this parsimony as an advantage: Models based on a small set of assumptions are more robust than those that depend on a long list of special requirements.

At first glance, this aspect of economic methodology may not seem to be very important. What I now argue, however, is that this change in how economics defines itself is meaningful in terms of economists' ability to frame problems and offer critical analyses of globalization and perhaps many other "economic" conditions and processes. If you cook only with greed, rationality, and equilibrium, you automatically, and perhaps unknowingly, exclude some dishes that might improve the menu.

Deep down, economics is about markets, and has been since the time of Adam Smith. Economics is even more about markets than it is about money, since money has value and significance only in exchange. The properties of greed, rationality, and equilibrium that condition all of economics have their roots in properties that economists find in markets. Economic knowledge begins with the market.

This property of economics is significant in that true globalization is correctly seen by economists as the logical expansion of markets from local institutions, to a regional, national, international, and finally global framework for production and distribution. Globalization, seen through the lens of economics, is therefore a highly efficient and altogether admirable process driven by greed (Solow) or the desire of wealth (Mill) or the love of money (Keynes) or purposeful behavior (Kreps). This process is rational; rational individuals interact through rational markets. It is also stable. Markets are inherently stable in economic analysis, tending toward stable equilibria.

Globalization, being the ultimate expansion of markets to a global scale, is therefore everything an economist believes in. To see why this matters, we need to examine briefly the economist's trinity: greed, rationality, and equilibrium.

GREED AND THE INVISIBLE HAND

How is it possible to believe in greed as a useful principle of social organization? Most noneconomists who confront the economic way of thinking are at least initially put off by the focus on greed or self-interest. Economists have a reputation for believing that "greed is good," not like Gordon Gecko in the movie *Wall Street*, however, for the thrill of it, nor like Keynes, who thought that love of money was a potentially less harmful vice than, say, love of power. Adam Smith (1723–1790) taught economists that greedy self-interest could be admirably connected with benevolent public interest. The key to understanding this was his famous "invisible hand."

Smith was a realist in thinking that people commonly put their self-interest above the public interest. In some cases, individual and public interest may be in conflict; however, there is a range of activities in which they are naturally aligned:

> Every Individual is continually exerting himself to find out the most advantageous employment for whatever capital he can command. It is his own advantage, indeed, and not that of society, which he has in view. But the study

of his own advantage naturally, or rather necessarily, leads him to prefer that employment which is most advantageous to society.[16]

When the butcher and the baker make business decisions, they think first of their own welfare. To succeed in competitive markets, however, they must please their customers and efficiently provide goods of a quality and price that are, at a minimum, no less desirable than their competitors. The invisible hand of market competition causes them to serve consumer interests while intending only to maximize their profits. The invisible hand doesn't always work, of course. The link between self-interest and public interest breaks down, for example, when competition is restricted. Smith the realist was as critical of monopoly and competitive restrains as he was favorably disposed toward the free market. As bad as monopoly, however, was government.

> The Statesman, who should attempt to direct private people in what manner they ought to employ their capitals, would not only load himself with a most unnecessary attention, but assume an authority which could safely be trusted, not only to no single person, but to no council or senate whatever, and which would nowhere be so dangerous as in the hands of a man who had folly and presumption enough to fancy himself fit to exercise.[17]

According to the tradition that derives from Smith, as long as competition exists, all participants are well informed, and a few other necessary conditions hold, markets serve both self-interest and the public interest. The expansion of these markets to a global scale, according to this logic, further increases both self-interest and public interest. This takes place without any sacrifice in national interest or national security, Smith argued, because self-interested individuals naturally include security issues in their decision making.

> He generally, indeed, neither intends to promote the public interest, nor knows how much he is promoting it. By preferring the support of domestic to that of foreign industry, he intends only his own security; and by directing that industry in such a manner as its own produce may be of the greatest value, he intends only his own gain, and he is in this, as in many other cases, led by an invisible hand to promote an end which was no part of his intention. Nor is it always the worse for the society that it was no part of it. By pursuing his own interest he frequently promotes that of society more effectually than when he really intends to promote it. I have never known much good done by those who affected to trade for the public good.[18]

The tradition within economics, therefore, is that markets, national markets, international markets, and now global markets, when driven by the invisible hand's competitive force, are nearly always unambiguously good. The extreme version of this view was best stated by David Ricardo (1772–1823), who is second only to Smith in his influence on how economists think about globalization. In one of my favorite passages of economics, Ricardo wrote that

> Under a system of perfectly free commerce, each country naturally devotes its capital and labour to such employments as are most beneficial to each. The pursuit of individual advantage is admirably connected with the universal good of the whole. By stimulating industry, by rewarding ingenuity, and by using most efficaciously the peculiar powers bestowed by nature, it distributes labour most effectively and most economically: while, by increasing the general mass of productions, it diffuses general benefit, and binds together, by one common tie of interest and intercourse, the universal society of nations throughout the civilized world.[19]

I call your attention to the last line of this famous quotation, because it provides a remarkably optimistic view of globalization. International trade stimulates industry and ingenuity, efficiently allocates jobs, creates material abundance, raises the general level of welfare, and leads to world peace. This view from the 1820s states very well how most economists today think about globalization.

My point, to conclude this brief section, is that the way that economists understand markets and the forces that drive them leads them to see markets in general as fundamentally positive factors in individual, national, and global welfare. When economists write about globalization, they focus on *particular* markets and industries—the ones their models are built for—not the general process of market expansion, which is taken as self-evidently stable and beneficial.[20]

RATIONAL PEOPLE, RATIONAL MARKETS

The second axiom of modern economics is rationality, or rational or purposeful behavior. Rationality is assumed as a principle of analysis, *not* as a description of the world. Economic analysis restricts itself to the domain of rational behavior. If behavior is not based on rationality, which in the real world it often isn't, then it is not economics—it is sociology or psychology or something else. As David Kreps has written, ". . . economists believe that behavior that does not accord with the standard model is irrational, unpredictable, and even somewhat unsavory—not a fit subject for serious discussion."[21]

It is one thing to define economics in a way that restricts it to situations in which individuals behave rationally or according to their known interests, subject to their knowledge of the universe. It is quite another, however, to think, as economists often do, that Adam Smith's invisible hand of self-interest extends to rationality—that actions considered rational for the individual are therefore also rational for society. There are too many counterexamples of this for us to feel comfortable with this assumption. To use an example from the classroom, it is well known that a good way to see better at a baseball game is to stand up. If everyone is rational and stands, however, no one sees better and some people cannot see at all.

Individual rationality and collective rationality don't line up. Keynes's famous *paradox of thrift* is another familiar example. If I am worried about hard economic times ahead, it is rational for me to spend less and save more, building up a cushion in case hard times come. If, however, everyone behaves rationally in this way, the result is a decline in total spending, surpluses of goods and services, and some combination of falling output and layoffs or falling prices and profits. The paradox of thrift is that it is rational for one individual to save but irrational for everyone to save.

The issue of market rationality is especially important to what I am saying in this book because irrational international capital markets represent a built-in limit to globalization. As I explained in Chapter 5, rational behavior under certain circumstances causes prices and quantities in international financial markets to behave in ways that defy normal notions of rationality. Sometimes the irrationality occurs through the Mexican peso-type mania-bubble-panic process that Charles Kindleberger and Hyman Minsky describe. In other cases, the cause may be a speculative attack as studied by Paul Krugman and others. But it is clear that, in the real world, market rationality breaks down at particular times and places, especially in the financial markets that are closely associated with globalization. Rationality may be a good general working assumption for much of economics, but it is a mistake to make it a definitional axiom of economics and assume that it applies everywhere.

Irrational markets get no respect in economics, except in the months immediately after a stock market crash (e.g., in 1987) or currency bubble (e.g., in 1997). Before too long, however, the rational market axiom reasserts its hegemony. Irrational markets, as I noted earlier, are considered unserious and simply not part of economics, so they get little professional attention. Kreps wrote of a conference on organizational theory in which a well-known labor economist spoke against labor market models that assumed that workers were "irrationally" motivated by relative wage rates—how their wages compared to those of their fellow workers (as opposed to those of "rational" workers, who think only of their own absolute purchasing power). He then explained that his own colleagues behaved in just such an irrational way. His real world observation of irrationality was then dismissed as "just an anecdote," whereas the theoretical concern was deemed "something serious."[22]

One problem with irrational markets is that, if the invisible hand fails, a visible (government) hand is perhaps needed. In the case of irrational international financial markets, for example, Charles Kindleberger has written of the need for a "lender of last resort" to provide the public good of stability. Economists since Adam Smith, however, have been distrustful of the government in particular and collective action in general. If the choice is between the extreme of perfectly free markets and the irrational but regulated ones, there is no question that typical economics will support and even believe in the former. Such a dichotomy is, of course, totally false, but this does not stop questions from being framed this way.[23]

Kindleberger found that discussions within the economics profession are often framed this way, with predictable results. He wrote that

> Frequently the argument seems to be between two polar positions, one which holds that no market is ever rational, the other that all markets are always so. In a meeting on the influence of expert networks, Harry G. Johnson offered this description of the difference between the "Bellagio group" of older economists, interested in international monetary reform, and a younger one from Chicago-Rochester-Manchester-Dauphine-Geneva:
>
>> The difference can be encapsulated in the proposition that whereas the older generation of economists is inclined to say "the floating rate system does not work the way I expected, therefore the theory is wrong, the world is irrational and we can only regain rationality by returning to some fixed rate system to be achieved by cooperation among national governments," the younger generation is inclined to say "the floating rate system is a system that should be expected to operate rationally, like most markets; if it does not seem to work rationally by my standards, my understanding of how it ought to work is probably defective; and I must work harder at the theory of rational maximizing behavior and the empirical consequences of it if I am to achieve understanding." This latter approach is the one that is being disseminated, and intellectually enforced through the [younger] network.[24]

This observation by Harry G. Johnson is interesting because it gives us insight into why rationality is so important to economics. At first glance, it seems that the addition of the axiom of rationality is limiting and narrowing. It takes Mill's social science of the desire of wealth and restricts it to a necessarily narrower set of problems, those where greed *and* rationality are the central factors. But this was neither the intent nor the effect of the rationality axiom. Rather, the idea was to convert economics from the narrow study of greed to the universal science of rational behavior.

Rationality makes economics more like physics than like sociology because if agents are rational, then theories can predict their behavior and the predictions can be evaluated. Specific hypotheses can be derived from the axiom of rational maximizing behavior, as well as those institutional factors that bear on an issue, and the hypothesis can be tested against real world data.

Without rationality, none of this is possible. Without rationality, economics is not a science.

In adopting the rationality axiom, neoclassical economics became part of a bigger project—the program of a grand unified theory of science based on the methodology of logical positivism. The desire to make economics a science is thus embedded in the rationality axiom. As a result, there is much to lose if irrational markets exist, and especially if they exist where they may restrict the largest market process of all—globalization.

ILLUSIVE EQUILIBRIUM

Modern economics is built on the axioms of greed and rationality, which, I have argued in the last two sections, render most economists unexpectedly insensitive to possible difficulties with the global expansion of markets. Economists are predisposed to see global markets as the beneficial, rational outcome of natural processes.

The third axiom of neoclassical economics is equilibrium; like greed and rationality, the notion that economic processes are (stable) equilibrium processes is not an empirical statement or the outcome of a logical analysis of greed and rationality, but a free-standing maxim or self-evident truth. Economics, by definition, is the study of equilibrium. The essence of contemporary economics is contained in general equilibrium theory, which is the highly formal mathematical analysis of equilibrium-maximizing behavior. Few economists specialize in general equilibrium theory, but this theory forms the base from which economists approach virtually all problems.

That equilibrium should be at the unquestioned heart of economics is not obvious. Daniel Hausman talks about the "hegemony" of equilibrium theory: "Whether equilibrium theory is the best way to proceed is an empirical question; and there is little reason to reject other approaches because they cannot be integrated into a unified theory of an economic realm."[25] But by beginning from the self-evident truth of equilibrium, economists necessarily limit their domain. In particular, they exclude problems involving nonlinear dynamics and chaos. In effect, they exclude the possibility that chaotic international financial markets might exist to limit globalization.

The equilibrium axiom is as uncontroversial to economists as is the consumption of raw fish for breakfast for a resident of Japan. Equilibrium is how we were raised—brought up within the discipline. It *is* controversial, however, to "civilians" who have reason to closely examine the methods of economics. One such is David Ruelle, a physicist whose work on nonlinear dynamics helped open physics to the study of chaotic processes. In a chapter on economics in his book *Chance and Chaos,* he criticizes harshly the equilibrium axiom.

Let me state things somewhat more brutally. Textbooks of economics are largely concerned with equilibrium situations between economic agents with perfect foresight. The textbooks may give you the impression that the role of the legislators and government officials is to find and implement an equilibrium that is particularly favorable for the community. . . . The examples of chaos in physics teach us, however, that certain dynamical situations do not produce equilibrium but rather a chaotic, unpredictable time evolution. Legislators and government officials are thus faced with the possibility that their decisions, intended to produce a better equilibrium, will in fact lead to wild and unpredictable fluctuations, with possibly quite disastrous effects. The complexity of today's economics encourages such chaotic behavior, and our theoretical understanding of this domain remains very limited.[26]

Ruelle's critique unfortunately demonstrates his lack of understanding of the way economists think. Ruelle seems to believe that economics is about the making of rational equilibrium government policy (visible hand economics), whereas economists know that it is about rational equilibrium self-interest (invisible hand economics). Ruelle's commentary is therefore unlikely to substantially influence the way economists think about what they do. His point, however, is extremely important. By *assuming* equilibrium, economists necessarily eliminate the possibility of *not* equilibrium when there is no particular reason to do so. Globalization, the increasing integration of the international economy, for example, need not be an equilibrium process.

A standard piece of economics wisdom is that suppressing economic barriers and establishing a free market makes everyone better off. Suppose that country A and country B both produce toothbrushes and toothpaste for local use. Suppose also that the climate of country A allows toothbrushes to be grown and harvested more profitably than in country B, but that country B has rich mines of excellent toothpaste. Then, if a free market is established, country A will produce cheap toothbrushes, and country B cheap toothpaste, which they will sell to each other for everyone's benefit. More generally, economists show (under certain circumstances) that a free market economy will provide the producers of various commodities with an equilibrium that will somehow optimize their well-being. But, as we have seen, the complicated system obtained by coupling together various local economies is not unlikely to have a complicated, chaotic time evolution rather than settling down to a convenient equilibrium.[27]

Ruelle, a physicist, argues that globalization itself might be inherently unstable, particularly as the dynamical interaction of the nonlinear economic processes of national economies increases. This hypothesis goes well beyond what I argued in Chapter 5, namely, that international financial markets may be chaotic. Ruelle's hypothesis, striking in its clarity and startling in its consequences, remains fundamentally uninvestigated by economists. The equilibrium axiom's powerful influence persists.

I do not want to leave you with the impression that economists *never* consider the possibility of nonequilibrium processes. Rather I want to suggest that the fundamental influence of equilibrium theory overwhelms them. One of the most important economic problems of the first half of the twentieth century, for example, was the business cycle problem. This was the problem of explaining how an economy could go through a macroeconomic cycle as pronounced as the Great Depression—a good question indeed!

Joseph Schumpeter, the celebrated Austrian-American economist, addressed this important problem in his 1939 book, *Business Cycles*.[28] Schumpeter found empirical evidence of three cycles: a Kondratieff long wave of 45–60 years due to technological change among other things; a Juglar medium wave of 8–11 years, caused by cycles in fixed investment, and a Kitchin short wave due to inventory fluctuations.[29] It is the dynamical interaction of these cycles, Schumpeter argued, that creates macroeconomic cycles. Recently it has been argued that what Schumpeter had in mind in this analysis was that these three cycles created a nonlinear dynamic process highly sensitive to initial conditions that tended toward chaos over time. Wolfgang Stopler, a former student of Schumpeter, writes that

> His "vision" was that the capitalistic process, which really encompassed all that was economic and social and even cultural in the history of the Western world at least as far back as the twelfth and the beginning of the thirteenth century when banking started in southern Europe, was a process never at rest. Equilibrium described only a small part of reality. It never has been reached. Various temporary "equilibria" existed at discrete intervals. They were never maintained for long and never repeated exactly.[30]

Schumpeter's vision of economics was dynamic, Stopler argues, and ultimately chaotic. Stopler argues that Schumpeter lacked the sophisticated mathematical tools necessary to make his vision of a theory of nonlinear dynamical economics a reality.[31]

UNSTABLE FOUNDATIONS

Ironically, it was another of Schumpeter's students, Paul A. Samuelson, who did perhaps the most to raise the equilibrium axiom to its exalted place in economic methodology. Samuelson is generally considered the most influential economist since Keynes. According to Philip Mirowski, "It is a testimony to his verve, his breadth, and his lucid writing style that his opinions were to be found in nearly every corner of neoclassical analysis from roughly the 1930s to the 1980s. . . . It was Samuelson . . . who by both word and deed was responsible for the twentieth-century self-image of the neoclassical economist as scientist."[32]

Samuelson, as a Harvard graduate student under Schumpeter in the 1930s and 1940s, wrote the book that essentially defined the program of neoclassical economics in the postwar period (it was published in 1947). The book was called *Foundations of Economic Analysis,*[33] and its influence has been enormous, as Mirowski just noted.

Samuelson's intent in *Foundations* was simply to raise economics to the level of a science. This meant changing the way economists thought about and did their work. The ambitious goal of the project, as stated in the opening lines of the first chapter, was to show that *"The existence of analogies between central features of various theories implies the existence of a general theory which underlies the particular theories and unifies them with respect to those central features"* [italics in the original].[34] The language used here is important and was certainly carefully chosen. Samuelson aims to develop a general theory of economics in the same way that Keynes had sought a "general theory" of macroeconomics. In both cases, I think, the term *general theory* was meant to suggest a grand unified theory, rather than, say, an incomplete or "special theory" like Einstein's special theory of relativity. If you reread the quote you will notice that Samuelson does not specifically refer to economics in his opening statement. He suggests, I think, that there is in fact a general theory of science that underlies the particular theories of the different areas of science (including economics). Samuelson's *Foundations* was an attempt to work out the economic aspects of this general theory while linking economic science to the larger theoretical program.

Actually, Samuelson intended two ambitious outcomes from *Foundations*. Together they would make economics a science.

1. To explore the implications for theoretical and applied economics of the existence of a *general theory*—that is, a theory that underlies all the particular theories.
2. To derive *operationally meaningful theorems* from this general theory. A meaningful theorem is a hypothesis about empirical data that could conceivably be refuted.

I remember reading *Foundations* in 1972, as a first-year graduate student at Purdue University enrolled in Mathematical Economics. In no way did I find Samuelson's ambitious agenda controversial. In fact, I don't think I even noticed it, so accepted were these theoretical considerations. Instead, we all dove headlong into the guts of the book, where the mathematical theories of consumer, producer, and welfare analysis are developed. I was so interested in finally getting to *do* economic science that I gave no thought to what that meant and how it affected the way I approached economic problems. I suspect that few of my fellow students gave these issues much more consideration than I did. For us, *Foundations* was about technique, and we accepted unthinkingly, I believe, the conditions that came with that technique. Most of all, we accepted the equilibrium axiom.

We may not have known just what we were doing when we studied *Foundations*, but Samuelson knew what he was doing when he wrote it. He did not see equilibrium as a defining axiom of economic analysis. Although much of the book focuses on equilibrium and the characteristics of movements from one equilibrium to another (which is called *comparative statics analysis*), the climax of *Foundations* occurs in the final chapters, where the first steps are made toward a *dynamical* theory of economics.

In the conclusion, in fact, Samuelson holds that the real goal of economic science should be to develop a theory of *comparative dynamics*, which would consider how the dynamical evolution of the economy is affected by various events and policies.[35] Along the way, he examines the properties of various dynamical systems and, through the economic examples he cites, makes clear that some of the most important problems in economics are really problems of dynamical analysis. He even discusses the problems of nonlinear dynamical systems, calling them by this name. Such systems are obviously important to economics, he says, "However, for now formal difficulties of solution are so great that very much remains to be done. . . . It is not unexpected that the simplest empirical notions may lead to the most complicated mathematical problems. This is a fact to inspire humility in both literary and mathematical investigators, but should prove discouraging to neither."[36]

The vision of economics found at the end of Samuelson's *Foundations* is thus clearly in the spirit of his mentor, Joseph Schumpeter. The goal of economics should be to understand *change*, not static states. So it is intensely ironic, I think, that the effect of Samuelson's *Foundations* probably was to focus economic analysis instead on the concept of equilibrium.

The reason that equilibrium became so embedded in economic analysis goes back to Samuelson's original goal of producing a *general* theory of economics from which one could derive *operationally meaningful theorems*. If Samuelson could have built a general theory on the axioms of greed and rationality, I suppose he would have tried. In fact, greed and rationality *are* enough for some kinds of economic theorems, such as those having to do with the profit-maximizing behavior of an individual firm or the utility-maximizing behavior of an individual consumer. But greed and rationality are not enough to predict how markets or systems of markets work:

> When we leave single economic units, the determination of unknowns is found to be unrelated to an extremum position. In even the simplest business cycle theories there is lacking symmetry in the conditions of equilibrium so that there is no possibility of directly reducing the problem to that of a maximum or minimum. Instead the dynamical properties of the system are specified, and the hypothesis is made that the system is in "stable" equilibrium or motion. By means of what I have called the *Correspondence Principle* be-

tween comparative statics and dynamics, definite *operationally meaningful* theorems can be derived from so simple a hypothesis.[37]

In other words, a "hypothesis" that soon became an axiom needed to be *added* to make the system work. The hypothesis that Samuelson needed was that the system was in stable equilibrium motion. Without this added assumption, the project of a general theory of economics would have failed. He called this hypothesis the *Correspondence Principle*, a name surely borrowed from the correspondence principle that Niels Bohr developed for quantum physics.[38] Bohr's correspondence principle was the assumption that the quantum behavior of particles could be approximated by the predictions of classical or nonquantum physics. Without Bohr's correspondence principle, an analysis of quantum behavior was impossible. Samuelson's correspondence principle was that the behavior of dynamical systems could be approximated by the behavior of equilibrium systems. Without this assumption, as we just saw, there was "no possibility" of attacking the problem on the basis of rationality and greed.

Samuelson immediately recognized that the correspondence principle was problematic, but he could not proceed without it. Critical sections of *Foundations* are therefore devoted to defending the equilibrium hypothesis. On page five, for example, having introduced the correspondence principle, he accepts its theoretical problems while simultaneously arguing its intuitive appeal.

> The empirical validity or fruitfulness of the theorems, of course, cannot surpass that of the original hypothesis. Moreover, the stability hypothesis has no teleological or normative significance; thus, the stable equilibrium might be at fifty per cent unemployment. The plausibility of such a stability hypothesis is suggested by the consideration that positions of unstable equilibrium, even if they exist, are transient, nonpersistent states, and hence on the crudest probability calculation would be observed less frequently than the stable states. How many times has the reader seen an egg standing upon its end? From a formal point of view it is often convenient to consider the stability of nonstationary motions.[39]

It is my sense that Samuelson is a little desperate here, and it is easy to see why. He wants to make economics a science, but to do this he is forced to rely on the uncertain center of gravity of an egg. The last sentence of this paragraph is the important one: From a *formal* point of view it is often *convenient* to consider the stability of *nonstationary* motions. The motion of economic systems may not be stable, Samuelson is telling us, but it is convenient to pretend that they are if you want to perform rigorous analysis.

From this basis, it is possible to imagine economics developing along two lines: one of "economic science" founded on the correspondence principle, relying heavily on the equilibrium assumption; and the other of "political economy," unrestricted by equilibrium conditions. This second line of thought would have been less formal, more literary, more "historical" or descriptive, and well prepared to consider problems such as globalization from the ground up.

This bifurcation of economics was possible but was not part of Samuelson's plan; it would have separated not just economic science from political economy but also economics from science. As Samuelson wrote in an early paper, "Technically speaking, we theorists hoped not to introduce hysteresis phenomena into our model, as the Bible does when it says: 'We pass this way only once' and, in so saying, takes the subject out of the realm of science and into the realm of genuine history."[40] So Samuelson was forced into further efforts to defend the correspondence principle. He was so successful in this that for 40 years it was impossible, or nearly so, to do serious economics without equilibrium.

Writing in the chapter on "Fundamentals of Dynamical Theory," for example, Samuelson argues that different economic processes proceed at much different speeds (they do), with some much "faster" and others much "slower."[41] There is no harm in assuming that the slower ones are constants, he argues, and assuming that the faster ones are heavily damped, so that what remains can be assumed to be an equilibrium system. Thus a non-equilibrium system is approximated by an equilibrium system by squeezing all the dynamics out of it, so to speak.

> It may be argued that so general a connotation is at variance with traditional usage of the word equilibrium. Is it not straining language to think of a cannon ball as being at equilibrium not only after it has fallen to the ground at rest, but also at every point in its flight, when it is on its mean trajectory as well as in its precession around this path? Perhaps such terminology may occasionally lead to confusion; however, with carefully stated qualifications it may be convenient.[42]

What Samuelson said was "convenient" soon became "necessary." Neoclassical economy theory *became* equilibrium theory, as Hausman has noted.[43]

PHYSICS ENVY?

The problem with economics, according to Philip Mirowski, the self-described *enfant terrible* of the discipline, is physics envy. Economics sold its social science soul to gain the status of a real science. The Faustian bargain backfired. Mirowski writes: "one might quibble over the details, but I think most would agree that the mid-20th century Classical-style program of a unified science of economics has run out of steam."[44] He makes a surprisingly strong case for this position in his interesting and controversial 1989 book, *More Heat than Light: Economics as Social Physics, Physics as Nature's Economics*.[45] The gist of the argument is that by the middle of the nineteenth century, physics looked like it had the potential to be a general theory of the natural world. Economics aspired to be the general theory of the social world. By treating utility like energy, economics could be social physics. Thus, economics patterned itself on the physics of the 1860s, adopting the same types of principles, techniques, and mathematical models.

Mirowski's case may be based to a considerable extent on circumstantial evidence, but it is persuasive nonetheless. Rereading Samuelson's *Foundations*, it is difficult not to notice the many references to the method and results of natural science in general and physics (and biology) in particular. The giants of neoclassical economics, Nobel Prize–winners such as Paul Samuelson and Robert Solow, have pretty consistently denied that they suffer from physics envy. Solow, for example, argues that economists have stuck with their methodology, including equilibrium theory, because it works so well.[46] It is such a good way of doing social science, in fact, that it has invaded political science and sociology successfully, Solow argues. However,

> there is no doubt that economists are attracted to the style of explanation they see (or think they see) in physics. That is at least clear in the externals. Economists feel at home with equilibrium conditions deduced from first principles or from reliable empirical statements. Similarly, they are used to deducing dynamics from local assumptions or generalizations; economics is full of differential or finite difference equations. All this seems fairly harmless, as long as it works.[47]

The question of physics envy aside, there is the related question of why Samuelson's vision of a science of comparative dynamics has not been realized in economics while the ideas of nonlinear dynamics *have* been integrated fairly rapidly into physics. This question is especially puzzling given that some of the most important early work on chaos theory (e.g., Beriot Mandelbrot's key findings on fractals) derived from work with economic data (e.g., Mandelbrot's study of price movements).[48]

Randall Bausor has recently studied the history of how nonlinear dynamical analysis has been treated by both physicists and economists, to try to understand why chaos is embraced by one group and shunned, for the most part, by the other.[49] Bausor concludes that the difference is based on different empirical and evidentiary foundations and by the distinct cultural and metaphorical backgrounds of the disciplines. Compared with physics, nonlinear dynamical theories in economics are likely to be discounted as ad hoc, counter-intuitive, and empirically unsupported.

In physics it was easy to accept nonlinear dynamics and chaos because there was solid theoretical ground on which to build. The Navier-Stokes equations for fluid dynamics were uncontroversial and were considered a valid contribution because they generated chaotic outcomes. In economics, on the other hand, there is no similar solid core of theory. That is, whereas most economic models are based on the three axioms discussed in this chapter, there is little else that is standardized or accepted. Your model of wheat supply behavior is probably different from my model of wheat supply behavior if we are studying somewhat different aspects of the problem. If my model generates some chaotic patterns over time, it is likely that they result from the peculiarities of my model, not the peculiarities of wheat supply behavior itself. Because economics lacks a hard core of theory, any behavior that is at odds with the axioms can easily be dismissed as ad hoc. So it has been hard to get nonlinear dynamics to be taken seriously by economists. It would be hard to get *any* theory taken seriously that produces novel hypotheses.

Second, Bausor argues that economists and physicists have different attitudes toward stability. Physicists observe instability in nature frequently and can produce it in the laboratory easily:

> By inclination and training, however, economists abhor instability. . . . To most economists competitive processes that rule the economy are inherently dynamically stable. Mathematically interesting dynamics and certainly "chaos," in contrast, *require* instability somewhere. . . . Few economists are keen on any of this. For them instability of competitive processes manifests only a palsied malfunctioning of the invisible hand. Their most cherished attitudes towards markets and their most central presumptions about how the economy should be governed are all profoundly challenged by analyses conditioned on systemic instability.[50]

Finally, there are differences in the empirical standards in economics and physics that bear on this issue. Scientists are generally able to experiment under controlled conditions. They are able, therefore, to test for stability and instability. The empirical test of nailing down chaos is much harder for economists, however, as we saw in the discussion of chaotic exchange rate evidence in Chapter 5. "Empirically, economists cannot begin with a controlled phenomenon but must go straight to the wild, as it were. It is as if the student of fluid mechanics had to begin with Niagara," according to Bausor.

If economists *do* have physics envy, then, it does not go so far as to allow them to comfortably embrace the theory and consequences of nonlinear dynamics, as their physicist colleagues have done unconditionally. The good news is that in the past 10 years more economists have begun to work within this framework, and preliminary results, such as those noted in Chapter 5, are being reported. Given the problems that Bausor outlines, however, it may be some time before there is general acceptance of these ideas in economics.

Until such acceptance, the theory of chaotic financial markets and the critique of globalization as I have used them in this book will be viewed by mainstream economists as ad hoc, counterintuitive, and empirically unsupported whereas the general theory of the stable, rational, socially beneficial global market system is true *by definition.*

Felix Martin, the young scholar who was my research associate at the Bologna Center, has suggested that the differences between economics and the natural sciences that Bausor outlines are more philosophical than practical.[51] Martin argues that the philosophy of economics diverged from the philosophy of science in the 1930s; while the philosophy of science changed and adapted to new discoveries, the philosophy of economics remained unchanged, trapped in a methodology of logical positivism. Martin explains that

> the dramatic scope of the logical positivist philosophy proved its undoing, and in particular the extension of the reductive method it implied from the natural sciences to the social sciences. It was in there that the cracks began to open. Partly in consequence of this, analytical philosophers began to move away from logical positivism during the 1930s and 40s, and by the 1950s new orthodoxies were emerging. A similar development in the philosophy of science can be traced, through Popper to Kuhn and Lakatos, forced on scientists through the inability of the logical positivist framework to cope with the expansion of the natural sciences. But in economics, no such process of methodological evolution was evident. In fact, neoclassical economic methodology was if anything recusant—after the war it became more positivist than it had been before, when it had at least enjoyed a variety of schools and methods and a Keynesian debate.[52]

Martin argues that Mirowski's physics envy thesis is too narrow. What economics embraced at the end of the nineteenth century was not so much physics as it was the analytical philosophy of logical positivism that seemed to underlie it and seemed to be the philosophy of nature. When analytical philosophy and the natural sciences moved on to postpositivist methodology, however, economics did not. Neoclassical economists, according to Martin, "have proved particularly uninterested in delving into the epistemological basis for their research programmes, and partly as a result of this, have generally and unintentionally become stuck with a logical positivist view of science and knowledge."[53]

By holding firm to logical positivism, Martin asserts, economics has fallen steadily away from the natural sciences and analytical philosophy, and hence steadily away from the fundamental goal of equilibrium theory, to make economics a science. An assault on equilibrium theory, therefore, shakes the discipline of economics clear to its deepest roots.

GLOBALIZATION AND THE END OF ECONOMICS

Globalization is not the end of history, the end of culture, or the end of the nation-state. But is it the end of economics? Well, no. As Felix Martin just noted, economists are pretty impervious to deep philosophical questions. They will likely continue doing what they do regardless of the final verdict on globalization, equilibrium, and logical positivism.

But it is a question worth thinking about. As global markets become increasingly integrated, I argued in Chapter 5, there is reason to think that chaotic fluctuations in international capital markets will increase. If this occurs—and there is no "proof" that it will, just as there are no guarantees that it will not—then neoclassical economics and its assumption of stable equilibrium will become irrelevant in precisely the most important market system in the world. Is this not the death of economics as a practical guide to business and public policy, if not as an academic industry?[54]

No, to repeat myself, I don't think so; I don't believe that economics is in any more danger than the other institutions that are supposedly doomed by globalization's destructive force. Ironically, the failure of the equilibrium axiom in global markets will limit globalization, as I argued earlier, and thus also limit the extent to which globalization can generate real world movements that shake the general theory of economics down to its axiomatic roots. But this does not mean that economics will be *unchanged* by globalization and the international financial market chaos that I have associated with it.

Recently the general theory of economics has been sharply criticized from both the outside and the inside. George Soros, arguably the world's most successful currency speculator, has attacked the axioms of economics from what I term a *political economy framework;* in this chapter's epigram, for example, he compared the pseudo-science of economics to Marxism![55]

The attack from the inside is less dramatic but more severe. Paul De Grauwe, Hans Dewachter, and Mark Embrechts have derived qualitatively realistic chaotic market behavior within the context of models based on greed and rationality.[56] Equilibrium in these models, they argue, is an ad hoc assumption as it is in other models of rationality. By accusing economic theory of "ad hocness," they aim an arrow at the heart of economic science. I'll explain the more technical "inside" argument first, so that the chapter can conclude as it began, with Soros and the outside argument.

De Grauwe and colleagues focus their criticism on rational expectations theory, the pinnacle of neoclassical theory, which extends the rationality and equilibrium axioms to the extreme. Empirical support of the rational expectations theory is weak, but empirical economics suffers built-in problems that limit its credibility. Rational expectations theory exists and thrives within economics because it is a pure statement of what economics *is* in the postwar period.

When models of rational expectations are analyzed closely, however, it becomes clear that equilibrium is an axiom, not a result. This is especially true in models of financial markets, where chaos and crisis are often observed:

The rational expectations models produce an infinite number of explosive paths (speculative bubbles). It is customary in the rational expectations literature to ignore these bubbles. . . . One rationalization has been that since all (observed) bubbles explode at some time, rational agents, with perfect foresight, will be able to forecast the exact timing of this future explosion. Since this would allow them to make infinite profits by taking the right speculative position just prior to the explosion of the bubble, all speculators would do this, thereby bringing the time of the burst in the bubble closer to today. Repeating this reasoning, one arrives at the conclusion that the bubble cannot start. . . .

This rationalization is unsatisfactory because it brings into the model an idea that is external to the functioning of the model, i.e., that every bubble must burst. . . . This problem is a very general one that appears in all rational expectations models. In all these models there is an infinity of possible solutions, most of which are unstable. The need then arises to select one particular solution. This selection will necessarily be based on information not contained in the model. Thus, even in rational expectations models, *ad hoc* assumptions will be necessary. . . . In a sense it can be said that rational expectations models introduce *ad hoc* assumptions at a higher level of abstraction than non-rational expectations models. . . . *Ad hoc* assumptions cannot be avoided.[57]

I do not want the significance of this statement to be lost. To an important degree, rational expectations theory *is* neoclassical economics. If it is ad hoc, then neoclassical economics is ad hoc and therefore not really science. This is not the end of economics, but it is the end of a certain vision of economics. Ad hoc economics would be more of a craft, like dentistry, in which different problems are approached using different tools and paradigms, with no single general theory to unite or justify them. This would not necessarily be bad for economics—it is after all what Keynes thought economics should aspire to— but it would make economics a very different animal, much more like sociology than physics despite its formalism and rigor.

This new characterization of economics would be a good thing, according to George Soros, whose outside attack on economic science appeared in an *Atlantic Monthly* article titled "The Capitalist Threat." In this article Soros, who has used his fortune to finance prodemocracy initiatives in formerly communist countries, takes aim at the equilibrium axiom in economics. Although it is economic science that he critiques, it is the invisible hand that he is ultimately concerned with. He writes that, "The main scientific underpinning of the laissez-faire ideology is the theory that free and competitive markets bring supply and demand into equilibrium and thereby ensure the best allocation of resources. This is widely accepted as an eternal verity, and in a sense it is one. Economic theory is an axiomatic system: as long as the basic assumptions hold, the conclusions follow. But when we examine the assumptions closely, we find that they do not apply to the real world."[58]

The markets in the real world, he argues, are characterized by "reflexivity," which is his term for a feedback mechanism that creates nonlinear dynamical behavior. It is like the feedback between the chartists and the fundamentalists in the exchange rate models discussed in Chapter 5. Action produces reaction. "There is a two-way feedback mechanism between the market participants' thinking and the situation they think about—'reflexivity.' It accounts for both the imperfect understanding of the participants (recognition of which is the basis of the concept of the open society) and the indeterminacy of the process in which they participate."[59]

The open society that Soros mentions here is what is behind his critique. If we cannot scientifically know how to best organize society, then it is best to have an "open society," open to ideas and influences and organized democratically, not according to some scientific principle. The notion of the open society derives from Karl Popper's 1945 book *The Open Society and Its Enemies*. In a way, Soros is engaging in a political use of chaos. He is using the fact of chaotic behavior of financial markets to promote his political interest in an open society. He opposes all theories of everything that would enslave society to a theory or principle, whether communist or capitalist. His open society is a world in which such knowledge is impossible, so it is better to work things out on an ad hoc basis. Soros's basic argument is summed up as follows:

> If we look at the behavior of financial markets, we find that instead of tending toward equilibrium, prices continue to fluctuate relative to the expectations of buyers and sellers. There are prolonged periods when the prices are moving away from any theoretical equilibrium. . . .Yet the concept of equilibrium endures. It is easy to see why: without it, economics could not say how prices are determined. . . .
>
> In the absence of equilibrium, the contention that free markets lead to the optimum allocation of resources loses its justification. The supposedly scientific theory that has been used to validate it turns out to be an axiomatic structure whose conclusions are contained in its assumptions and are not necessarily supported by the empirical evidence. The resemblance to Marxism, which also claimed scientific status for its tenets, is too close for comfort.[60]

Financial market crisis and chaos, therefore, seem to have surprisingly broad and important implications. My argument, which probably seemed extreme at the start but is by now beginning to look rather moderate, is that market chaos is a self-limiting factor of globalization. As globalization proceeds, financial markets become increasingly unstable, which limits the further spread of global markets.

In this chapter, however, we have seen that this tendency can also be interpreted to have much larger impacts: the end of economics as a science and the end of *laissez faire*—the ideology of global markets—as a valid political philosophy.

NOTES

1. George Soros, "The Capitalist Threat," *The Atlantic Monthly* (February 1997), p. 50.

2. Paul R. Krugman, *Pop Internationalism* (Cambridge, MA: MIT Press, 1996).

3. David Sousa, "Converging on 'Competitiveness': Garbage Cans and the Global Economy" (University of Puget Sound, Tacoma, WA, March 1997, mimeo). The original idea of the garbage can is found in Michael Cohen, James March, and Johan Olsen, "A Garbage Can Model of Organizational Choice," *Administrative Science Quarterly* 17:1 (1972), pp. 1–25.

4. Michael Veseth, *Mountains of Debt: Crisis and Change in Renaissance Florence, Victorian Britain, and Postwar America* (New York: Oxford University Press, 1990).

5. Sousa, "Converging on 'Competitiveness,'" p. 7.

6. Paul Krugman, *Peddling Prosperity: Economic Sense and Nonsense in the Age of Diminished Expectations* (New York: W. W. Norton & Co., 1994), p. xiii.

7. The numbers generated by the search are only roughly indicative of economists' interest in globalization, however. These figures indicate the number of books, articles, and working papers in which the terms *globalization* or *globalisation* appeared in either title or abstract. Context is important; many of these articles were only tangentially concerned with globalization processes.

8. Krugman, *Pop Internationalism,* pp. viii–ix.

9. Krugman's *Slate* column, the "Dismal Scientist," was recently joined by another called "Global Vision" that is written by a faceless team of international management consultants. It is unclear, therefore, if sound economic ideas (about globalization and other matters) have made more than temporary gain via the Internet.

10. Krugman, *Pop Internationalism;* see "Competitiveness: A Dangerous Obsession," pp. 3–24.

11. At least this is how I defined it years ago in my *Introductory Economics* (New York: Academic Press, 1981), p. 5.

12. George Ackerlof, as quoted in Daniel M. Hausman, *The Inexact and Separate Science of Economics* (Cambridge, UK: Cambridge University Press, 1992), p. 260.

13. John Stuart Mill, *A System of Logic,* quoted in F. Martin, "The Development of General Equilibrium Theory," Part II, p. 7.

14. Political economy did not become economics until Alfred Marshall made it so at the close of the nineteenth century in an attempt to distill science (economics) from moral philosophy (political economy).

15. David M. Kreps, "Economics—The Current Position," *Daedalus* (winter 1997), p. 59.

16. Adam Smith, *The Wealth of Nations* (New York: Dutton, 1964), p. 398.

17. Ibid., p. 400.

18. Ibid., p. 400.

19. David Ricardo, *The Principles of Political Economy and Taxation* (London: Dent, 1993), p. 81.

20. This fact accounts for the structure of the present study, which tries to make economic sense of globalization through synthesis of the studies of particular aspects of the process.

21. Kreps, "Economics—The Current Position," p. 79.

22. Ibid., p. 79.

23. This is how Greider presented the issue of global markets, for example (see Chapter 6).

24. Charles P. Kindleberger, *Manias, Panics and Crashes: A History of Financial Crises* (New York: Basic Books, 1978), p. 26.

25. Daniel M. Hausman, *The Inexact Science*, p. 247.

26. David Ruelle, *Chance and Chaos* (Princeton, NJ: Princeton University Press, 1991), pp. 84–85.

27. Ibid., p. 84.

28. Joseph A. Schumpeter, *Business Cycles*, 2 vols. (New York: McGraw-Hill, 1939).

29. Wolfgang F. Stopler, *Joseph Alois Schumpeter: The Public Life of a Private Man* (Princeton, NJ: Princeton University Press, 1994), p. 65.

30. Ibid., p. 58.

31. Although theories of business cycles based on Schumpeter's analysis are still used in some areas of business economics, his fundamental idea did not survive the influence of equilibrium theory. The mainstream theory of business cycles today—the real business cycle theory—is based on cycles that result from rational equilibrium behavior.

32. Philip Mirowski, *More Heat than Light: Economics as Social Physics, Physics as Nature's Economics* (Cambridge, UK: Cambridge University Press, 1989), p. 378.

33. Paul A. Samuelson, *Foundations of Economic Analysis* (Cambridge, MA: Harvard University Press, 1947).

34. Ibid., p. 3.

35. Ibid., Chapter 12.

36. Ibid., p. 340.

37. Ibid., p. 5

38. This is discussed in Mirowski, *More Heat Than Light*, p. 379.

39. Samuelson, *Foundations*, p. 5.

40. Quoted in Mirowski, *More Heat Than Light*, p. 390.

41. Samuelson, *Foundations*, pp. 330–332 for the discussion referred to here.

42. Ibid., pp. 331–332.

43. Hausman, *The Inexact Science*, p. 272.

44. Philip Mirowski, "Do You Know the Way to Santa Fe? Or, Political Economy Gets More Complex" (University of Notre Dame, Notre Dame, IN, December 1994, mimeo), p. 13.

45. Mirowski, *More Heat Than Light*.

46. Robert M. Solow, "How Did Economics Get That Way? What Way Did It Get?" *Daedalus* (winter 1997), pp. 55–56.

47. Ibid., p. 55.

48. Mirowski, *More Heat Than Light*, pp. 386–387.

49. Randall Bausor, "Qualitative Dynamics in Economics and Fluid Mechanics: A Comparison of Recent Applications," in *Natural Images in Economic Thought*, ed. Philip Mirowski (New York: Cambridge University Press, 1994), pp. 109–127.

50. Ibid., p. 121.

51. Felix Martin, "The Development of General Equilibrium Theory" (Johns Hopkins School of Advanced International Studies Bologna Center, Bologna, Italy, May 1997, mimeo).

52. Ibid., Part II, p. 2.

53. Ibid., Part II, p. 19.

54. If the unsettled *Foundations* of economic science give way, then all we will be left with is political economy.

55. George Soros, "The Capitalist Threat," *The Atlantic Monthly* (February 1997), pp 45–58.

56. Paul De Grauwe, Hans Dewachter, and Mark Embrechts, *Exchange Rate Theory: Chaotic Models of Foreign Exchange Markets* (Oxford: Blackwell Publishers, 1993). This model and its results were surveyed in Chapter 5.

57. Ibid., pp. 68–69.

58. Soros, "The Capitalist Threat," p. 48.

59. Ibid., pp. 48–50.

60. Ibid., p. 50.

8

Rethinking Globalization

The social process is really one indivisible whole. Out of its great stream the classifying hand of the investigator artificially extracts economic facts.
—Joseph A. Schumpeter[1]

There is something important happening in the world today, and we call it globalization. Having spent so much effort trying to debunk the myths surrounding globalization, I want to be very clear now that the forces we see and sense are real. But if the process called globalization is important — and it is — then it is even *more* important that we begin to understand what it really is, what is left when the rhetoric is edited out and the smokescreen is stripped away. When this rethinking is done, I suggest, we will both understand globalization more clearly and be able to conceive of a better name for what it is.[2]

THE ARGUMENT SO FAR

So far in *Selling Globalization* I have argued that globalization in practice is very much different from globalization in theory and especially the visions of globalization that drive political choices today. Actual global firms are relatively rare and the process of globalization is far less developed than most people imagine. By some measures, the world is less thoroughly integrated today than it was in the period before World War I that Keynes has idealized.

When I examined case studies of four "global" firms—Nike, Boeing, Microsoft, and Frank Russell—only Nike seemed to fit the definition of a footloose truly global business, floating effortlessly in a virtual market world, drawing on global resources for its production and global markets for its sales. When people think of globalization, for good or for bad, they think about a world of Nike, which is an unequal, envious, performance-oriented, capitalist world.

The other "global" businesses I studied were as unlike Nike as you can get. Boeing is a creature of the state and in the process of negotiating with states has become one, or nearly so. Microsoft is market driven, but it *needs* strong states to enact and enforce intellectual property rights laws; it cannot exist as a profitable enterprise without strong states to enforce its copyrights. Microsoft's product lines illustrate the durability of local language, culture, and history (distinct national differences) by the extent to which they are tailored or customized to fit local markets. The Frank Russell Company, which looks from the outside like the quintessential virtual financial firm, turns out on the inside to be based on trust that is built through face-to-face personal relations, for which no electronic perfect substitute exists.

Globalization exists as a process, but it is less complete than many people think and of a different nature than is commonly assumed. Globalization in practice turns out not to be the triumph of the irresistible market force over all that stands in its way. The rumors of the deaths of distance and the state and culture and the individual all are exaggerated. These forces, which have always limited global market integration, still limit it today.

Among the many forces that limit the extent to which true globalization can happen is the fundamental instability of global financial markets. If globalization is to happen, I argue, it must draw on and perhaps be driven by global financial markets, which provide the economic means by which resources move around the globe. But these markets are an unstable foundation for globalization. Global financial markets are subject to both big instabilities caused by currency crises and to smaller but fundamentally more troublesome chaotic movements. Globalization can only proceed so far if exchange rates are as fundamentally unstable as I think they are. There is reason to believe that as global financial markets expand they become increasingly unstable. At some point, the instability is great enough to halt the forces of economic integration and perhaps to reverse them. If my analysis is correct, globalization is a self-limiting process. The world economy may never be much more "global" in a real sense than it is today or was in Keynes's day.

If globalization is not new, not ubiquitous, and not unstoppable, then why does it get so much attention? I have provided two answers to this question. First, globalization gets attention because it is a useful concept. Politicians, policymakers, and intellectuals link their pet projects to the promise or threat of globalization and then sell globalization to us. Because globalization is such a large and vague idea, all sorts of policies and projects can be easily attached to it. And it is easy to sell this vague idea to the public during a period when there are many reasons for anxiety and concern. Globalization is such a useful concept that if it did not exist, it would have to be invented—again, not to describe the way the world works, but as a delivery device for all sorts of good and bad ideas that are packaged with it.

The second reason that globalization has been so effectively marketed is that attempts to provide a sound economic critique of this concept have thus far been ineffective. In some cases the economic analysis has been done, but it didn't matter because economists tend to communicate using highly specialized and symbolic language and methods. Noneconomist "civilians" simply cannot understand what economists say for the most part, so a meaningful economic critique of globalization by a certified economist might as well be written in Martian on the back side of the moon for all the good it will do. More to the point, however, is the notion (which I advanced in the last chapter) that postwar economics has unintentionally defined itself in a very narrow way that effectively excludes the sort of analysis that leads to theoretical questions about global market forces. Crisis and complexity, which are the basis of my analysis of global financial markets, are not economics as most economists understand it. Expecting a critique of global markets from the economics profession, therefore, is like expecting a defense of usury from a group of Islamic clerics.

The bottom line here is that globalization is not what it seems to be. The question, then, is what is it?

GLOBALIZATION AND COMPLEXITY

The process that we call globalization is really a complex set of changes. It is driven by a number of forces that interact with one another in endlessly fascinating ways. Such a process is called *complex* in the language of nonlinear dynamics, and what we are seeing now is an example of complexity. There is no generally accepted definition of complexity, according to M. Mitchell Waldrop, whose bestselling book by that name helped to popularize the concept.[3] The subtitle of his book, however—*The Emerging Science at the Edge of Order and Chaos*—suggests a definition. If this is a definition of complexity, then globalization certainly seems to fit.

The key to misunderstanding globalization is to ignore its complexity. If you artificially extract facts about globalization in a simple way (to paraphrase Schumpeter's epigraph to this chapter), then you will understand it as a simple process (e.g., demonic global market, impotent state, borderless world) and succeed in misconstruing what is going on. Worse, your misunderstanding will serve to confirm your highest hopes and worst fears.

The problem with complex social processes is that it is difficult to understand them in their complexity. So we simplify. This process is artificial, however, as Schumpeter says, and arbitrary. We must pick and choose the facts that we emphasize and those that we ignore. It is possible to see anything you want to see, if the process is complex enough. So we tend to choose what we want to choose and see what we want to see. This is a serious problem. When we misunderstand the forces of change, mistaking them for angels or devils of our own creation, we lose contact with reality. It becomes all too easy to mistake friend for foe and good effect for bad.

More to the point of this book, because global complexity has so many interrelated elements, it is easy for political and intellectual entrepreneurs to pick and choose their facts to suit their agendas. It is hard to understand global complexity but easy to sell "globalization" as the cure for this or the enemy of that. So long as globalization is thus misunderstood, it can be too easily abused and misused.

The historian David Cannadine has written about this problem—misunderstanding complex social processes—in the case of the industrial revolution.[4] The industrial revolution in England was like globalization is today in that it was a complex event of great importance, but also of great complexity. If we can manage to misunderstand the industrial revolution, even given the improved perspective of hindsight, then we clearly can misunderstand globalization today.

The way that historians, economists, and the informed public viewed the industrial revolution changed dramatically during the one hundred years after Toynbee's *Lectures on the Industrial Revolution*. Without much change in the "facts" available, each generation was able to see in the industrial revolution a different image.[5] In each case it was an image of startling clarity and relevance to the contemporary situation. In each case it was the image that viewers wanted to see. Cannadine found four "phases" between 1880 and 1980.

In the 1920s, for example, historians saw the industrial revolution in terms of the social conditions of urban workers and the unemployed. The "facts" chosen were those that best reflected the then-current concern over social condition and poverty in England. What they (historians, citizens, and officials) saw in the Industrial Revolution was a mirror of their own times, and their reading of this history probably also influenced their reading of current events and policy.[6] The lesson of history was that industry is hard on the weak and devastating to the poor. Something should be done to change things before it is too late.

Economic historians who wrote from the mid-1920s to the mid-1950s saw a different industrial revolution. What they saw were the cycles in the economy, the ups and downs of the business cycle that seemed to characterize industrial capitalism. In this, of course, they were guided by the experience of their own times. The crash of the Great Depression and the effects of world war were on their minds and so appeared before their eyes in the form of history. The lesson of history was that capitalism is unstable—it booms and crashes, but especially it crashes. Something should be done to change things before it is too late.

Those who studied the industrial revolution from the mid-1950s to the 1970s, the period of the great postwar economic expansion, saw growth, not poverty and not cycles. They saw the rise of a static economy to self-sustaining economic growth. The famous *stages of growth* theory that guided economic policies around the world in the 1960s was the product of W. W. Rostow's examination of the economic history of the industrial revolution. Improved data (better facts) make us think today that Rostow's theory of the need of a "leading sector" was as wrong in its interpretation of the industrial revolution as it seems to have been wrong in the form of advice to less developed countries. But the lesson of history was that economic growth could be attained by promoting a leading sector. A great leap forward is needed.

Finally, Cannadine noted that those who have studied the industrial revolution during the current "Age of Diminished Expectations" have also perceived it as a distant mirror of the contemporary condition.[7] It was an *industrial evolution,* not revolution, with many evolutionary false starts and dead ends:

> Instead of being presented as the paradigmatic case, the first and most famous instance of economic growth, the British Industrial Revolution, is now depicted in a more negative light, as a limited, restricted, piecemeal phenomenon, in which various things did *not* happen or where, if they did, they had far less effect than was previously supposed.[8]

The lesson of history here is that dramatic economic growth is an illusion, or at least not something to be expected. The past is pretty much like the present—mired in the doldrums. You'd better get used to it.

It should now be obvious to you that the industrial revolution was a pretty complicated process—at least as complicated as globalization, not in the least because it including a dramatic global expansion of trade. The industrial revolution was clearly all of the things that these four generations of historians and citizens perceived: unequal, unstable, dynamical, and evolutionary. It was more, too. But the point is that we select the facts to suit our uses, to mirror the times. Cannadine's analysis forces us to consider whether our verdict on the industrial revolution says more about Britain in the period 1780–1840 or about our own view of contemporary social and economic conditions.

The main points I want to make here are these. First, what we call globalization is not a new process, even though we think of it as new. Second, globalization seems to be complex, with many causes and effects, some quite unexpected. Finally, because globalization is so complex, it can be viewed in many ways, and there is always the chance that we are missing the most important action through a poor selection of "facts." With these points in mind, let us turn from past tense to present.

CRUMBLING WALLS, COMPLEX INTERACTIONS

What we call *globalization* is the complex process that results from breaking down the walls that separate and distinguish many of the important institutions that we use to define the world we live in. In our attempt to understand a complex world, we necessarily try to conceptualize it in simple ways. We put various elements of society into pigeonholes or mental compartments. During periods of economic and social stability, this simplified framework is useful. During periods of rapid change, however, the old mental framework prevents us from understanding the nature of the change itself. The walls of the pigeonholes must be broken down and rebuilt to reflect the new reality.

The fact that the borders that define the geographical boundaries of nation-states are now less important than they were 30 years ago is only the most obvious aspect of this general process of crumbling walls. Unfortunately, it has given the entire process its name—globalization. Globalization *is* about the need to rethink states and markets in terms other than those defined by geographic borders, but it is about much more than this. Globalization is about a general breaking down of borders and the processes that result from this. To illustrate and motivate this point, let me draw on analytical frameworks developed by Kenneth N. Waltz, James N. Rosenau, and Susan Strange.

Kenneth N. Waltz is the author of one of the most useful intellectual frameworks for understanding international relations. In his influential 1959 book *Man, the State, and War*, he proposed a three-level analytical framework.[9] Human individuals exist within the nation-state, which exists within an international system. Each element—individual, state, system—has its own nature and motivations and is conditioned by the next higher level of analysis. In writing about the problem of war, for example, Waltz said that war and peace are complex matters that depend on all three levels and their interactions. To understand war and peace, you must understand human individuals and their motivations; the state, its motivation, and how it conditions the actions of individuals; and the international system, its structure, and how it conditions the actions of states.[10]

Writing in the 1950s, it was probably relatively easy to conceive of a framework in which individuals could be considered separately from states and from systems in structural and motivational terms. In fact, I think this three-level approach is still useful in considering many problems. But the clean distinction among the three levels of analysis has broken down. Individuals, states, and systems now interact in a variety of complex ways that in part define the world around us. The brief case studies I presented in Chapter 3 do not prove this point, but they provide a few examples that I hope will illustrate and motivate it. Boeing, for example, would be considered within the individual level of Waltz's analysis, since it is a firm made up of and controlled by individuals and lacking the authority that traditionally defines states. But, as we have seen, Boeing acts like a state in its negotiations with nation-states and is even treated like a nation-state for some purposes. In the negotiations that we studied, the nation-states were most often concerned with profits and jobs while the enterprises were most often concerned with security and autonomy—a role reversal. Both were caught in a competitive environment that brought their interests together in new combinations. The difference between the first two levels of analysis is thus no longer distinct, and their interactions are complex.

The Microsoft case study illustrated another breakdown in this framework. Who determines the *system*? For Microsoft, the system—at least the parts of it that affect intellectual property rights—is terribly important, and so Microsoft invests heavily in technology and legal resources to try to define the system within which states and individuals operate. To be successful, Microsoft must help create and sustain a global system that protects it from the self-interested competitive actions of the individuals and states within that system. In a certain sense, Microsoft must *be* the system, or at least be *of* the system, since it has the strongest interest in defining and enforcing it. (I mean this in the larger sense, but of course, "being the system" is also Microsoft's strategy concerning their Windows-based operating system and products.) It is increasingly hard to separate the system from the individuals who comprise it and their actions and motivations.

It is interesting to consider how much globalization is associated with technology, despite the fact that international trade and finance are not much more technology intensive than other aspects of contemporary life. One reason for this association is that the microelectronic revolution of recent years has been an important element in the breakdown of barriers among individuals, states, and systems, which we mistakenly call globalization. More rapid and efficient communications have clearly helped insert individual interests and motivations into state-level and system-level issues. On the Internet, in fact, states and systems are almost but not quite irrelevant. The resulting framework is not global and systemic, however, but local and individual, which is the main message I found in Bill Gates's book, *The Road Ahead*.

Susan Strange has recently developed a similar theme in her book *The Retreat of the State*, in which she frames the issue in terms of the breakdown of traditional structures of authority and the creation of new combinations that embody authority in new ways.

Strange perceives that the dynamic that we call globalization is conditioned by the diffusion of authority *within* society, not just *between* nation-states, which creates different patterns of influence and behavior. Using the terms of international relations, we might say that there are more actors in the international political economy today and more levels of analysis are necessary. Strange makes the point by arguing that traditional international political economy is based on the "Gilpin equation":

$$S + M = P/E$$

States + Markets = Political Economy[11]

This equation suggests a state-level analysis focusing on a small set of actors. It is consistent with an international relations–based approach to international political economy. This way of thinking must now be replaced, she suggests, with the sort suggested by the "Strange equation":[12]

$$A(n) \div M(n) + M(n) \div A(n) = V(n) \div Soc(n)$$

The interaction of many sources of authority with many markets plus the interaction of many markets with many sources of authority, equal the distribution of values within a complex, multilayered society.

This equation stresses the complexity of the interactions: more levels, more actors, and more different social valuations to influence. It is not so much that states are less powerful and markets are more powerful, it is that the whole *process* of determining whose values count and where they count is now far more complex and at the same time far more dynamic. What is most important here is not the left-hand side of this equation but the right-hand side. The diffusion of power is significant only because it allows a change in the distribution of values within society. People who fear value change within their social systems find in globalization a convenient external villain.

James N. Rosenau has taken this idea of crumbling walls and complex behaviors and used it to develop models of *Turbulence in World Politics* that mirror, at least metaphorically, the formal mathematical models of hydrodynamic turbulence that were the original chaos theory.[13] Like Waltz, Rosenau develops a three-level framework of analysis. He proposes that there are three *dimensions* of global politics. The first dimension operates at the microlevel of individuals and "consists of the orientations and skills by which citizens of states and members of nonstate organizations link themselves to the macro world of global politics."[14] The second dimension operates at the level of "collectives," which include both state and nonstate actors and where structural parameters are particularly relevant. The third dimension is relational and is a mixture of the first two. Rosenau's analytical framework is not as easy to state briefly or to understand quickly as are Waltz's three levels, but a deep understanding of this theory is not necessary here. It is what Rosenau says about his framework and what he does with it that I find interesting.

Rosenau argues that all three dimensions of his analysis are undergoing rapid change and are interacting in increasingly complex ways. That is, the orientations and skills of individuals are changing rapidly within a system of collectives that is experiencing fundamental structural change, and during a period when the nature of relationships between and among individuals and collectives is also in flux. The result, he argues, is conceptually similar to the fluid dynamical flows that produce turbulence and chaos in nature.

Rosenau's work, apart from his relatively formal attempt to apply chaos theory to politics, leads to an interesting observation that brings us back to the globalization issue. When the three dimensions of political change are mixed, the result is a *bifurcation*, which is a common occurrence in naturally chaotic systems. That is, the world does not settle into a simple and unique equilibrium but develops a pair of "strange attractors." In Rosenau's analysis, the bifurcation is toward political issues that are *too big* for the nation-state ("global" issues such as ozone depletion and ocean environmental pollution, and regional issues such as trading blocs) and those that are *too small* for the nation-state (many security issues, many economic issues). In Rosenau's model of political turbulence, the nation-state is the missing middle in the bifurcation of politics.

This political bifurcation hypothesis is interesting because it argues that the "death of the nation-state" that has been so loudly proclaimed is *not* caused by the rise of the all-powerful global markets (which I think is impossible). Rather, it is due to the rise of new combinations of opportunities and constraints within the world of politics itself.[15] Rosenau finds the cause of political change in politics itself, which is refreshing.

We should press beyond even Rosenau's analysis, to consider the economic and social as well as the political implications of crumbling walls, mixed levels, diffused authority, scrambled dimensions, and new combinations of the institutional elements that we use to define our world. This is my notion of the complex global dynamic that is reshaping society today. It affects a wide variety of structural relationships and is driven by a number of forces, and its dynamic interaction make it difficult to describe and to understand. It is *globalization* and a whole lot more. When we choose to consider it without accounting for its complexity, we make a simple error at the very least but also risk making enormous and important errors. Understanding this complex situation is difficult, but misunderstanding it is easy.

Before you sharpen your pen and begin to list the problems with the preceding analysis, you should know that there is a better analysis than mine. Joseph Schumpeter wrote it in 1911, when he gave this complex process a simple name, *economic development*.

NEW COMBINATIONS

The best theoretical analysis of global complexity, as I perceive it, is found in Joseph Schumpeter's first book, *The Theory of Economic Development*, which he wrote (in German) in 1911. A second German edition was published in 1926 and appeared in English translation in 1934. What makes Schumpeter's theory so appealing in the present context is its focus on forces that seem especially relevant today: the tension between the static and the dynamic and an emphasis on the importance of intellectual creativity. In 1911, as he looked back at the Victorian globalization period from the perspective of Vienna, Schumpeter saw these as critical elements of social change. The power of this idea in the present context surprises and fascinates me.

Schumpeter's analysis begins with a biological metaphor for society and social change: Society is like a plant or an animal, with the dual nature to both sustain (equilibrium) and grow and change (development). Although Schumpeter did not say so, this metaphor may be a fractal property of biology, existing on every scale from the cell to the individual to the species to the ecological system. Social systems of humans fit in there somewhere.

Schumpeter's economic analysis is divided into a study of equilibrium, the "circular flow," and a study of change, or "economic development." He conceived of

> a "circular flow" running on in channels essentially the same year after year—similar to the circulation of the blood in an animal organism. Now this circular flow and its channels do alter in time . . . continuously, that is by steps which one can choose smaller than any assignable quantity, however small, and always within the same framework. Economic life experiences such changes too, but it also experiences others which do not appear continuously and which change the framework, the traditional course itself. They cannot be understood by means of any analysis of the circular flow, although they are purely economic and although their explanation is obviously among the tasks of pure theory.[16]

Schumpeter's analysis of economic activity—that it comprised a static equilibrium circular flow and a dynamical process of economic development—parallels Paul Samuelson's later division of economic analysis into comparative statics and comparative dynamics. This similarity is unsurprising, since Samuelson was Schumpeter's student. Because the relevant mathematical tools were already available, Samuelson focused his attention on comparative statics, and the profession largely followed his lead. In *The Theory of Economic Development*, however, Schumpeter makes clear that it is economic development—comparative dynamics—that deserve the most attention.

> Development in our sense is a distinct phenomenon, entirely foreign to what may be observed in the circular flow or in the tendency towards equilibrium. It is spontaneous and discontinuous change in the channels of the flow, dis-

turbance of equilibrium, which forever alters and displaces the equilibrium state previously existing.[17]

The pattern of economic development derives from intellectual creativity, which Schumpter describes simply as the ability to undertake "new combinations." Globalization, in this reduced form model, and global complexity, is all about new combinations within firms, within nations, and among nations. But the sort of development that Schumpeter is interested in is endogenous, not exogenous. That is, it is not the result of an *outside* force but rather is generated by *internal* events. This way of thinking is consistent with the biological metaphor and also consistent with my understanding of *globalization*. Schumpeter writes that these new combinations come in five types: new goods, new methods, new markets, new sources, and new forms of organization.[18] Schumpeter's ideas are as current as today's *Wall Street Journal.* You could find these ideas in a story about Nike or a "borderless world" column by Kenichi Ohmae.

What is important about Schumpeter's analysis, however, is that these new combinations act to stimulate intellectual creativity, because it is ideas that count, along with the values that those ideas embody. The clear hero of *The Theory of Economic Development* is the entrepreneur, the person who reacts to changing circumstances by taking risks, trying out new combinations, creating change. Change flows from the individual, through markets, to society. This change diffuses authority and produces new distributions of values. It is dynamic and creative, in Schumpeter's vision.

The obvious weakness in this analysis is that Schumpeter works on two levels without providing a way to connect them. On the one hand, he claims that "the social process is really one indivisible whole,"[19] but then his theory ends up looking at new combinations from within a relatively narrow market-based framework. How can I find this way of thinking more useful or revealing than *globalization*? I do not know what Schumpeter would think of this, but I believe that the new *economic* combinations that he describes here are only part of the dynamic process. That is, the new markets that stimulate entrepreneurs to create new changes are an example of the process of social change. New combinations need not be economic or solely economic.[20] These new combinations take many forms, as Susan Strange has suggested, and they produce not just new profits, but new values. And values are what count. These changes can result in new political orders, including Rosenau's turbulent political bifurcation.

The strength of this way of thinking is that it challenges us to consider *globalization* as something old, not something new, as something human and intellectual, not inhuman and geographical, and that it encourages us to perceive it as the cause or the effect of the opening of new opportunities. These opportunities are made real only when acted on by creative intellect. Schumpeter characterized this process by the famous term *creative destruction*. And it is both creative and destructive because it is change.

NOTES

1. Joseph A. Schumpeter, *The Theory of Economic Development,* trans. Redvers Opie (New Brunswick, NJ: Transactions Publishers, 1983), p. 3.

2. Thanks to Dave Balaam, who encouraged me to give this chapter a clearer and bolder focus.

3. M. Mitchell Waldrop, *Complexity: The Emerging Science at the Edge of Order and Chaos* (New York: Simon and Schuster, 1992), p. 9.

4. David Cannadine, "The Present and the Past in the English Industrial Revolution 1880–1980." *Past and Present* 103 (May 1984), pp. 131–172. Thanks to my colleague David Smith for pointing me to this article.

5. The "facts" have changed too, however, especially in recent years, as improved data about wages, production, and trade have been produced.

6. Perhaps one of the factors that influenced Churchill in his disastrous 1927 decision to return Britain to the gold standard at the prewar parity was a perception of the success of Britain's gold policy during the industrial revolution.

7. In my book *Mountains of Debt,* for example, I compared the industrial revolution to a mountain glacier, which is powerful, because although it moves slowly and unevenly, the landscape that surrounds it does not move at all.

8. Cannadine, "Present and Past in the Industrial Revolution," p. 162.

9. Kenneth N. Waltz, *Man, the State, and War: A Theoretical Analysis* (New York: Columbia University Press, 1959). Waltz writes about three "images" in this book, which is the basis of the "levels-of-analysis" approach to international relations.

10. States act differently in a bipolar world system, for example, than in a hegemonic system or a balance of power system.

11. Susan Strange, *The Retreat of the State: The Diffusion of Power in the World Economy* (Cambridge, UK: Cambridge University Press, 1997), p. 37. Robert Gilpin is the author of the standard text on international political economy, *The Political Economy of International Relations* (Princeton, NJ: Princeton University Press, 1987).

12. Strange, *The Retreat of the State*, p. 38.

13. James N. Rosenau, *Turbulence in World Politics* (Princeton, NJ: Princeton University Press, 1990).

14. Ibid., p. 10.

15. Obviously, however, many of the new orientations, skills, structures, and relations that Rosenau discusses involve technological and economic factors.

16. Schumpeter, *Economic Development*, p. 61.

17. Ibid., p. 64

18. Ibid., p. 65.

19. Ibid., p. 3.

20. Indeed, the very idea that we should examine these issues as questions of international political economy is an example of the importance of new intellectual combinations.

Bibliography

Abu-Lughod, Janet L. *Before European Hegemony: The World System A.D. 1250–1350.* New York: Oxford University Press, 1989.

Akyüz, Yilmaz. "Financial Globalization and Instability." In *Change: Threat or Opportunity for Human Progress.* Vol. III: *Globalization of Markets,* edited by Üner Kirdar, pp. 39–84. New York: United Nations, 1992.

Angell, Norman. *The Great Illusion.* New York: G. P. Putnam's Sons, 1911.

Arthur, Brian W. "Self-Reinforcing Mechanisms in Economics." In *The Economy As an Evolving Complex System. SFI Studies in the Sciences of Complexity.* Vol. V, pp. 9–31. Redwood City, CA: Addison-Wesley, 1988.

Axford, Barrie. *The Global System. Economics, Politics, and Culture.* New York: St. Martin's Press, 1995.

Bagehot, Walter. *Lombard Street: A Description of the Money Market.* Philadelphia: Orion Editions, 1991.

Bagehot, Walter. "What a Panic Is and How It Might Be Mitigated." In *The Collected Works of Walter Bagehot.* Vol. 10, edited by Norman St. John-Stevas, pp. 88–92. London: The Economist, 1978.

Bairoch, Paul. "Globalization Myths and Realities: One Century of External Trade and Foreign Investment." In *States Against Markets: The Limits of Globalization,* edited by Robert Boyer and Daniel Drache, pp. 173–192. London: Routledge: 1996.

Balaam, David N., and Michael Veseth (editors). *Introduction to International Political Economy.* Upper Saddle River, NJ: Prentice Hall, 1996.

Baumol, William J., and Jess Benhabib. "Chaos: Significance, Mechanism, and Economic Applications." *Journal of Economic Perspectives* 3:1 (1989), pp. 77–105.

Bausor, Randall. "Qualitative Dynamics in Economics and Fluid Mechanics: A Comparison of Recent Applications." In *Natural Images in Economics Thought,* edited by Philip Mirowski, pp. 109–127. New York: Cambridge University Press, 1994.

Bean, Charles, and Nicholas Crafts. "British Economic Growth Since 1945: Relative Economic Decline . . . and Renaissance?" In *Economic Growth in Europe Since 1945,* edited by N.F.R. Crafts and Gianni Toniolo, pp. 131–172. Cambridge, UK: Cambridge University Press, 1996.

Bernstein, Peter L. *Against the Gods: The Remarkable Story of Risk.* New York: John Wiley, 1996.

Boyer, Robert. "State and Market: A New Engagement for the Twenty-First Century?" In *States Against Markets: The Limits of Globalization,* edited by Robert Boyer and Daniel Drache, pp. 84–116. New York: Routledge, 1996.

Boyer, Robert, and Daniel Drache. *States Against Markets: The Limits of Globalization.* New York: Routledge, 1996.

Braun, Michael J. *An Imperfect Union: The Maastricht Treaty and the New Politics of European Integration.* Boulder, CO: Westview Press, 1996.

Briggs, John, and F. David Peat. *Turbulent Mirror.* New York: Harper & Row, 1989.

Brittan, Samuel. *Capitalism with a Human Face.* Cambridge, MA: Harvard University Press, 1995.

Brock, William A. "Nonlinearity and Complex Dynamics in Economics and Finance." In *The Economy As an Evolving Complex System. Santa Fe Institute Studies in the Sciences of Complexity.* Vol. V. edited by P. W. Anderson, K. Arrow, and D. Pines, pp. 77–97. Redwood City, CA: Addison-Wesley, 1988.

Bryan, Lowell, and Diana Farrell. *Market Unbound: Unleashing Global Capitalism.* New York: John Wiley, 1996.

Cameron, Rondo. *A Concise Economic History of the World: From Paleolithic Times to the Present* (2nd ed.). New York: Oxford University Press, 1993.

Cannadine, David. "The Present and the Past in the English Industrial Revolution 1880–1980." *Past and Present* 103 (May 1984), pp. 131–172.

Carlin, Wendy. "West German Growth and Institutions, 1945–90." In *Economic Growth in Europe Since 1945,* edited by N.F.R. Crafts and Gianni Toniolo, p. 460. Cambridge, UK: Cambridge University Press, 1996.

Chitty, Andrew (guest editor). "The Direction of Contemporary Capitalism." *Review of International Political Economy* 4:3 (special issue; autumn 1997).

Cleaveland, Harold Van Buren. "Europe in the Economic Crisis of our Time: Macro-economic Policies and Microeconomic Constraints." In *Recasting Europe's Economies: National Strategies in the 1980s,* edited by David P. Calleo and Claudia Morgenstern, pp. 197–229. Lanham, MD: The Washington Foundation for European Studies, 1990.

Cohen, David. *The Misfortunes of Prosperity: An Introduction to Political Economy.* Cambridge, MA: MIT Press, 1995.

Cohen, Michael, James March, and Johan Olsen. "A Garbage Can Model of Organizational Choice." *Administrative Science Quarterly* 17:1 (1972), pp. 1–25.

Conley, Tom. "The Politics of International Finance." *Flinders Journal of History and Politics* (conley.htm at http://www.ssn.flinders.edu.au, accessed October 24, 1996), pp. 1–11.

Cox, Robert W. "A Perspective on Globalization." In *Globalization: Critical Reflections,* edited by J. H. Mittleman, pp. 21–30. Boulder, CO: Lynne Rienner Publishers, 1996.

Cox, Robert W. "Civilisations in World Political Economy." *New Political Economy* 1:2 (July 1996), pp. 141–156.

Davidson, James Dale, and Lord William Rees-Mogg. *The Great Reckoning: Protect Yourself in the Coming Depression* (revised ed.). New York: Simon & Schuster, 1993.

Davis, Dwight B. "Building a Global Network on a Shoestring." *Datamation* (May 15, 1993), p. 59.

Day, Richard H. *Complex Economic Dynamics.* Vol. 1. Cambridge, MA: MIT Press, 1994.

De Grauwe, Paul. *The Economics of Monetary Integration* (2nd ed.). New York: Oxford University Press, 1994.

De Grauwe, Paul. *International Money: Postwar Trends and Theories.* New York: Oxford University Press, 1989.

De Grauwe, Paul. "Towards European Monetary Union Without the EMS." *Economic Policy* 18 (April 1994), pp. 147–185.

De Grauwe, Paul, and Hans Dewachter. "Chaos in the Dornbusch Model of the Exchange Rate." *Kredit und Kapital* 25:1 (1992), pp. 26–54.

De Grauwe, Paul, and Hans Dewachter. "A Chaotic Model of the Exchange Rate: The Role of Fundamentalists and Chartists." *Open Economics Review* 4 (1993), pp. 351–379.

De Grauwe, Paul, Hans Dewachter, and Mark Embrechts. *Exchange Rate Theory: Chaotic Models of Foreign Exchange Markets.* Oxford, UK: Blackwell Publishers, 1993.

Dornbusch, Rudiger. "Euro Fantasies," *Foreign Affairs* 75:5 (September/October 1996), pp. 110–125.

Dornbusch, Rudiger. "International Financial Crises." In *The Risk of Economic Crisis,* edited by Martin Feldstein, pp. 116–123. Chicago: University of Chicago Press, 1991.

Drache, Daniel. "From Keynes to K-Mart: Competitiveness in a Corporate Age." In *States Against Markets: The Limits of Globalization,* edited by Robert Boyer and Daniel Drache, pp. 31–61. New York: Routledge, 1996.

Drucker, Peter F. "Trade Lessons from the World Economy." In *Readings in International Political Economy,* edited by David N. Balaam and Michael Veseth, pp. 90–96. Upper Saddle River, NJ: Prentice-Hall, 1996.

Eichengreen, Barry. *Elusive Stability: Essays in the History of International Finance, 1919–1939.* Cambridge MA: Cambridge University Press, 1990.

Eichengreen, Barry. *Globalizing Capital: A History of the International Monetary System.* Princeton, NJ: Princeton University Press, 1996.

Eichengreen, Barry. "One Money for Europe? Lessons from the US Currency Union." *Economic Policy* 10 (April 1990), pp. 118–187.

Eichengreen, Barry, and Jeffry A. Frieden. "The Political Economy of Monetary Unification." In *International Political Economy* (3rd ed.), edited by Jeffry A. Frieden and David A. Lake, pp. 273–274. New York: St. Martin's Press, 1995.

Eichengreen, Barry, and Peter H. Lindert (editors). *The International Debt Crisis in Historical Perspective.* Cambridge, MA: MIT Press, 1989.

Eichengreen, Barry, Andrew K. Rose, and Charles Wyplosz. "Contagious Currency Crises," *National Bureau of Economic Research Working Paper* no. 5681, July 1996.

Eichengreen, Barry, Andrew W. Rose, and Charles Wyplosz. "Exchange Rate Mayhem: The Antecedents and Aftermath of Speculative Attacks." *Economic Policy* (October 1995), pp. 251–312.

Epstein, Gerald. "International Capital Mobility and the Scope for National Economic Management." In *States Against Markets: The Limits of Globalization,* edited by Robert Boyer and Daniel Drache, pp. 211–226. New York: Routledge, 1996.

Erdman, Paul. *Tug of War: Today's Global Currency Crisis.* New York: St. Martin's Press, 1996.

Favre, Alexandre, Henri Guitton, Jean Guitton, Andre Lichnerowicz, and Etienne Wolf. *Chaos and Determinism: Turbulence as a Paradigm for Complex Systems Converging Towards Final States,* trans. by Bertram Eugene Schwarzbach. Baltimore: Johns Hopkins University Press, 1988.

Feldstein, Martin (editor). *The Risk of Economic Crisis.* Chicago: University of Chicago Press, 1991.

Feltenstein, Andrew, and Stephen Morris. "Fiscal Stabilization and Exchange Rate Instability." *Journal of Public Economics* 42 (1990), pp. 329–356.

Galbraith, John Kenneth. "Preface." *New Political Economy* 2:1 (March 1997), pp. 5–10.

Gallarotti, Guilio M. *The Anatomy of an International Monetary Regime: The Classical Gold Standard 1880–1914.* New York: Oxford University Press, 1995.

García Márquez, Gabriel. *One Hundred Years of Solitude.* New York: Harper & Row, 1970.

Gargan, Edwarde A. "Speculators Shake Currencies and Poise of Asians." *New York Times,* July 29, 1997.

Gates, Bill, with Nathan Myhrvold and Peter Rinearson. *The Road Ahead.* New York: Viking, 1995.

Geisst, Charles R. *Exchange Rate Controls: Twenty-Five Years of Finance and Consumer Democracy.* London: Routledge, 1995.

Ghashghaie, S., W. Breymann, J. Peinke, P. Talkner, and Y. Dodge. "Turbulent Cascades in Foreign Exchange Markets." *Nature* 381 (27 June 1996), pp. 767–770.

Gill, Stephen. "Globalization, Democratization, and the Politics of Indifference." In *Globalization: Critical Reflections,* edited by J. H. Mittleman, pp. 205–228. Boulder, CO: Lynne Rienner Publishers, 1996.

Gills, Barry K. (editor). "Globalization and the Politics of Resistance." *New Political Economy* 2:1 (special issue; March 1997).

Gilpin, Robert. *The Political Economy of International Relations.* Princeton, NJ: Princeton University Press, 1987.

Gleick, James. *Chaos: Making a New Science.* New York: Viking, 1987.

Goldthwaite, Richard A. *Wealth and the Demand for Art in Italy, 1300–1600.* Baltimore: Johns Hopkins University Press, 1993.

Greider, William. *One World, Ready or Not: The Manic Logic of Global Capitalism.* New York: Simon and Schuster, 1997.

Grunberg, Leon. "The Changing IPE of the Multinational Corporation." In *Introduction to International Political Economy,* edited by David N. Balaam and Michael Veseth, pp. 338–359. Upper Saddle River, NJ: Prentice Hall, 1996.

Hannon, Bruce, and Matthias Ruth. *Dynamic Modeling.* New York: Springer Verlag, 1994.

Hausman, Daniel M. *The Inexact and Separate Science of Economics.* Cambridge, UK: Cambridge University Press, 1992.

Helleiner, Eric. "Explaining the Globalization of Financial Markets: Bringing States Back In." *Review of International Political Economy* 2:2 (spring 1995), pp. 315–341.

Helleiner, Eric. "Post-Globalization: Is the Financial Liberalization Trend Likely to be Reversed?" In *States Against Markets: The Limits of Globalization,* edited by Robert Boyer and Daniel Drache, pp. 193–210. New York: Routledge, 1996.

Helleiner, Eric. *States and the Reemergence of Global Finance: From Bretton Woods to the 1990s.* Ithaca, NY: Cornell University Press, 1994.

Hirst, Paul, and Grahame Thompson. *Globalization in Question.* Cambridge, UK: Polity Press, 1996.

Hodgson, Geoffrey M. "Varieties of Capitalism and Varieties of Economic Theory." *Review of International Political Economy* 3:3 (autumn 1996), pp. 380–433.

Horgan, John. "From Complexity to Perplexity." *Scientific American* (June 1995), pp. 104–109.

Huntington, Samuel P. *The Clash of Civilizations and the Remaking of World Order.* New York: Simon and Schuster, 1996.

Huntington, Samuel P. "The West: Unique, Not Universal." *Foreign Affairs* 75:6 (November/December 1996), pp. 28–46.

Hutton, Will. "Relaunching Western Economies: The Case for Regulating Financial Markets." *Foreign Affairs* 75:6 (November/December 1996), pp. 8–12.

James, Harold. *International Monetary Cooperation Since Bretton Woods.* New York: Oxford University Press, 1996.

Kahler, Miles (editor). *The Politics of International Debt.* Ithaca, NY: Cornell University Press, 1986.

Kapstein, Ethan B. *Governing the Global Economy: International Finance and the State.* Cambridge, MA: Harvard University Press, 1994.

Kellert, Stephen H. *In the Wake of Chaos.* Chicago: University of Chicago Press, 1993.

Kenen, Peter B. (editor). *Understanding Interdependence: The Macroeconomics of the Open Economy.* Princeton, NJ: Princeton University Press, 1995.

Kennedy, Paul. *Preparing for the Twenty-First Century.* New York: Random House, 1993.

Keylor, William R. *The Twentieth Century World: An International History* (3rd ed.). New York: Oxford University Press, 1996.

Keynes, John Maynard. *The Economic Consequences of the Peace.* New York: Penguin, 1988.

Kindleberger, Charles P. *A Financial History of Western Europe* (2nd ed.). New York: Oxford University Press, 1993.

Kindleberger, Charles P. *International Capital Movements.* Cambridge, UK: Cambridge University Press, 1987.

Kindleberger, Charles P. *Manias, Panics, and Crashes: A History of Financial Crises.* New York: Basic Books, 1978.

Kindleberger, Charles P. *World Economic Primacy 1500–1990.* New York: Oxford University Press, 1996.

Kirshner, Jonathan. *Currency and Coercion: The Political Economy of International Monetary Power.* Princeton, NJ: Princeton University Press, 1995.

Korzeniewicz, Miguel. "Commodity Chains and Marketing Strategies: Nike and the Global Athletic Footwear Industry." In *Commodity Chains and Global Capitalism,* edited by Gary Gereffi and Miguel Korzenicwics. Westport, CT: Praeger, 1994.

Kreps, David M. "Economics—The Current Position." *Daedalus* (winter 1997).

Krugman, Paul R. *Currencies and Crises.* Cambridge, MA: MIT Press, 1992.

Krugman, Paul R. "Dutch Tulips and Emerging Markets." *Foreign Affairs* 74:4 (July/August 1995), pp. 28–44.

Krugman, Paul R. *Exchange Rate Instability.* Cambridge, MA: MIT Press, 1989.

Krugman, Paul R. "Financial Crises in the International Economy." In *The Risk of Economic Crisis,* edited by Martin Feldstein, pp. 85–109. Chicago: University of Chicago Press, 1991.

Krugman, Paul R. *Geography and Trade.* Cambridge, MA: MIT Press, 1991.

Krugman, Paul R. *Peddling Prosperity: Economic Sense and Nonsense in the Age of Diminished Expectations.* New York: W. W. Norton & Co., 1994.

Krugman, Paul R. *Pop Internationalism.* Cambridge, MA: MIT Press, 1996.

Krugman, Paul R. "What Do We Need to Know About the International Monetary System?" In *Understanding Interdependence,* edited by P. Kenen, pp. 273–307. Princeton, NJ: Princeton University Press, 1995.

Larsen, Erik Reimer, John D. W. Morecroft, Jesper Skovhus Thomsen, and Erik Mosekilde. "Devil's Staircase and Chaos from Macroeconomic Mode Interaction." *Journal of Economic Dynamics and Control* 17 (1993), pp. 759–769.

Lauwerier, Hans. *Fractals: Endlessly Repeated Geometrical Figures,* trans. Sophia Gill-Hoffstädt. Princeton, NJ: Princeton University Press, 1991.

Lever, Harold, and Christopher Huhne. *Debt and Danger: The World Financial Crisis.* Boston: Atlantic Monthly Press, 1986.

Lorenz, Edward N. *The Essence of Chaos.* Seattle: University of Washington Press, 1993.

Mackkay, Charles. *Extraordinary Popular Delusions and the Madness of Crowds.* New York: Farrar, Straus and Giroux, 1932.

Markusen, James R. "The Boundaries of Multinational Enterprises and the Theory of International Trade." *Journal of Economic Perspectives* 9:2 (spring 1995), pp. 149–168.

Martin, Felix. "The Development of General Equilibrium Theory." SAIS Bologna Center, Bologna, Italy, May 1997, mimeo.

McCallum, Bennett T. *International Monetary Economics.* New York: Oxford University Press, 1996.

Medio, Alfredo. *Chaotic Dynamics: Theory and Application to Economics.* Cambridge, UK: Cambridge University Press, 1992.

Microsoft Corporation. *1996 Annual Report.* Redmond, WA: Microsoft Corporation, 1996.

Mirowski, Philip. "Do You Know the Way to Santa Fe? Or Political Economy Gets More Complex." University of Notre Dame, Notre Dame, IN, December 1994, mimeo.

Mirowski, Philip. *More Heat than Light: Economics As Social Physics: Physics As Nature's Economics.* Cambridge, UK: Cambridge University Press, 1989.

Mittleman, James H. "How Does Globalization Really Work?" In *Globalization: Critical Reflections,* edited by J. H. Mittleman, pp. 229–240. Boulder, CO: Lynne Reinner Publishers, 1996.

Mittleman, James H. "The Dynamics of Globalization." In *Globalization: Critical Reflections,* edited by J. H. Mittleman, pp. 1–19. Boulder, CO: Lynne Rienner Publishers, 1996.

Mizrach, Bruce. "The State of Economic Dynamics: A Review Essay." *Journal of Economic Dynamics and Control* 6 (1992), pp. 175–190.

Murphy, R. Taggart. *The Weight of the Yen.* New York: W. W. Norton, 1996.

Naím, Moisés. "Latin America the Morning After." *Foreign Affairs* 74:4 (July/August 1995), pp. 45–61.

Neal, Larry. *The Rise of Financial Capitalism: International Capital Markets in the Age of Reason.* Cambridge, MA: Cambridge University Press, 1990.

Nordhaus, William. "The Political Business Cycle." *Review of Economics Studies* 43 (1975), pp. 169–190.

Norman, Alfred, and David W. Shimer. "Risk, Uncertainty, and Complexity. *Journal of Economic Dynamics and Control* 18 (1994), pp. 231–249.

O'Brien, Richard. *Global Financial Integration: The End of Geography.* New York: Council on Foreign Relations, 1992.

Obstfeld, Maurice. "International Capital Mobility in the 1990s." In *Understanding Interdependence,* edited by P. Kenen, pp. 201–261. Princeton: Princeton University Press, 1995.

Obstfeld, Maurice. "Models of Currency Crises with Self-Fulfilling Features." National Bureau of Economic Research Working Paper no. 5285, 1995.

Obstfeld, Maurice, and Kenneth Rogoff. "Exchange Rate Dynamics Redux." *Journal of Political Economy* 103:3 (June 1995), pp. 624–660.

Ohmae, Kenichi. *The Borderless World: Power and Strategy in the Interlinked Economy.* New York: HarperPerennial, 1990.

Ohmae, Kenichi (editor). *The Evolving Global Economy.* Cambridge, MA: Harvard University Press, 1995.

Ohmae, Kenichi. "Putting Global Logic First." In *The Evolving Global Economy: Making Sense of the New World Order,* edited by K. Ohmae, pp. 129–137. Cambridge MA: Harvard Business Review, 1995.

Padoa-Schioppa, Tommaso, and Fabrizio Saccomanni "Managing a Market-Led Global Financial System." In *Managing the World Economy: Fifty Years After Bretton Woods,* edited by Peter B. Kenen, pp. 235–268. Washington, DC: Institute for International Economics, 1994.

Perraton, Jonathan, David Goldblatt, David Held, and Anthony McGrew, "The Globalization of Economic Activity." *New Political Economy* 2:2 (July 1997), pp. 257–277.

Petrella, Ricardo. "Globalization and Internationalization: The Dynamics of the Emerging World Order." In *States Against Markets: The Limits of Globalization,* edited by Robert Boyer and Daniel Drache, pp. 62–83. London: Routledge: 1996.

Porter, Michael. *The Competitive Advantage of Nations.* New York: The Free Press, 1990.

Ramey, Garey, and Valerie A. Ramey. "Cross-Country Evidence on the Link Between Volatility and Growth." *American Economic Review* 85:5 (1995), pp. 1138–1151.

Reich, Robert B. *The Work of Nations: Preparing Ourselves for 21st-Century Capitalism.* New York: Alfred A. Knopf, 1991.

Ricardo, David. *The Principles of Political Economy and Taxation.* London: Dent, 1993.

Rodrik, Dani. *Has Globalization Gone Too Far?* Washington, DC: Institute for International Economics, 1997.

Rogoff, Kenneth. "The Purchasing Power Parity Puzzle." *Journal of Economic Literature* 34 (June 1996), pp. 647–668.

Rosecrance, Richard. "The Rise of the Virtual State." *Foreign Affairs* 75:4 (July/August 1996), pp. 45–61.

Rosenau, James N. *Turbulence in World Politics.* Princeton, NJ: Princeton University Press, 1990.

Rosser, J. Barkley, Jr. *From Catastrophe to Chaos: A General Theory of Economic Discontinuities.* Boston: Kluwer Academic Publishers, 1991.

Ruelle, David. *Chance and Chaos.* Princeton, NJ: Princeton University Press, 1991.

Sachs, Jeffrey, Aaron Tornell, and Andrés Velasco, "Financial Crises in Emerging Markets: The Lessons from 1995." National Bureau of Economic Research Working Paper no. 5576, 1996.

Sachs, Jeffrey, Aaron Tornell, and Andrés Velasco. "The Collapse of the Mexican Peso: What Have We Learned?" *Economic Policy* 22 (April 1996), pp. 13–64.

Samuelson, Paul A. *Foundations of Economic Analysis.* Cambridge, MA: Harvard University Press, 1947.

Sasakura, Kazuyuki. "Political Economics Chaos?" *Journal of Behavior and Organization* 27 (1995), pp. 213–221.

Schroeder, Manfred. *Fractals, Chaos, Power Laws: Minutes from an Infinite Paradise.* New York: W. H. Freeman & Co., 1991.

Schumpeter, Joseph A. *Business Cycles.* 2 vols. New York: McGraw-Hill, 1939.

Schumpeter, Joseph A. *Capitalism, Socialism, and Democracy.* New York: Harper & Brothers, 1942.

Schumpeter, Joseph A. *The Theory of Economic Development,* trans. Redvers Opie. New Brunswick, NJ: Transactions Publishers, 1983.

Schwartz, Herman M. *In the Dominions of Debt: Historical Perspective on Dependent Development.* Ithaca, NY: Cornell University Press, 1989.

Shelton, Judy. *Money Meltdown: Restoring Order to the Global Currency System.* New York: The Free Press, 1994.

Smale, Steve. *The Mathematics of Time: Essays on Dynamical Systems, Economics Processes, and Related Topics.* New York: Springer-Verlag, 1980.

Smith, Adam. *The Wealth of Nations.* New York: Dutton, 1964.

Solow, Robert M. "How Did Economics Get That Way? What Way Did It Get?" *Daedalus* (winter 1997), pp. 39–58.

Soros, George. "Can Europe Work?" *Foreign Affairs* 75:5 (September/October 1996), pp. 8–14.

Soros, George. "The Capitalist Threat." *The Atlantic Monthly* 279:2 (February 1997), pp. 45–58.

Sousa, David. "Converging on 'Competitiveness': Garbage Cans and the Global Economy." University of Puget Sound, Tacoma, WA, March 1997, mimeo.

Sousa, David. "Democracy and Markets: The IPE of NAFTA." In *Introduction to International Political Economy,* edited by David N. Balaam and Michael Veseth, pp. 241–258. Upper Saddle River, NJ: Prentice Hall, 1996.

Ssicsic, Pierre, and Charles Wyplosz. "France, 1945–92." In *Economic Growth in Europe Since 1945,* edited by N.F.R. Crafts and Gianni Toniolo, p. 236. Cambridge: Cambridge University Press, 1996.

Stauffer, Dietrich, and H. Eugene Stanley. *From Newton to Mandelbrot* (2nd ed.). Berlin: Springer-Verlag, 1996.

Stopford, John, and Susan Strange, with John S. Henley. *Rival States, Rival Firms: Competition for World Market Shares.* Cambridge, UK: Cambridge University Press, 1991.

Stopler, Wolfgang F. *Joseph Alois Schumpeter: The Public Life of a Private Man.* Princeton, NJ: Princeton University Press, 1994.

Stoppard, Tom. *Arcadia.* London: Faber and Faber, 1993.

Strange, Susan. *Casino Capitalism.* London: Basil Blackwell, 1986.

Strange, Susan. "States, Firms, and Diplomacy." In *International Political Economy: Perspectives on Global Power and Wealth* (3rd ed.), edited by Jeffry A. Frieden and David A. Lake. New York: St. Martin's Press, 1995.

Strange, Susan. *The Retreat of the State: The Diffusion of Power in the World Economy.* Cambridge, UK: Cambridge University Press, 1997.

Streek, Wolfgang. "From Market Making to State Building? Reflections on the Political Economy of European Social Policy." In *European Social Policy: Between Fragmentation and Integration,* edited by Stephan Leibfried and Paul Pierson, pp. 389–431. Washington, DC: The Brookings Institution, 1995.

Summers, Lawrence. "Planning for the Next Financial Crisis." In *The Risk of Economic Crisis,* edited by Martin Feldstein, pp. 135–158. Chicago: University of Chicago Press, 1991.

Tabellini, Guido. "Money, Debt and Deficits in a Dynamic Game." *Journal of Economic Dynamics and Control* 10 (1986), pp. 427–442.

Taylor, Mark P. "The Economics of Exchange Rates." *Journal of Economic Literature* 32 (March 1995), pp. 13–47.

Thurow, Lester. *The Future of Capitalism: How Today's Economic Forces Shape Tomorrow's World.* New York: William Morrow, 1996.

United Nations Conference on Trade and Development. *World Investment Report 1996: Investment, Trade, and International Policy Arrangements.* New York: United Nations, 1996.

Veseth, Michael. *Introductory Economics.* New York: Academic Press, 1981.

Veseth, Michael. *Mountains of Debt: Crisis and Change in Renaissance Florence, Victorian Britain, and Postwar America.* New York: Oxford University Press, 1990.

Wade, Robert. "Globalization and Its Limits: Reports of the Death of the National Economy Are Greatly Exaggerated." In *National Diversity and Global Capitalism,* edited by Suzanne Berger and Ronald Dore, pp. 60–88. Ithaca, NY: Cornell University Press, 1996.

Waldrop, M. Mitchell. *Complexity: The Emerging Science at the Edge of Order and Chaos.* New York: Simon and Schuster, 1992.

Waltz, Kenneth N. *Man, the State, and War: A Theoretical Analysis.* New York: Columbia University Press, 1959.

Warnecke, H. J. *The Fractal Company: A Revolution in Corporate Culture.* Berlin: Springer-Verlag, 1993.

Weber, Axel. "Reputation and Credibility in the European Monetary System." *Economic Policy* 12 (April 1991), pp. 57–102.

Westerman, Jonathan. "Microsoft Windows 95: A Product of India." University of Puget Sound, Tacoma, WA, 1995 typescript.

World Investment Report 1996: Investment, Trade, and International Policy Arrangements. New York, United Nations, 1996.

Zysman, John. "The Myth of a 'Global Economy': Enduring National Foundations and Emerging Regional Realities." *New Political Economy* 1:2 (July 1996), pp. 157–184.

Index

About the Book

Michael Veseth makes a colorful and contrarian argument: The reality of globalization is both quantitatively and qualitatively different from the images that intellectuals, politicians, and business leaders promote; the globalization myth persists, however, because the notion of invincible global markets serves so many often contradictory interests.

Veseth's investigation of international financial markets finds strong evidence of systematic crisis and chaos conditions that limit the degree and also influence the nature of truly global business behavior. Critiquing exaggerated claims of global market power and providing insightful case studies of "global" firms, he examines the political and intellectual interests that promote the globalization myth for their own purposes. The book concludes with a speculative essay on the prospects for and consequences of real globalization in the international political economy of the twenty-first century.

Michael Veseth is professor of economics and director of the Political Economy Program at the University of Puget Sound. His numerous books include *Mountains of Debt; Introductory Economics; Public Finance;* and most recently, *Introduction to International Political Economy* (coauthored with David Balaam).